CONTENTS

Cover Picture: Dale Head Hall Lakeside Hotel, Keswick, Cumbria (page 98)

Key to symbols 2

Foreword 3

Map of Great Britain & Ireland 4

Johansens 2000 Awards for Excellence 5

How to use this guide 7

Introduction from Ashelford
Winner of the Johansens 2000 Most Excellent Country House Award *(see page 66)* 8

Introduction from Rylstone Manor
Winner of the Johansens 2000 Most Excellent Value for Money Award *(see page 97)* 10

Introduction from Glebe Farm House
Winner of the Johansens 2000 Most Excellent Service Award *(see page 164)* 12

Johansens Recommended Country Houses and Small Hotels in the Channel Islands 15–19

Johansens Recommended Country Houses and Small Hotels in England 25–181

Johansens Recommended Country Houses and Small Hotels in Ireland 182–193

Johansens Recommended Country Houses and Small Hotels in Scotland 194–217

Johansens Recommended Country Houses and Small Hotels in Wales 218–232

'Mini Listings' of Johansens Recommended Traditional Inns, Hotels & Restaurants
(published in full in the Johansens Recommended Traditional Inns, Hotels
& Restaurants Guide 2001) 235

Indexes 237–240

Johansens Guide Order Forms and Guest Survey Reports 247–256

KEY TO SYMBOLS

Total number of rooms	Nombre de chambres	Anzahl der Zimmer
MasterCard accepted	MasterCard accepté	MasterCard akzeptiert
Visa accepted	Visa accepté	Visa akzeptiert
American Express accepted	American Express accepté	American Express akzeptiert
Diners Club accepted	Diners Club accepté	Diners Club akzeptiert
Quiet location	Un lieu tranquille	Ruhige Lage
Access for wheelchairs to at least one bedroom and public rooms	Accès handicapé	Zugang für Behinderte

(The 'Access for wheelchairs' symbol (♿) does not necessarily indicate that the property fulfils National Accessible Scheme grading)

Chef-patron	Chef-patron	Chef-patronn
Meeting/conference facilities with maximum number of delegates	Salle de conférences – capacité maximale	Konferenzraum – Höchstkapazität
Children welcome, with minimum age where applicable	Enfants bienvenus	Kinder willkommen
Dogs accommodated in rooms or kennels	Chiens autorisés	Hunde erlaubt
At least one room has a four-poster bed	Lit à baldaquin dans au moins une chambre	mindestens 1 Zimmer mit Himmelbett
Cable/satellite TV in all bedrooms	TV câblée/satellite dans les chambres	Satellit-und Kabelfernsehen in allen Zimmern
CD player in bedrooms	Lecteur CD dans les chambres	CD-Player im Zimmer
Video players in bedrooms	Lecteur video dans les chambres	Videogerät im Zimmer
ISDN/Modem point in bedrooms	Ligne ISDN / point modem dans les chambres	ISDN-/Modemanschluss im Zimmer
No-smoking rooms (at least one no-smoking bedroom)	Au moins une chambre non-fumeur	mind. 1 Zimmer für Nichtraucher
Lift available for guests' use	Ascenseur	Fahrstuhl
Indoor swimming pool	Piscine couverte	Hallenbad
Outdoor swimming pool	Piscine en plein air	Freibad
Tennis court at hotel	Tennis à l'hôtel	Hoteleigener Tennisplatz
Croquet lawn at hotel	Croquet à l'hôtel	Krocketrasen
Fishing can be arranged	Pêche	Angeln
Golf course on site or nearby, which has an arrangement with the hotel allowing guests to play	Golf sur site ou à proximité	hoteleigener oder nahegelegener Golfplatz
Shooting can be arranged	Tir	Schiessen
Riding can be arranged	Équitation	Reiten
Hotel has a helicopter landing pad	Helipad	Hubschrauberlandeplatz
Licensed for wedding ceremonies	Licencé pour cérémonies de mariage	Konzession für Eheschliessungen

FOREWORD

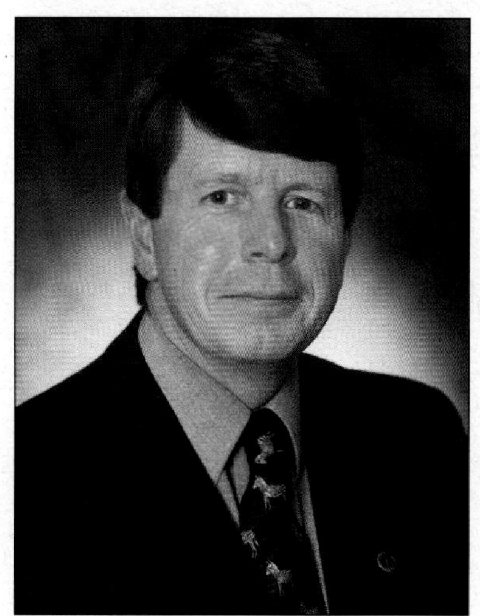

Welcome to the 12th edition of 'Johansens Recommended Country Houses & Small Hotels – Great Britain & Ireland'.

Our team of inspectors have spent the past twelve months revisiting the country houses and hotels that we recommended last year and inspecting new establishments for consideration in this, the 2001, edition. A number have been rejected, and new recommendations can be identified by a red disc at the top of their entry page.

To maintain and monitor standards, we encourage constructive comments and observations through the 'Guest Survey Forms' printed at the back of this guide. This information is invaluable, and whether it contains criticism or praise, we are always pleased to hear from you.

Our first Guide to 'Recommended Hotels & Lodges – Australia, New Zealand, The Pacific' is also published this year, which means that Johansens now recommend over 1400 Hotels, Country Houses, Traditional Inns, Game Lodges and Business Meeting Venues throughout four continents.

Order forms to purchase all Johansens titles are provided at the back of this guide together with a list of our other recommendations which can also be found by location or 'keyword' search on our website: www.johansens.com.

Direct reservations can be made on our website and many recommendations display a 'Call Free Now' facility enabling you to speak directly to the hotel at no cost to yourself.

You will also find some wonderful 'Historic Houses, Castles & Gardens' to visit throughout the UK and Europe. In addition, you can enjoy the benefits of 'Special Offers' and 'Famous Chefs' Recipes'!

We very much hope that you appreciate our recommendations for 2001 as much as you have enjoyed using our guides in the past.

Finally, your experience has proved that to mention Johansens when you make your booking and again when you arrive will make you a most welcome guest.

Andrew Warren
Managing Director

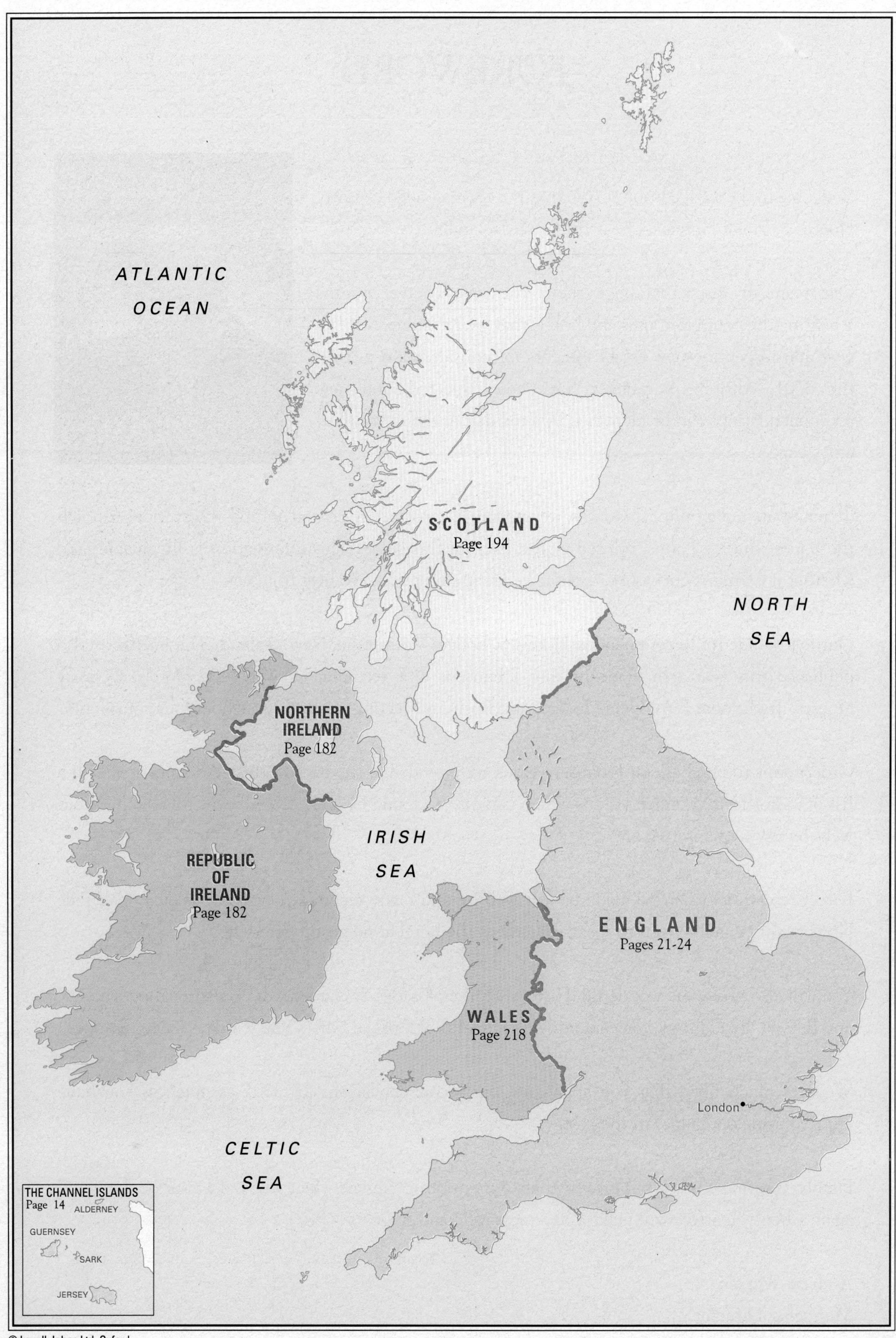
ATLANTIC
OCEAN
SCOTLAND
Page 194
NORTH
SEA
NORTHERN
IRELAND
Page 182
IRISH
SEA
REPUBLIC
OF
IRELAND
Page 182
ENGLAND
Pages 21-24
WALES
Page 218
London
CELTIC
SEA
THE CHANNEL ISLANDS
Page 14
ALDERNEY
GUERNSEY
SARK
JERSEY

JOHANSENS AWARDS FOR EXCELLENCE 2000

The 2000 Awards for Excellence winners at the Dorchester

The Johansens Awards for Excellence were presented at the Johansens Annual Dinner held at The Dorchester on November 1st, 1999.

Each year we rely on the appraisals of Johansens guests, alongside the nominations of our team of inspectors, as a basis for making all our awards, not only to our Recommended Hotels but also to our Country Houses and Inns with Restaurants in Great Britain & Ireland, Recommended Hotels – Europe and the Mediterranean and Recommended Hotels & Inns – North America, Bermuda & The Caribbean. In these categories the award winners for 2000 were:

Johansens Most Excellent Country Hotel Award:
Lucknam Park, Bath, England

Johansens Most Excellent City Hotel Award:
The Merrion, Dublin, Ireland

Johansens Most Excellent Country House Award:
Ashelford, Devon, England

Johansens Most Excellent Traditional Inn Award:
Pool House Hotel, Inverness, Scotland

Johansens Most Excellent London Hotel Award:
The Cliveden Town House

Johansens Most Excellent Value for Money Award:
Rylstone Manor, Isle of Wight, England

Johansens Most Excellent Service Award:
Glebe Farm House, Warwickshire, England

Johansens Most Excellent Restaurant Award:
The Vineyard at Stockcross, Newbury, England

Johansens – Europe: The Most Excellent City Hotel:
Hotel Claris, Barcelona, Spain

Johansens – Europe: The Most Excellent Country Hotel:
Relais la Suvera, Pievescola-Siena, Italy

Johansens – Europe: The Most Excellent Waterside Resort:
Hôtel du Palais, Biarritz, France

Johansens – North America: Most Excellent Inn:
Antrim 1844, Maryland, USA

Johansens – North America: Most Excellent Hotel:
Nob Hill Lambourne, California, USA

Johansens – North America: Special Award for Excellence:
The Swag Country Inn, North Carolina, USA

Knight Frank Award for Outstanding Excellence and Innovation:
Jonathan Wix of 42, The Calls and his newly-formed The Scotsman Group

Published by
Johansens Limited, Therese House, Glasshouse Yard, London EC1A 4JN
Tel: 020 7566 9700 Fax: 020 7490 2538
Find Johansens on the Internet at: **www.johansens.com**
E-Mail: info@johansens.com

Publishing Director:	Peter Hancock
P.A. to Publishing Director:	Carol Sweeney
Regional Inspectors:	Geraldine Bromley
	Robert Bromley
	Julie Dunkley
	Pat Gillson
	Martin Greaves
	Joan Henderson
	Marie Iversen
	Pauline Mason
	John O'Neill
	Mary O'Neill
	Fiona Patrick
	Brian Sandell
Production Director:	Daniel Barnett
Production Controller:	Kevin Bradbrook
Production Assistant:	Rachael Gasiorowski
Sub-editor:	Stephanie von Selzam
Senior Designer:	Michael Tompsett
Designers:	Sue Dixon
	Kerri Bennett
Copywriters:	Simon Duke
	Norman Flack
	Debra Giles
	Rozanne Paragon
	Leonora Sandwell
Sales and Marketing Manager:	Laurent Martinez
Marketing Executive:	Adam Crabtree
Sales Administrator:	Susan Butterworth
P.A. to Managing Director :	Joanne Jones
Managing Director:	Andrew Warren

Johansens is a subsidiary of the Daily Mail & General Trust plc

ISBN 1 86017 7425

Printed in England by St Ives plc
Colour origination by Catalyst Creative Imaging

Distributed in the UK and Europe by Johnsons International Media Services Ltd, London (direct sales) & Portfolio, Greenford (bookstores). In North America by Hobsons DMI, Cincinnati (direct sales) and Hunter Publishing, New Jersey (bookstores). In Australia and New Zealand by Bookwise International, Findon, South Australia. In Southern Africa by Liquid Amber Distributions, Gillitts, South Africa.

HOW TO USE THIS GUIDE

If you want to find a Country House or Small Hotel in a particular area you can:

- Turn to the Maps on pages 4, 14, 21–24, 182, 194 and 218.

- Search the Index on pages 237–240.

- Look for the Town or Village where you wish to stay in the main body of the Guide. This is divided into countries. Place names in each country appear at the head of the pages in alphabetical order.

The Index lists the Country Houses and Small Hotels by countries and by counties, and also shows those with amenities such as fishing, conference facilities, swimming, golf, etc.

The maps cover all regions. Each Country House and Small Hotel symbol (a green square) relates to a property in this guide situated in or near the location shown.

If you cannot find a suitable country house near where you wish to stay, you may decide to choose one of Johansens Recommended Traditional Inns, Hotels & Restaurants as an alternative. These establishments are all listed by place names on page 235.

Properties which did not feature in our last (2000) edition are identified with a "NEW" symbol at the top of the page.

The prices, in most cases, refer to the cost of one night's accommodation, with breakfast, for two people. Prices are also shown for single occupancy. These rates are correct at the time of going to press but always should be checked with the hotel before you make your reservation.

We occasionally receive letters from guests who have been charged for accommodation booked in advance but later cancelled. Readers should be aware that by making a reservation with a hotel, either by telephone or in writing, they are entering into a legal contract. A hotelier under certain circumstances is entitled to make a charge for accommodation when guests fail to arrive, even if notice of the cancellation is given.

All guides are obtainable from bookshops or by Johansens Freephone 0800 269397 or by using the order coupons on pages 247–256.

AWARD WINNER 2000

Ashelford, Combe Martin, Devon
Winner of the 2000 Johansens Most Excellent Country House Award

Yes, Ashelford is special! We knew that the first day we walked into it back in 1993. For nearly 40 years, the property had laid 'dormant' but the 70 acres of land had been farmed. There were springs and streams everywhere, and water was even running through the house. There was no sink, just a hand pump above a drain which was the only item to denote a kitchen! The day we moved in (14th February) the digger arrived and went through our only 'proper' water supply...and it snowed!

Looking back on the renovations, we are pleased that we lived in the house while the work went on, as this enabled us to 'get the true feel' of the home that we hoped would evolve. We never bought 'new' but scoured the local paper for second hand slates, oak beams, slate flooring, sinks etc. We renovated the water pump which still gives water straight from the spring at the back of the house. We took the fireplaces 'back' to the originals, one with a superb bread oven and the other with a 'salt drying cupboard'. There was a toilet, but you crossed your fingers when pulling the chain until we installed a plastic tank. The barns were full of old farming items, and our next door neighbour (half a mile away), Farmer Phillips, spent much time advising us on what to keep.

We have retained the old pens in one of the barns, which we now use for the Exmoor ponies. One barn is still being used for storage, and the other, a traditional Devon 'Hill Barn' which faces the moor, has been converted to the same standard as the house... with the help of the same work team.

We can honestly say we have never once regretted our move here, and each time new guests arrive, we derive vicarious enjoyment from their pleasure and appreciation of all that we have achieved. It is a lovely way of living and we now have a home of which we are proud and which we enjoy sharing.

Tom & Erica McClenaghan

A foundation for the future

The Hildon Foundation will provide a helping hand for young people from all walks of life to realise their full potential

Since its launch in 1999, Hildon Sport has become the mineral water of choice for young, sporty, dynamic and health-orientated individuals. At the beginning of the year 2000 Hildon Sport looked at new ways of enhancing the bond that existed between itself and those who enjoy it.

The conclusion was that a charitable foundation would be the ideal vehicle and it now gives Hildon Sport great pleasure to announce the creation of The Hildon Foundation.

Courtesy of Retna

For each bottle of Hildon Sport sold, a donation of 1p will be made to the Foundation, with the intention of raising at least £100,000 in the first year alone. Any shortfall will be met by Hildon Limited and, unlike many charities, 100 per cent of the money raised will go directly to the Foundation as all of the administrative costs will be met by Hildon Limited itself.

The beneficiaries of the Foundation will be needy young people – both individuals and youth projects. There will be no 'preferred' cause, with applications welcome from all areas: budding musicians, sports students needing funds to continue training, disabled causes, science and technology projects; deserving cases from all walks of life will be considered by the Foundation.

It's important that the Foundation has a 'face' and a short list of suitable personalities was drawn up for the role of patron – the role requires someone who possesses the qualities that embody the Foundation and what it hopes to achieve; someone who can relate to the needs of the children involved and has demonstrated the drive to succeed in their own life. It's important, also, to note that the patron will receive no financial rewards for his or her time and efforts on behalf of the Hildon Foundation.

We're thrilled that the former English cricket captain **David Gower OBE** has agreed to be our first patron. Since retiring from professional cricket, David has become an accomplished broadcaster on radio and TV, and a witty, interesting motivational and after dinner speaker. A keen sportsman in his spare time – he is a talented tennis player and skier on snow and water – David is the ideal figure to encourage youngsters, wherever their individual talents may lie.

As well as supporting and helping to communicate the concept, David and his successors will hold key roles in deciding who the first beneficiaries should be. He will have a junior counterpart, who will also reflect the aims of the Foundation, and the two will hold their positions for one year, from June 2000.

The first awards ceremony will take place in June 2001 when David will present the recipients with the first year's funds. Handing over the reins to his successor, David will remain available to provide valuable advice as the Hildon Foundation enters its second year.

Hildon Sport – creating a better future for the next generation.

AWARD WINNER 2000

Rylstone Manor, Isle of Wight, England
Winner of the 2000 Johansens Most Excellent Value for Money Award

We are just into our third year at Rylstone, and so we felt honoured and proud to be awarded the Johansens accolade of Most Excellent Value for Money Award, which has recognised what we wanted to achieve, but in a very short time. After being restaurateurs for 25 years, the progression to a hotel seemed natural, and finding Rylstone made it even more so. The house soaked up our collection of antiques and china like a sponge – it all looked as if it was bought for here. We opened the doors and the guests started to appear, including locals.

Rylstone Manor was built in 1863 and has Tudor and Gothic influences. It sits on a cliff top with a natural chine winding through to the sea, making it a wonderful setting for all seasons.

The island itself has a laid back atmosphere with winding leafy lanes leading to a hamlet or village around every corner and being surrounded by the sea, a feeling of security is installed.

The Manor has nine en suite bedrooms, all with an individual feel, from a gentleman's study to a pretty four-poster room.

You can relax with tea on the terrace with a good book, take a stroll to the beach or visit the many places of interest – the choices are numerous but Rylstone is timeless.

Whether at home or abroad, a Johansens hotel is a must. We wish you a most enjoyable stay.

Neil Graham
Alan Priddle

AWARD WINNER 2000

Glebe Farm House, Stratford-upon-Avon, Warwickshire, England
Winner of the 2000 Johansens Most Excellent Service Award

To be the recipient of this award has thrilled us here at Glebe Farm House.

From the moment we first opened the doors of our Country House to the discerning customers of Johansens, we were determined that our guests would enter the 'Glebe Farm House Experience' founded on traditional values, namely service in the old-fashioned sense of the word.

Glebe Farm House is not grand and ostentatious but intimate and welcoming. Having driven through our entrance gates you become our house guest, not a room number, and enter our world where hospitality abounds.

Glebe Farm House is only two miles from Stratford-upon-Avon, and is therefore locally positioned for visiting this historic town and its theatres. Alternatively with Warwick Castle only ten minutes away and the Cotswolds on the doorstep, there is plenty to see and do.

Be sure to pack plenty into your day so that we can pamper you on your return.

We look forward to the coming year, and to meeting up again with many regular visitors, now friends, and the opportunity to make new friends.

The award is all the more special because it is our customers who have taken time out from their busy schedules to show their appreciation for our efforts. This is evident from the generous comments in our visitors' book and letters of thanks.

We look forward to you enjoying the Glebe Farm House Experience.

Kate McGovern

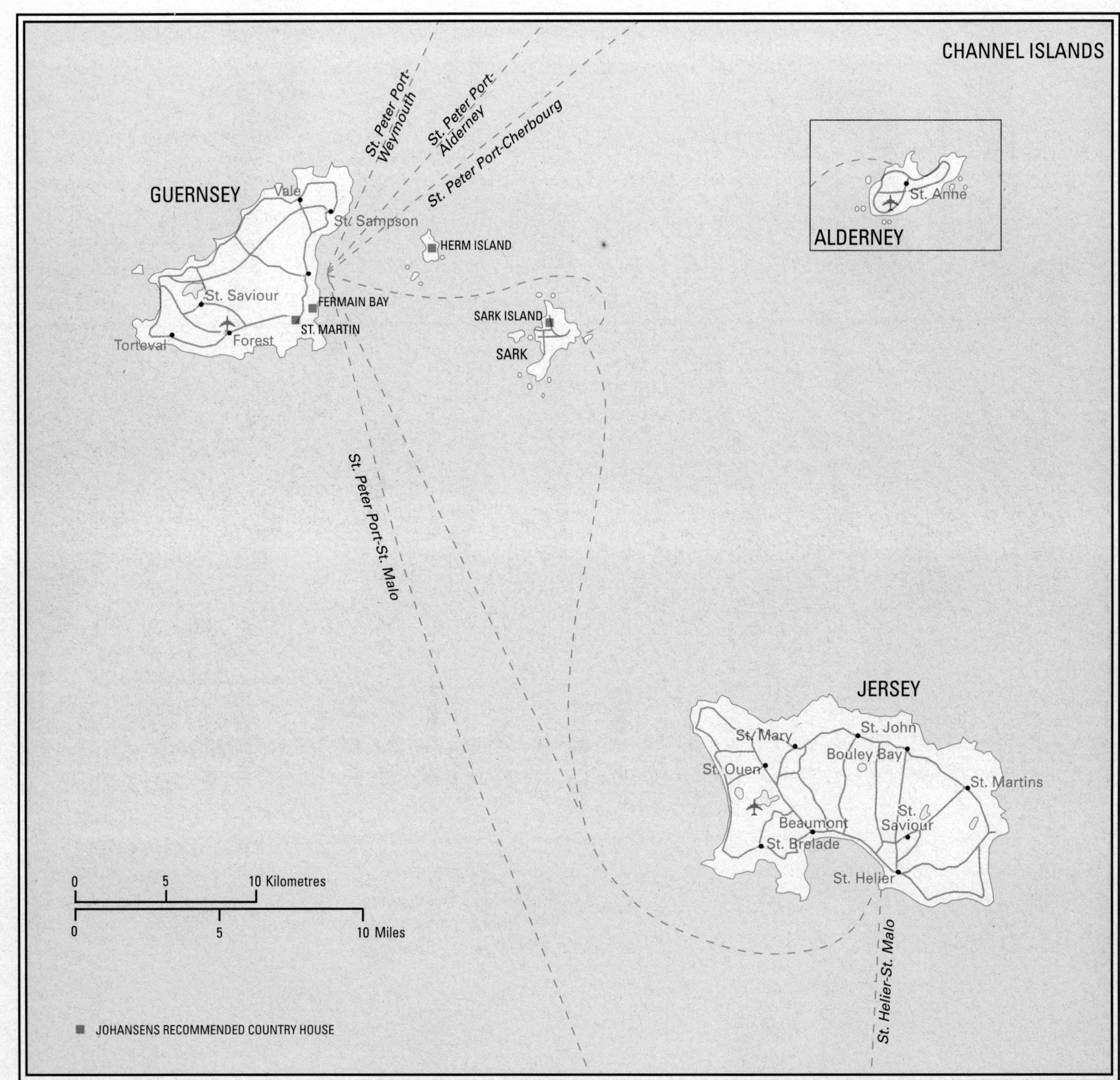
CHANNEL ISLANDS
GUERNSEY
Vale
St. Sampson
St. Saviour
FERMAIN BAY
ST. MARTIN
Torteval
Forest
HERM ISLAND
SARK ISLAND
SARK
St. Peter Port-Weymouth
St. Peter Port-Alderney
St. Peter Port-Cherbourg
St. Peter Port-St. Malo
ALDERNEY
St. Anne
JERSEY
St. Mary
St. John
Bouley Bay
St. Ouen
St. Martins
St. Saviour
Beaumont
St. Brelade
St. Helier
St. Helier-St. Malo
0 5 10 Kilometres
0 5 10 Miles
JOHANSENS RECOMMENDED COUNTRY HOUSE

Johansens Recommended Country Houses & Small Hotels

Channel Islands

Visit the Channel Islands and experience the classic combination of clifftop views, locally caught seafood, picturesque cobbled streets, unique shopping boutiques and pristine gardens – all of which can be enjoyed whilst staying in recommended luxurious accommodation!

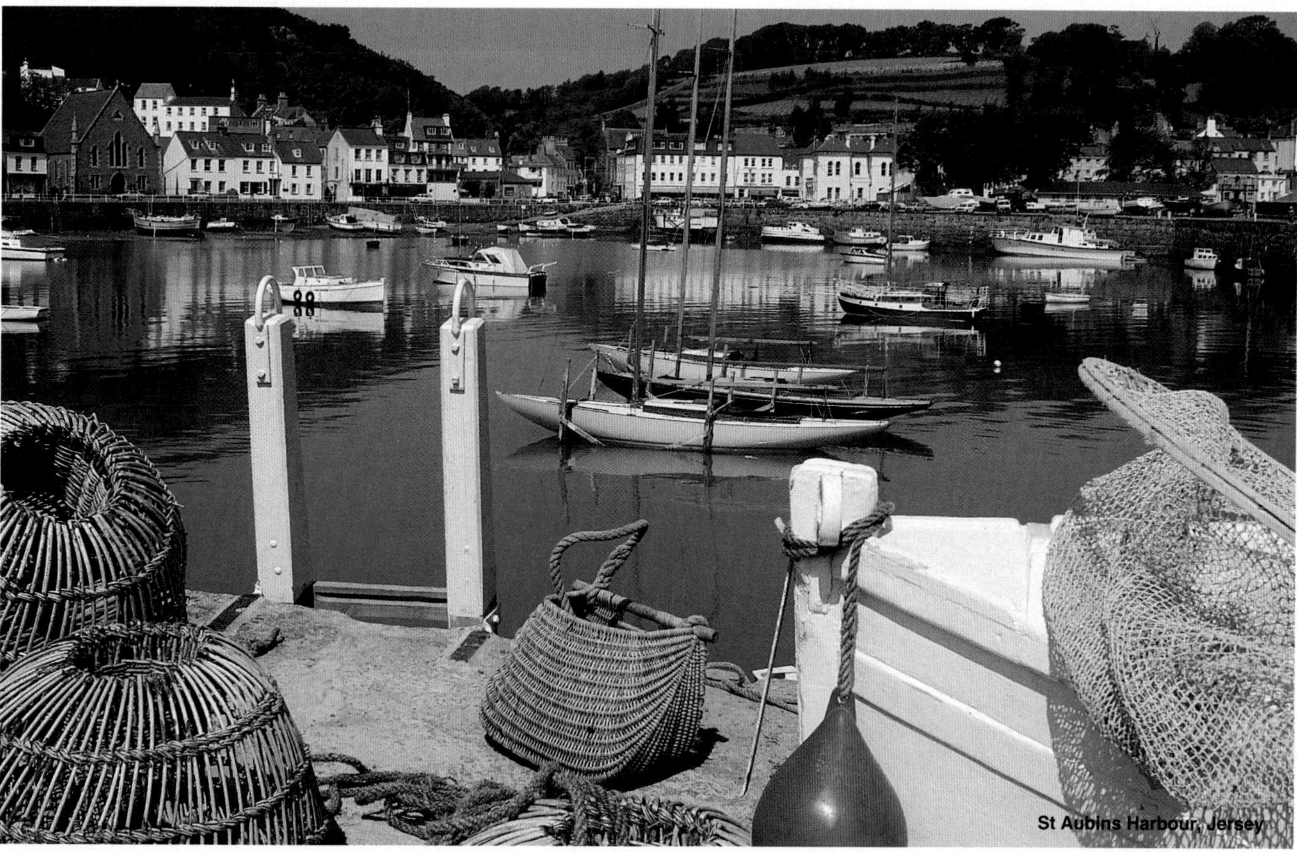

St Aubins Harbour, Jersey

What's happening in Guernsey?

• **Festival of Food and Wine** – throughout March to mid April, restaurants, bistros and pubs compete for the acclaimed title 'The Guernsey Eating Experience'. The festival features mouth-watering menus to suit all tastes, many of which use local produce. The event comes to its conclusion with the 'Salon Culinaire' finale where chefs give demonstrations and hold competitions For more information call 01481 713583 or visit www.gourmet.guernsey.net.

• **Floral Guernsey Show** – this three day show gives visitors the opportunity to view the island's vast array of beautiful flowers and gardens. For more information call the Tourist Information Centre on 01481 723552.

What's happening in Jersey?

• **Jersey Jazz Festival** – held annually at various venues around the Island, this event is a must for visitors to Jersey. Held on 9th August. For more information call 01534 500700.

• **Jersey Battle of Flowers** – in celebration of the island's outstanding flowers, this parade boasts floats with floral tributes, musicians dancers and much more. Held on 9th August. For more information call 01534 500700.

For further information, please contact:-

Guernsey Tourist Board
PO Box 23
St Peter Port
Guernsey GY1 3AN
Tel: 01481 723557

Jersey Tourism
Liberation Square
St Helier
Jersey JE1 1BB
Tel: 01534 500700

La Favorita Hotel

FERMAIN BAY, GUERNSEY, CHANNEL ISLANDS GY4 6SD
TEL: 01481 235666 FAX: 01481 235413 E-MAIL: info@favorita.com

OWNERS: Simon and Helen Wood

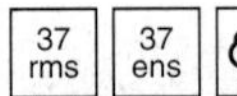

S: from £46.50
D: from £77

Once a fine private country house, La Favorita retains all the charm and character of those former days. The hotel is comfortable and fully licensed. Set in its own grounds, a few minutes walk from Guernsey's famous Fermain Bay, it enjoys spectacular views over the sea towards Jersey.

The bedrooms, all non smoking, are comfortable and provide every modern amenity, including colour television, radio and refreshment tray. Guernsey's mild climate means that it has much to offer out of season and the hotel also has a full range of facilities to satisfy the extra needs of spring, autumn and winter guests, including the indoor pool.

La Favorita has an excellent reputation for traditional English cooking and island seafood specialities. The restaurant is strictly no smoking. A coffee shop serves a wide range of lunch dishes and bar suppers for those who enjoy a more informal meal.

St Peter Port is within easy walking distance, whether taking the woodland walk which follows the coastline or the more direct route past Victor Hugo's house.

Places of interest nearby: The coast of Guernsey and all the island's attractions. Boat trips to Jersey, Alderney, Herm and Sark can easily be arranged. **Directions: Fermain Bay is 10 minutes from the airport and five minutes from St Peter Port on the east coast of Guernsey.**

Bella Luce Hotel & Restaurant

LA FOSSE, ST MARTIN, GUERNSEY, CHANNEL ISLANDS GY4 6EB
TEL: 01481 238764 FAX: 01481 239561 E-MAIL: info@bellalucehotel.guernsey.net

OWNER: Richard Cann
MANAGER: John Cockcroft

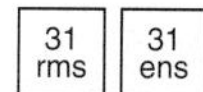  

S: From £30
D: From £60

The Bella Luce is one of Guernsey's original Norman manor houses. Set in splendid grounds on the most select side of the island, this perfectly preserved house includes extensions built in the 14th century. Happily the utmost care has been taken to maintain its period character during upgrading, so today's hotel offers excellent accommodation with every modern amenity.

Drinks are served throughout the day in the hotel's lounge bar, which dates back to the 11th century and is the oldest part of the building. Here, under the fine oak beamed ceiling, guests can enjoy a lunch and savour the cheerful and serene old world.

A varied table d'hôte menu, offering a wide range of English and Continental dishes, is provided in the restaurant which enjoys an excellent reputation throughout the island. A comprehensive à la carte menu featuring fresh seafood specialities is also available.

In a sun-trapped corner of the gardens there is a swimming pool surrounded by sun-beds and providing a perfect location for relaxation. Refreshments are served throughout the day and there is a sauna/solarium room nearby.

Places of interest nearby: Within easy reach of the three most beautiful south coast bays of Moulin Huet, Petit Port and Saints. Marine trips operate daily in season to Herm, Sark, Jersey and the nearby coast of France. **Directions: 5 minutes from the airport and St Peter Port.**

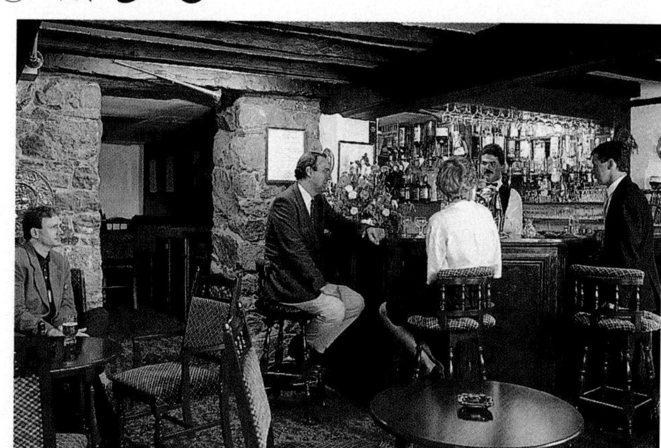

THE WHITE HOUSE

HERM ISLAND, GUERNSEY, CHANNEL ISLANDS GY1 3HR
TEL: 01481 722159 FAX: 01481 710066 E-MAIL: hotel@herm–island.com

OWNERS: Adrian and Pennie Heyworth
MANAGER: Sue Hester
CHEF: Chris Walder

39 rms | 39 ens | SMALL HOTEL

Room rate: from £59 per person (including dinner)

As wards of Herm Island, Adrian and Pennie Heyworth assume responsibility for the well-being of all visitors to their island home which is for all to enjoy at leisure. For an island just 1½ miles long its diversity is remarkable and during a two-hour stroll that takes in its cliff walks, white sandy coves and abundant wildlife no two moments are the same.

The magic starts to work from the moment of arrival at the pretty harbour, for in the absence of cars on Herm a tractor laden with guests' luggage chugs up from the jetty to The White House. Here, relaxation is the key, and guests can enjoy afternoon tea or a drink in its succession of homely lounges, in the bar or on the poolside patio.

In keeping with a cherished tradition there are no televisions, no clocks nor telephones in the hotel's 39 bedrooms, the best of which have balconies and sea views. Appointments are nonetheless faultless and all include spacious up-to-date private bathrooms. Families are made particularly welcome and high tea is a popular event with younger guests.

Seafood plays a prominent part on the menus: the hotel has its own oyster farm. Guernsey lobster, scallops and crab are landed regularly. Self-catering holiday cottages also available. **Places of interest nearby:** There is excellent fishing and snorkelling; yachts and cruisers can be chartered; and there are regular trips to Sark, Guernsey, Jersey and France. **Directions: Herm is reached by boat from Guernsey.**

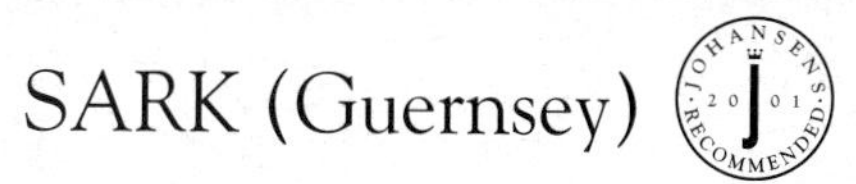

La Sablonnerie

LITTLE SARK, SARK, CHANNEL ISLANDS GY9 0SD
TEL: 01481 832061 FAX: 01481 832408

OWNER: Elizabeth Perrée

S: £77.50–£84.50
D: £148–£163.90
(including dinner)

Owner and manager Elizabeth Perrée considers La Sablonnerie an oasis of good living and courtesy rather than a luxury hotel. It is truly that – and more! It is an hotel of rare quality situated in a time warp of simplicity on a tiny, idyllic island where no motor cars are allowed and life ambles along at a peaceful, unhurried pace.

A vintage horse-drawn carriage collects guests from Sark's tiny harbour to convey them in style to the islands' southernmost tip - Little Sark. Crossing la Coupée, a narrow isthmus, guests can enjoy breathtaking views of the coast. Tranquil cosiness, friendliness and sophistication characterise this hotel with its low ceilings and 400 year old oak beams.

Opened in 1948 and retaining many of the characteristics of the old farmhouse, La Sablonnerie has been extended and discreetly modernised to provide 22 bedrooms which are charmingly individual in style and offer every amenity. The granite-walled bar, with its open fire, is a comfortable extra lounge where pre-dinner drinks can be enjoyed before sampling the delights of the candlelit restaurant. The hotel has a reputation for superb cuisine. Many of the dishes are prepared from produce grown on its own farm and gardens and enhanced by locally caught lobster and oysters.

Places of interest nearby: Many beauty spots such as Grande Grève, one of Sark's best sandy beaches, and the famous pools of Venus and Adonis. **Directions: By air or sea to Guernsey and then by ferry from St Peter Port.**

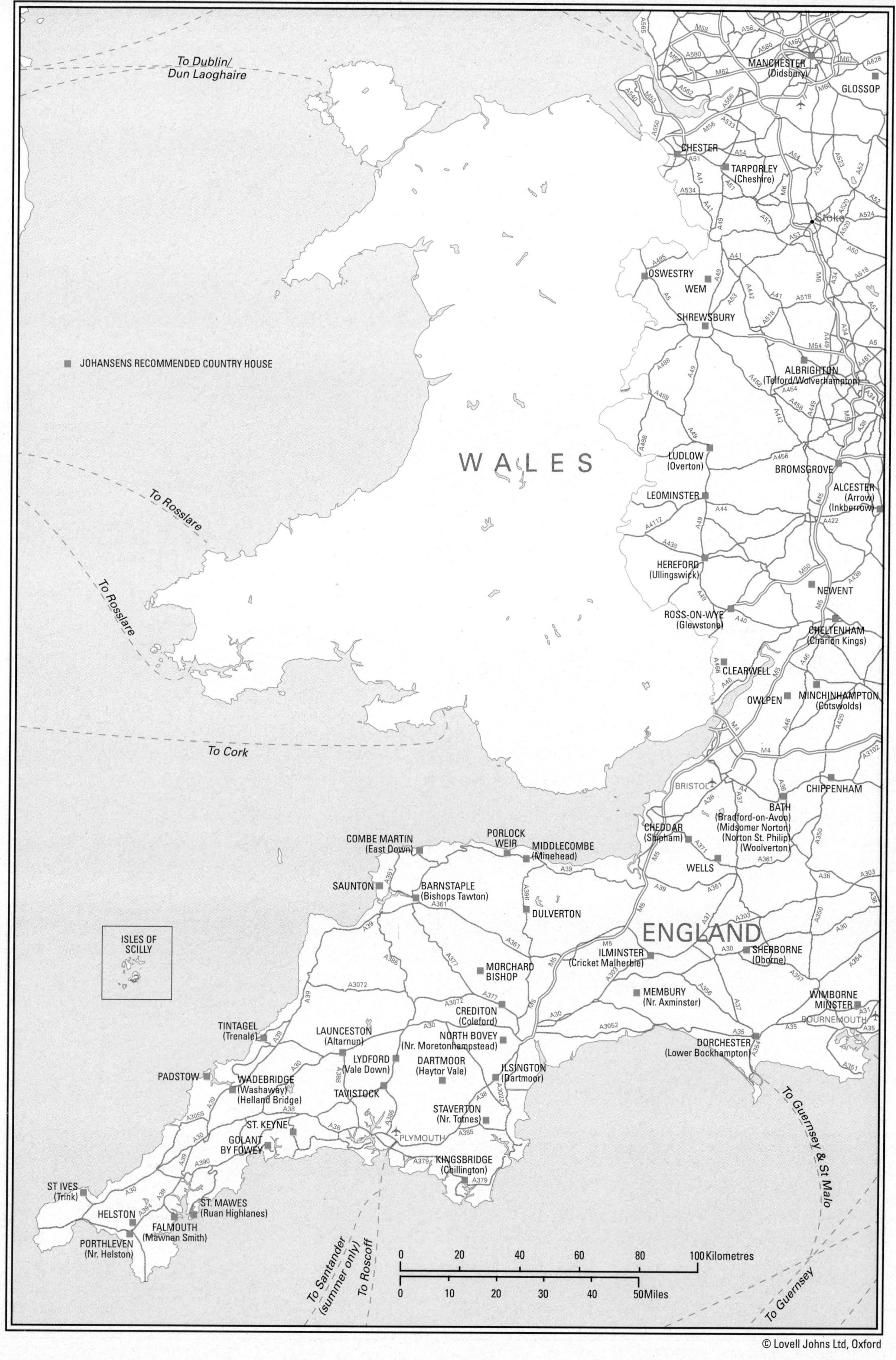
To Dublin/
Dun Laoghaire
JOHANSENS RECOMMENDED COUNTRY HOUSE
WALES
ENGLAND
To Rosslare
To Rosslare
To Cork
MANCHESTER
(Didsbury)
GLOSSOP
CHESTER
TARPORLEY
(Cheshire)
Stoke
OSWESTRY
WEM
SHREWSBURY
ALBRIGHTON
(Telford/Wolverhampton)
LUDLOW
(Overton)
BROMSGROVE
ALCESTER
(Arrow)
(Inkberrow)
LEOMINSTER
HEREFORD
(Ullingswick)
NEWENT
ROSS-ON-WYE
(Glewstone)
CHELTENHAM
(Charlton Kings)
CLEARWELL
OWLPEN
MINCHINHAMPTON
(Cotswolds)
BRISTOL
CHIPPENHAM
BATH
(Bradford-on-Avon)
(Midsomer Norton)
(Norton St. Philip)
(Woolverton)
CHEDDAR
(Shipham)
WELLS
COMBE MARTIN
(East Down)
PORLOCK
WEIR
MIDDLECOMBE
(Minehead)
SAUNTON
BARNSTAPLE
(Bishops Tawton)
DULVERTON
ILMINSTER
(Cricket Malherbie)
SHERBORNE
(Oborne)
MORCHARD
BISHOP
MEMBURY
(Nr. Axminster)
WIMBORNE
MINSTER
BOURNEMOUTH
CREDITON
(Coleford)
ISLES OF
SCILLY
TINTAGEL
(Trenale)
LAUNCESTON
(Altarnun)
NORTH BOVEY
(Nr. Moretonhampstead)
DORCHESTER
(Lower Bockhampton)
LYDFORD
(Vale Down)
DARTMOOR
(Haytor Vale)
ILSINGTON
(Dartmoor)
PADSTOW
WADEBRIDGE
(Washaway)
(Helland Bridge)
TAVISTOCK
STAVERTON
(Nr. Totnes)
ST. KEYNE
GOLANT
BY FOWEY
PLYMOUTH
KINGSBRIDGE
(Chillington)
ST IVES
(Trink)
HELSTON
ST. MAWES
(Ruan Highlanes)
FALMOUTH
(Mawnan Smith)
PORTHLEVEN
(Nr. Helston)
To Guernsey & St Malo
To Guernsey
To Santander
(summer only)
To Roscoff
0 20 40 60 80 100 Kilometres
0 10 20 30 40 50 Miles

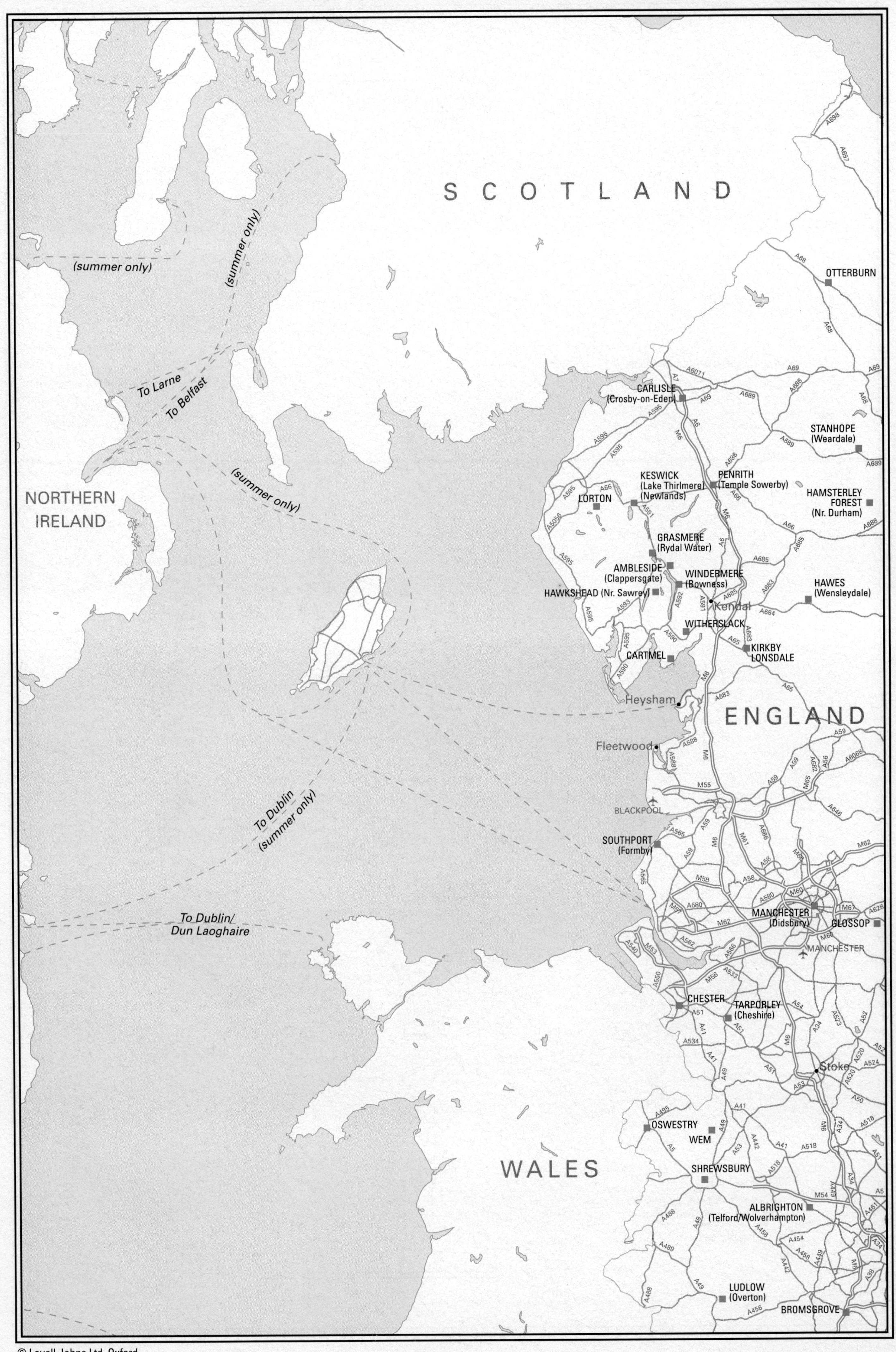
SCOTLAND
ENGLAND
WALES
NORTHERN IRELAND
(summer only)
(summer only)
To Larne
To Belfast
(summer only)
To Dublin (summer only)
To Dublin/ Dun Laoghaire
OTTERBURN
CARLISLE (Crosby-on-Eden)
STANHOPE (Weardale)
KESWICK (Lake Thirlmere) (Newlands)
PENRITH (Temple Sowerby)
HAMSTERLEY FOREST (Nr. Durham)
LORTON
GRASMERE (Rydal Water)
AMBLESIDE (Clappersgate)
WINDERMERE (Bowness)
HAWES (Wensleydale)
HAWKSHEAD (Nr. Sawrey)
Kendal
WITHERSLACK
KIRKBY LONSDALE
CARTMEL
Heysham
Fleetwood
BLACKPOOL
SOUTHPORT (Formby)
MANCHESTER (Didsbury)
GLOSSOP
MANCHESTER
CHESTER
TARPORLEY (Cheshire)
Stoke
OSWESTRY
WEM
SHREWSBURY
ALBRIGHTON (Telford/Wolverhampton)
LUDLOW (Overton)
BROMSGROVE

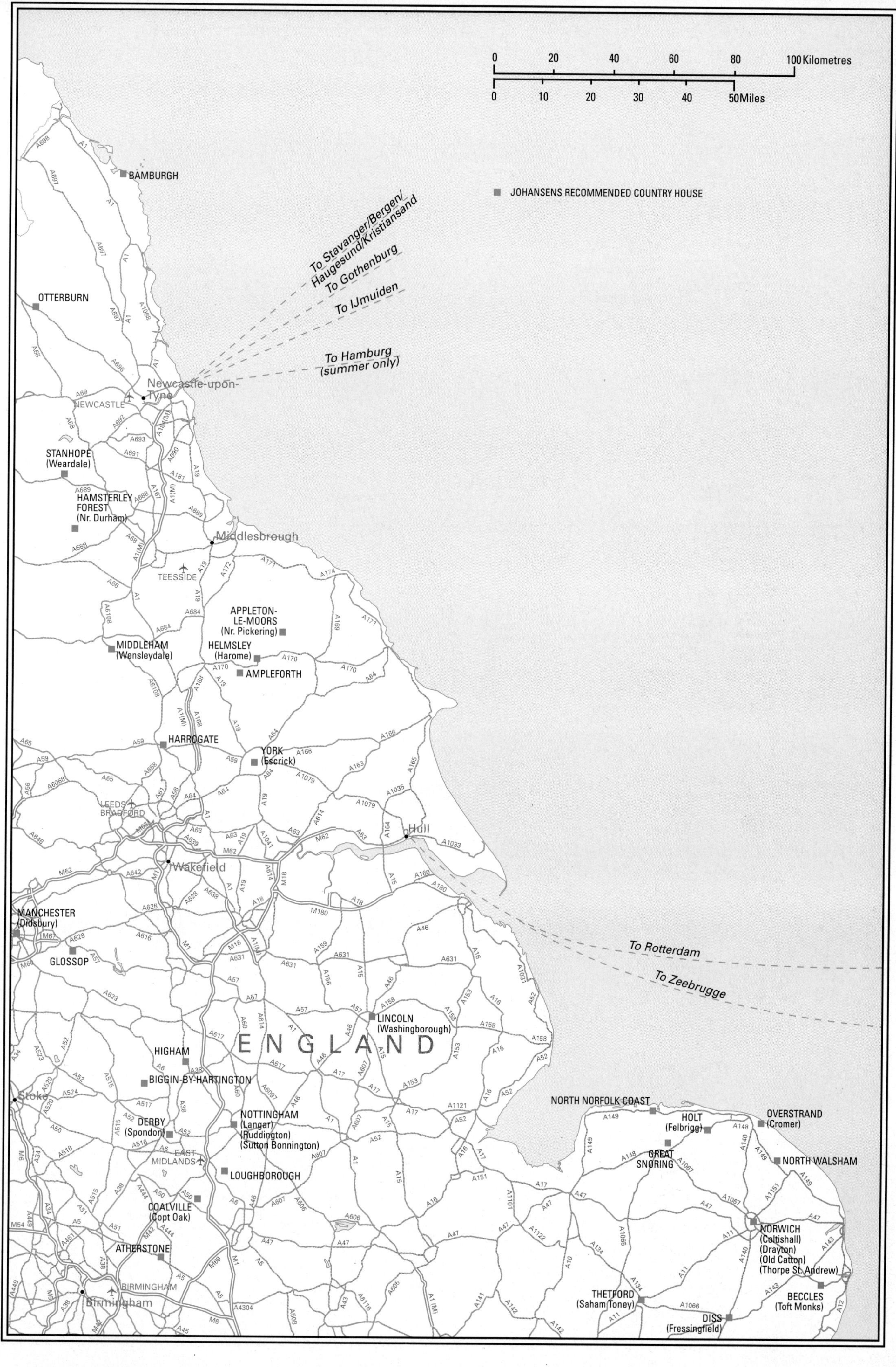

0 20 40 60 80 100 Kilometres
0 10 20 30 40 50 Miles
JOHANSENS RECOMMENDED COUNTRY HOUSE
BAMBURGH
OTTERBURN
To Stavanger/Bergen/
Haugesund/Kristiansand
To Gothenburg
To IJmuiden
To Hamburg
(summer only)
Newcastle-upon-
Tyne
NEWCASTLE
STANHOPE
(Weardale)
HAMSTERLEY
FOREST
(Nr. Durham)
Middlesbrough
TEESSIDE
APPLETON-
LE-MOORS
(Nr. Pickering)
MIDDLEHAM
(Wensleydale)
HELMSLEY
(Harome)
AMPLEFORTH
HARROGATE
YORK
(Escrick)
LEEDS
BRADFORD
Hull
Wakefield
MANCHESTER
(Didsbury)
GLOSSOP
To Rotterdam
To Zeebrugge
LINCOLN
(Washingborough)
ENGLAND
HIGHAM
BIGGIN-BY-HARTINGTON
Stoke
NOTTINGHAM
(Langar)
(Ruddington)
(Sutton Bonnington)
DERBY
(Spondon)
EAST
MIDLANDS
LOUGHBOROUGH
COALVILLE
(Copt Oak)
ATHERSTONE
BIRMINGHAM
Birmingham
NORTH NORFOLK COAST
HOLT
(Felbrigg)
OVERSTRAND
(Cromer)
GREAT
SNORING
NORTH WALSHAM
NORWICH
(Coltishall)
(Drayton)
(Old Catton)
(Thorpe St. Andrew)
THETFORD
(Saham Toney)
DISS
(Fressingfield)
BECCLES
(Toft Monks)

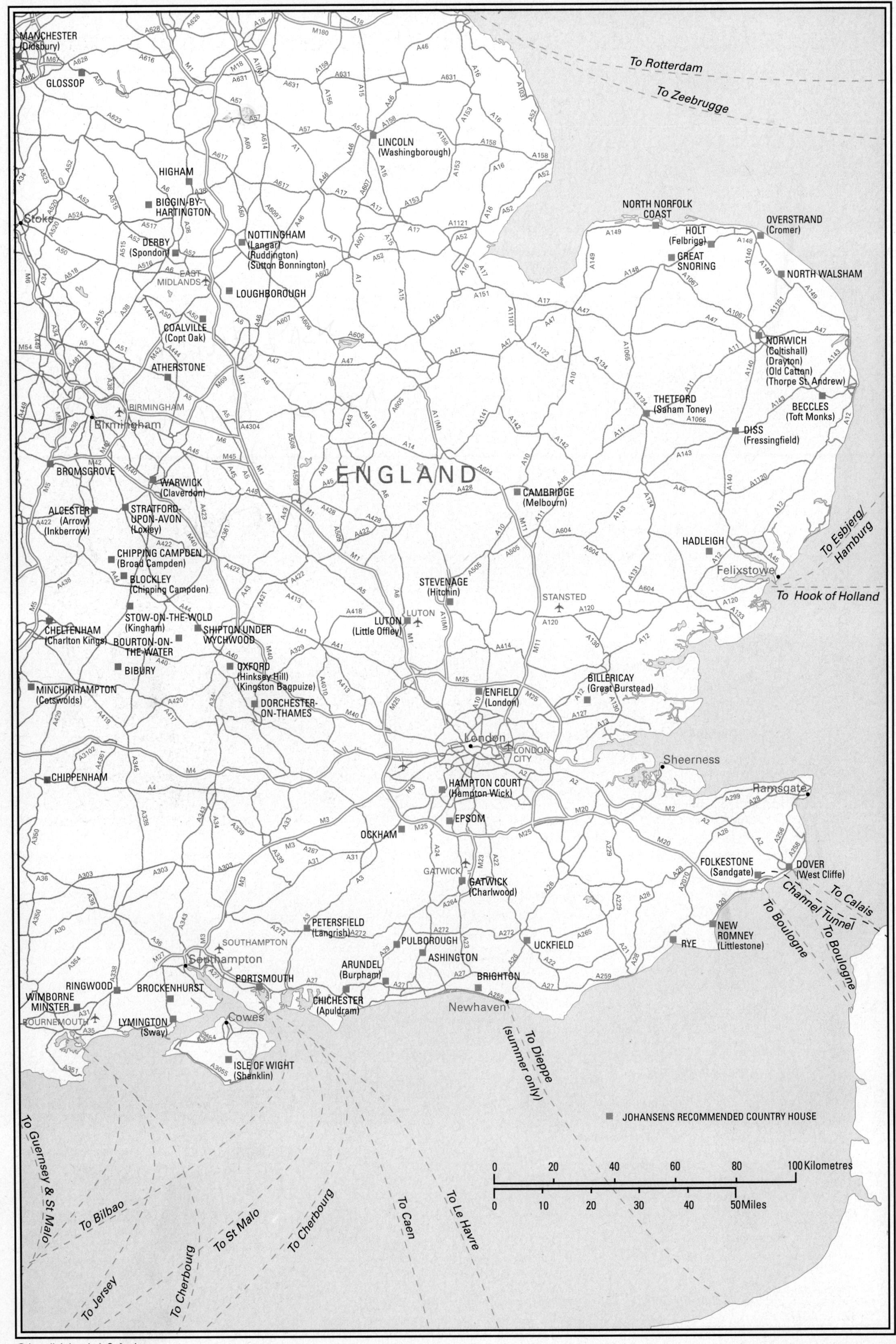

MANCHESTER (Didsbury)
GLOSSOP
To Rotterdam
To Zeebrugge
LINCOLN (Washingborough)
HIGHAM
BIGGIN-BY-HARTINGTON
Stoke
NORTH NORFOLK COAST
OVERSTRAND (Cromer)
HOLT (Felbrigg)
GREAT SNORING
NORTH WALSHAM
NOTTINGHAM (Langar) (Ruddington) (Sutton Bonnington)
DERBY (Spondon)
EAST MIDLANDS
LOUGHBOROUGH
COALVILLE (Copt Oak)
ATHERSTONE
NORWICH (Coltishall) (Drayton) (Old Catton) (Thorpe St. Andrew)
BECCLES (Toft Monks)
THETFORD (Saham Toney)
DISS (Fressingfield)
BIRMINGHAM
Birmingham
BROMSGROVE
WARWICK (Claverdon)
ENGLAND
CAMBRIDGE (Melbourn)
ALCESTER (Arrow) (Inkberrow)
STRATFORD-UPON-AVON (Loxley)
CHIPPING CAMPDEN (Broad Campden)
BLOCKLEY (Chipping Campden)
STOW-ON-THE-WOLD (Kingham)
SHIPTON UNDER WYCHWOOD
CHELTENHAM (Charlton Kings)
BOURTON-ON-THE-WATER
BIBURY
OXFORD (Hinksey Hill) (Kingston Bagpuize)
MINCHINHAMPTON (Cotswolds)
DORCHESTER-ON-THAMES
HADLEIGH
To Esbjerg/Hamburg
Felixstowe
To Hook of Holland
STEVENAGE (Hitchin)
STANSTED
LUTON (Little Offley)
LUTON
BILLERICAY (Great Burstead)
ENFIELD (London)
London
LONDON CITY
Sheerness
Ramsgate
CHIPPENHAM
HAMPTON COURT (Hampton Wick)
EPSOM
OCKHAM
GATWICK
GATWICK (Charlwood)
FOLKESTONE (Sandgate)
DOVER (West Cliffe)
To Calais
Channel Tunnel
To Boulogne
To Boulogne
PETERSFIELD (Langrish)
PULBOROUGH
ASHINGTON
UCKFIELD
RYE
NEW ROMNEY (Littlestone)
SOUTHAMPTON
Southampton
ARUNDEL (Burpham)
BRIGHTON
RINGWOOD
BROCKENHURST
PORTSMOUTH
CHICHESTER (Apuldram)
Newhaven
WIMBORNE MINSTER
BOURNEMOUTH
LYMINGTON (Sway)
Cowes
ISLE OF WIGHT (Shanklin)
To Dieppe (summer only)
JOHANSENS RECOMMENDED COUNTRY HOUSE
0 20 40 60 80 100 Kilometres
0 10 20 30 40 50 Miles
To Guernsey & St Malo
To Bilbao
To Jersey
To Cherbourg
To St Malo
To Cherbourg
To Caen
To Le Havre

England

Discover England's rich history by visiting an array of castles, cathedrals and gardens set amongst unique countryside.

Pulls Ferry, Norwich, Norfolk

Regional Tourist Boards

Cumbria Tourist Board
Ashleigh, Holly Road, Windermere
Cumbria LA23 2AQ
Tel: 015394 44444
England's most beautiful lakes and tallest mountains reach out from the Lake District National Park to a landscape of spectacular coasts, hills and dales.

East of England Tourist Board
Toppesfield Hall, Hadleigh
Suffolk IP7 5DN
Tel: 01473 822922
Cambridgeshire, Essex, Hertfordshire, Bedfordshire, Norfolk and Suffolk.

Heart of England Tourist Board
Woodside, Larkhill Road.
Worcester WR5 2EZ
Tel: 01905 763436
Lincolnshire, Gloucestershire, Hereford & Worcester, Shropshire, Staffordshire, Warwickshire, West Midlands, Derbyshire, Leicestershire, Northamptonshire, Nottinghamshire & Rutland. Represents the districts of Cherwell & West Oxfordshire in the county of Oxfordshire.

London Tourist Board
Glen House, Stag Place
London SW1E 5LT
Tel: 020 7932 2000
The Greater London area (see page 16)

Northumbria Tourist Board
Aykley Heads
Durham DH1 5UX
Tel: 0191 375 3000
The Tees Valley, Durham, Northumberland, Tyne & Wear.

North West Tourist Board
Swan House, Swan Meadow Road, Wigan Pier
Lancashire WN3 5BB
Tel: 01942 821222
Cheshire, Greater Manchester, Lancashire, Merseyside & the High Peak District of Derbyshire.

South East England Tourist Board
The Old Brew House, Warwick Park, Tunbridge Wells, Kent TN2 5TU
Tel: 01892 540766
East & West Sussex, Kent & Surrey

Southern Tourist Board
40 Chamberlayne Road, Eastleigh
Hampshire SO50 5JH
Tel: 01703 620006
East & North Dorset, Hampshire, Isle of Wight, Berkshire, Buckinghamshire & Oxfordshire.

West Country Tourist Board
60 St David's Hill, Exeter
Devon EX4 4SY
Tel: 01392 425426
Bath & NE Somerset, Bristol, Cornwall and the Isles of Scilly, Devon, Dorset (Western), North Somerset & Wiltshire.

Yorkshire Tourist Board
312 Tadcaster Road
York YO2 2HF
Tel: 01904 707961
Yorkshire and North & North East Lincolnshire.

Further Information

English Heritage
23rd Floor, Portland House, Stag Place
London SW1E 5EE
Tel: 020 7973 3000
Offers an unrivalled choice of properties to visit.

Historic Houses Association
2 Chester Street
London SW1X 7BB
Tel: 020 7259 5688
Ensures the survival of historic houses and gardens in private ownership in Great Britain

The National Trust
36 Queen Anne's Gate
London SW1H 9AS
Tel: 020 7222 9251
Cares for more than 590,000 acres of countryside and over 400 historic buildings.

TI 01722 334956

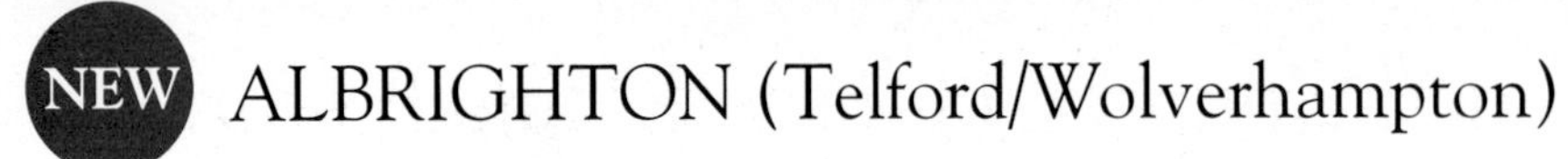

THE GRANGE HOTEL

PATSHULL PARK, BURNHILL GREEN, STAFFORDSHIRE WV6 7HY
TEL: 01902 701711 FAX: 01902 701791 E-MAIL: jo@serene.co.uk

OWNERS: John & Shirley Mathews

S: £65-115
D: £90-120

This little gem of a hotel is set in a truly idyllic location amidst acres of rolling parkland in the Patshull Estate with lakes and woodlands landscaped by Capability Brown.

Originally the coach house to Patshull Hall, this serene and tranquil hotel has recently undergone a substantial refurbishment programme to restore it to its original grandeur, and the result really is a triumph.

Every room is a delight to the eye, from the spacious en suite bedrooms with elegant drapes and canopied beds to the graceful dining room with lofty french doors – a glorious setting in which to enjoy the 7 course gourmet banquets. Guests may relax beside a log fire in the Drawing Room and admire the unspoilt views over the beautiful landscape.

The Mathews Family have masterminded this spectacular makeover, and have ensured that service has remained as immaculate as the décor. Issued with their own cordless phone on arrival, guests are aware that one quick phone call will answer their every need.

A range of stunning walks can be taken from the hotel doorstep, and riding, golf, and fishing can all be arranged from the hotel.

Places of interest nearby: Whitwick Manor, Boscobel House and Ironbridge are well worth a trip. **Directions: The hotel is just 7 miles from Telford and Wolverhampton and only 3 miles from the M54, coming from the M6. The Grange is the set in Patshull Estate, facing Patshull Hall.**

Arrow Mill Hotel And Restaurant

ARROW, NEAR ALCESTER, WARWICKSHIRE B49 5NL
TEL: 01789 762419 FAX: 01789 765170

OWNERS: The Woodhams Family

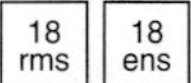    

  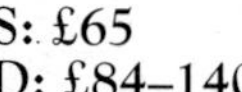

S: £65
D: £84–140

Once a working flour mill, Arrow Mill is proud of its listing in the Domesday Book, when it was valued at three shillings and sixpence. Since Norman times standards and inflation have risen. Today it remains a historic and charming building, although it offers its guests the most modern and comfortable accommodation.

Its rustic charm, enhanced by log fires and exposed beams, is complemented by a spectacular yet secluded riverside setting. Creature comforts are plentiful in the individually furnished bedrooms and panoramic views take in the mill pond, River Arrow and surrounding countryside.

A highly trained team of chefs uses only market-fresh ingredients in maintaining their uncompromising standards. The Millstream Restaurant incorporates the original working floor of the mill, with its wheel still driven by the flowing stream. It offers an à la carte menu and carefully selected wine list to satisfy the most discriminating palate. Similarly high standards are assured by the luncheons from the Miller's Table.

Residential conferences, business meetings, hospitality days and product launches can all be accommodated. **Places of interest nearby:** Stratford-upon-Avon, Warwick Castle and the Cotswolds are all nearby. Arrow Mill is closed from 26 December for two weeks. **Directions: Set back from the A435 1 mile south of Alcester.**

The Old Windmill

WITHYBED LANE, INKBERROW, WORCESTER WR7 4JL
TEL & FAX: 01386 792801 E-MAIL: sheila@theoldwindmill.co.uk

OWNERS: Sheila and Mike Dale

PRIVATE HOUSE

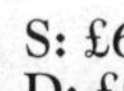

S: £60
D: £90

Built circa 1840, this Grade II listed former working mill and quarry is set in an attractive two-acre tree-lined garden with enchanting ponds and an abundance of wildlife. The friendly service afforded by the charming owners, Sheila and Mike Dale, adds to the pleasant ambience of The Old Windmill.

The four-storey house has an original and intriguing layout. The three en suite bedrooms are exceptional and have been individually decorated with dramatic drapes, soft pastel hues and luxurious furnishings. An open fireplace dominates the comfortable drawing room and is particularly inviting during winter. The property is unlicensed and guests may bring their own wine.

Nature enthusiasts will be delighted with the surrounding countryside that is home to song birds, squirrels, foxes, hare and badgers. The owners request arrivals after 4pm.

Places of interest nearby: This is an ideal base from which to explore the Malvern Hills, the surrounding Worcestershire countryside Stratford-upon-Avon the Cotswolds and Warwick Castle. Fans of the popular 'Archers' programme must visit The Old Bull pub in Inkberrow as it is claimed as the 'Bull in Ambridge'. **Directions: From the M40 out of London, head towards Oxford and then Birmingham. Exit at jct 15, take A46 to Stratford-upon-Avon. At the roundabout just before Alcester, turn right, then left at the next roundabout. Follow the A422 and signs to Inkberrow.**

NANNY BROW COUNTRY HOUSE HOTEL & RESTAURANT

CLAPPERSGATE, AMBLESIDE, CUMBRIA LA22 9NF
TEL: 015394 32036 FAX: 015394 32450 E-MAIL: reservations@nannybrowhotel.demon.co.uk

OWNERS: Michael and Carol Fletcher
MANAGER: David Lancaster
CHEF: Darren Priddeaux

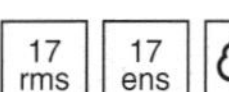

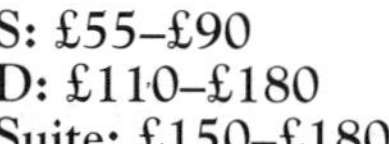

S: £55–£90
D: £110–£180
Suite: £150–£180

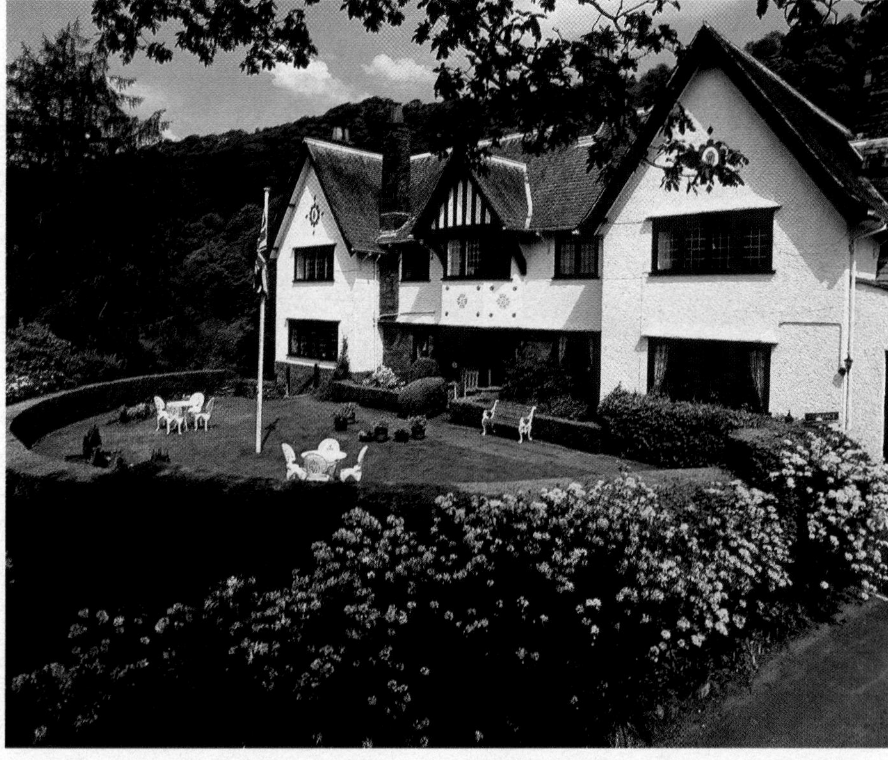

Away from the tourists visiting Ambleside at the northern end of Lake Windermere, a Victorian architect built Nanny Brow for himself on this magnificent site on Loughrigg Fell, which overlooks the dramatic Langdale Pikes and River Brathay. Set in five acres of landscaped gardens, the house has been converted into a comfortable elegant hotel whilst retaining its country house charm and has been awarded many accolades such as Hotel of the Year 1998 – Lancashire & Lake District Life, AA Romantic Hotel of the Year and holds two AA Red Rosettes. New arrivals appreciate the welcoming atmosphere of the lounge hall, filled with local antiques and find the drawing room with its graceful furniture and log fires very restful. The pretty bedrooms, individually decorated, have been thoughtfully equipped with many extras. The romantic Garden Suites have balconies or patios outside the sitting rooms. Guests mingle in the inviting Library Bar, before dining by candlelight in the RAC Merit Awards RHCC restaurant. The ever-changing five course menu features the chef's inspired rendition of traditional English dishes, complemented by the many fine wines. Fishing, putting and spa facilities, with membership of a private leisure club and a sailing cruiser on Lake Windermere are offered. Special breaks available. **Directions: From Ambleside A593 Coniston Road for 1m. Nanny Brow is on the right.**

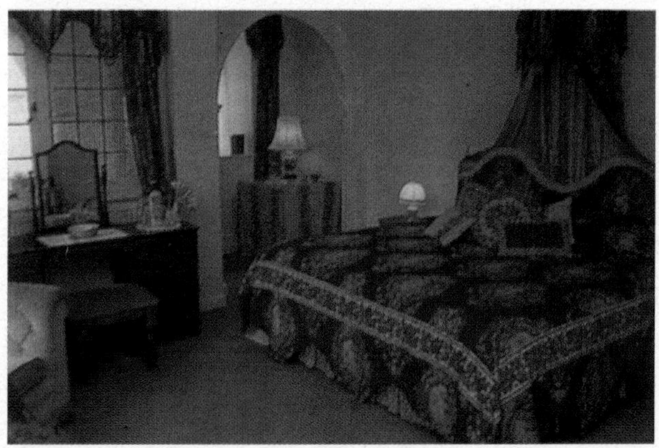

Shallowdale House

AMPLEFORTH, YORK, NORTH YORKSHIRE YO62 4DY
TEL: 01439 788325 FAX: 01439 788885

OWNERS: Anton Van Der Horst and Phillip Gill

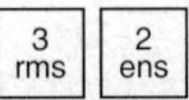 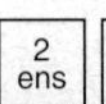 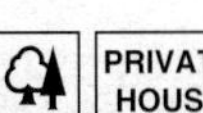

3 rms | 2 ens | PRIVATE HOUSE

S: £44–£55
D: £64–£80

With breathtaking views of unsullied countryside from every room, Shallowdale House is an elegant guest house, awarded five Diamonds and a Silver Award, situated at the edge of Ampleforth village, just inside the North York Moors National Park. Peace and tranquillity are the hallmarks and visitors can relax in the peaceful 2½ acre landscaped garden with its stunning views of the Coxwold Gilling Gap.

Guests relax in the drawing room, with its crackling log fire, or read in the comfortable sitting room, crammed with guide books and literature. Shallowdale House prides itself on the quality of its home-cooked food. Although self-taught, chef Phillip Gill concocts fare of remarkable flair and originality, all made with locally-produced goods. The bedrooms are comfortably decorated and have spacious bathrooms. The house is a totally non-smoking establishment. Special breaks available.

Places of interest nearby: Shallowdale House is a perfect base from which to explore the glorious routes of the North York Moors National Park. The historic town of York is nearby, while other towns of interest in the vicinity include Helmsley, Thirsk and Whitby. Visitors interested in the history of this culturally rich area should not miss Rievaulx Abbey, Castle Howard, or the Ryedale Folk Museum.

Directions: Shallowdale House is on the west side of Ampleforth. From York, take B1363, turning left at Brandsby. From Thirsk, take A170.

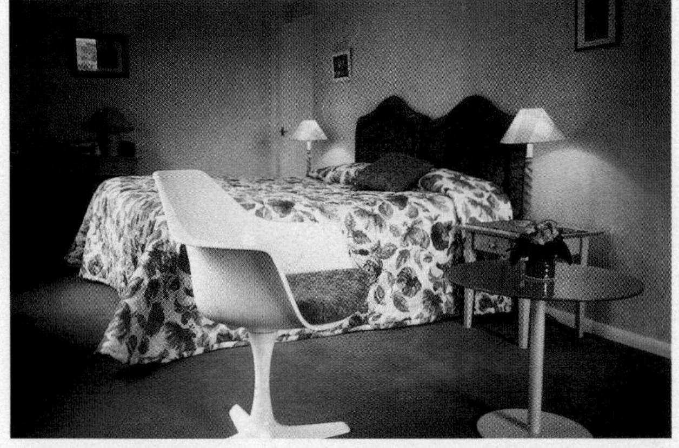

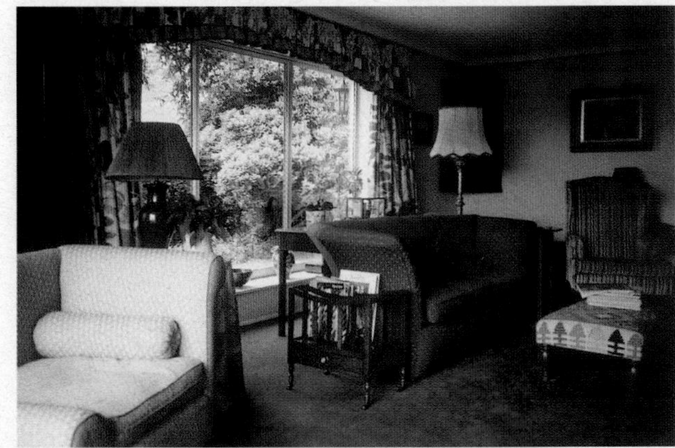

Appleton Hall

APPLETON-LE-MOORS, NORTH YORKSHIRE YO62 6TF
TEL: 01751 417227 FAX: 01751 417540

OWNERS: Edward and Wendy Horne

S: £70–£75
D: £140–£162
(including 5 course dinner)

Appleton Hall is a focal point of the historic Yorkshire village of Appleton-le-Moors, which lies on the southern side of the North Yorkshire Moors National Park. The hotel is surrounded by beautiful mature landscaped gardens where guests can sit and relax or stroll at their leisure. The spacious and elegant lounge and dining room both have open fires in winter. Visitors are heartened by the sense of peace and comfort this inviting country house offers. Edward, Wendy and their staff maintain a high standard of service and hospitality.

The nine en suite bedrooms have attractive views and are all fully equipped to provide modern comforts, two have their own lounges. One of the rooms has a four-poster bed. There is a cosy well-stocked bar in which to rest before dinner. The choice five-course table d'hôte menu is accompanied by a comprehensive selection of quality wines.

Places of interest nearby: The enchanting North York moors and steam railway, Castle Howard, Ryedales many attractions, the rugged East Coast and York. **Directions: Appleton-le-Moors is between Kirbymoorside and Pickering, just north off the A170. Leave the A1 near Thirsk from the north or from the south the A64 junction for York and Scarborough.**

M 16 12

BURPHAM COUNTRY HOUSE HOTEL

OLD DOWN, BURPHAM, NR ARUNDEL, WEST SUSSEX BN18 9RJ
TEL: 01903 882160 FAX: 01903 884627

OWNERS: George and Marianne Walker
CHEF: Stephen Piggott

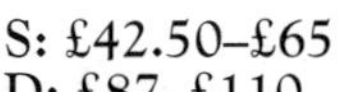

S: £42.50–£65
D: £87–£110

This charming Country House Hotel nestles in a fold of the Sussex South Downs – just perfect for a 'Stress Remedy Break'.

The ten en-suite bedrooms are all tastefully furnished with telephone, television, hairdryer, and tea/coffee facility. A lovely old world garden, with a croquet lawn, surrounds the hotel.

Drinks before dinner can be enjoyed by the open fire in the comfortable Cocktail Lounges. A good wine list is available with most countries represented. A fine new conservatory addition to the dining room makes a quite delightful setting in which to enjoy the excellent award-winning cuisine of Stephen Piggott. The Hotel has won a Silver award from the English Tourist Board for quality and the most prestigious Johansens 1999 award for 'Most Excellent Service'.

Special breaks are offered throughout the year. Golf, riding, fishing and sailing are all available in the locality. Racing at Goodwood and Fontwell.

Places of interest nearby: Burpham has a beautiful and historic Norman church, while Arundel, with its Wildfowl Sanctuary and renowned Castle, is three miles away. The coast lies within six miles. **Directions: The Hotel is signposted on the A27 east of Arundel railway bridge. Turn off here and follow this road for 2½ miles.**

THE MILL HOUSE HOTEL

MILL LANE, ASHINGTON, WEST SUSSEX RH20 3BX
TEL: 01903 892426 E-MAIL: mill1@netcomuk.co.uk

OWNERS: Simon and Maria Hudson

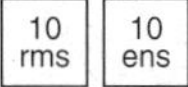    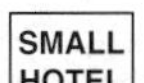

S: £49–£57
D: £79–£89

This charming Grade II listed building exudes warmth and character. Vestiges of the past are evident throughout the country house, and the original paintings adorning the walls and the antiques in the public rooms form a lasting testament to its 17th century past.

Following extensive renovation in 1997, the house combines the charm and attentive service associated with bygone days with the modern facilities of the present. The enthusiastic owners, Simon and Maria Hudson, and their gracious staff provide a helpful yet unobtrusive service. The bedrooms, some of which have recently been refurbished, are simple yet stylish.

Gastronomes will be impressed with the excellent cuisine which is complemented by a good selection of wines, liqueurs and Cognacs. The menu includes delights such as garlic roasted tenderloin of pork with a stem ginger risotto and a juniper berry sauce. Accommodating up to 30 people, the private dining room is ideal for small conferences and meetings and for private dining.

Places of interest nearby: Heritage enthusiasts will be delighted with the situation of this property as Parham House and Arundel Castle and Cathedral are within easy reach. Popular daytime excursions include trips to the pleasant beaches of Chichester and Brighton. **Directions: Ashington is west of the A24 and north of the junction with the A283. If travelling from the North, follow the large brown sign.**

Chapel House

FRIARS' GATE, ATHERSTONE, WARWICKSHIRE CV9 1EY
TEL: 01827 718949 FAX: 01827 717702

OWNERS: Chapel House (Atherstone) Ltd
MANAGING DIRECTOR: David Arnold

10 rms | 10 ens | SMALL HOTEL

S: £52.50–£70
D: £75–£90

A former dower house to the now demolished Atherstone Hall, Chapel House is discreetly tucked away in the corner of Atherstone's market square, within a walled garden that remains a particularly attractive feature of the property. With the oldest part of the house dating from about 1720, subsequent additions were made until 1879. Many original features have been retained and others carefully restored so that the house retains the elegance of an earlier age.

Holder of two AA Rosettes since 1995, the restaurant at Chapel House has acquired an enviable reputation for high quality, imaginative food and an extensive and adventurous wine cellar and most attentive service. Chef Adam Bennett uses the very best ingredients and changes the à la carte menu every five or six weeks. Speciality and themed evenings are noteworthy events and special dietary needs can be catered for by prior arrangement. Closed on Christmas Day and Boxing Day, Chapel House is just 25 minutes from the centres of Birmingham and Leicester and is most conveniently situated for those visiting the NEC or using Birmingham's International Airport.

Places of interest nearby: Bosworth Battlefield, Tamworth Castle, Arbury Hall, Lichfield and Coventry Cathedrals and the many industrial museums of the Midlands. Also close is the Belfry Golf Centre. **Directions: On A5 about 8 miles south-east of M42 Jct10. Chapel House is in the market square beside the church.**

WAREN HOUSE HOTEL

WAREN MILL, BAMBURGH, NORTHUMBERLAND NE70 7EE
TEL: 01668 214581 FAX: 01668 214484 E-MAIL: enquiries@warenhousehotel.co.uk

OWNERS: Peter and Anita Laverack
CHEFS: Paul Tindle

10 rms | 10 ens | SMALL HOTEL

S: £57.50–£67.50
D: £115–£135
Suite: £155–£185

"To visit the North East and not to stay here, would be foolish indeed". So says one entry in a visitors book that is filled with generous and justified praise for this delightful traditional country house which lives up to all its promises and expectations and beyond. The hotel is set in six acres of gardens and woodland on the edge of Budle Bay Bird Sanctuary overlooking Holy Island and two miles from the majestic Bamburgh Castle.

The owners, Anita and Peter, do not cater for children under 14, so they are able to offer a rare commodity of peace and tranquillity even during the busy summer months. Throughout the hotel, the antique furnishings and the immaculate and well-chosen décor evoke a warm, friendly and charming ambience.

Seated in the candlelit dining room, surrounded by family pictures and portraits, guests can select dishes from the daily changing menu and wines from over 250 bins. There is a boardroom for executive meetings. Dogs by prior arrangement. Special short breaks available all year.

Places of interest nearby: The Farne Islands are just a boat trip away, while Bamburgh, Alnwick and Dunstanburgh Castles along with Holy Island are nearby. Waren House is open all year. **Directions: There are advance warning signs on the A1 both north and south. Take B1342 to Waren Mill. Hotel (floodlit at night) is on south-west corner of Budle Bay just two miles from Bamburgh.**

M 25 14

DOWNREW HOUSE HOTEL

BISHOPS TAWTON, BARNSTAPLE, DEVON EX32 0DY
TEL: 01271 342497 FAX: 01271 323947 E-MAIL: downrew@globalnet.co.uk

OWNERS: Patrick and Fiona Byrne

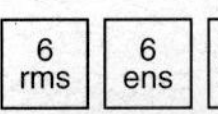

S: £55
D: £95–£130

Built in 1640 and enlarged in the early years of the 18th century, this Queen Anne-style house is surrounded by 12 acres of attractive meadowland and gardens and lies 500ft above sea level facing the slopes of Codden Hill.

Inside, the elegant air of an English country house blends harmoniously with a relaxed ambience, making this an ideal escape from the pressures of a hectic lifestyle. The well-appointed en suite bedrooms are peaceful and relaxing and overlook the beautiful grounds and countryside beyond.

The comfortable drawing room is ideal for reclining before feasting in the restaurant on succulent dishes made with fresh local produce and home-grown herbs and vegetables from the kitchen garden. The daily changing menu includes delicious West Country specialities.

Short breaks are available.

Places of interest nearby: Popular day trips include visits to the Maritime Museum at Appledore or exploring the many National Trust properties and gardens within the area, such as Tapeley Park, Rosemoor and Arlington Court. Walkers may follow the Tarka Trail or one of the many wonderful coastal paths. **Directions: From M5, exit at junction 27, and join A361 to Barnstaple. Then take A39 towards Bideford and at the next roundabout join A337. Follow through Bishops Tawton and at the garage on the right, join the lane directly opposite.**

M 40

Apsley House

141 NEWBRIDGE HILL, SOMERSET BA1 3PT
TEL: 01225 336966 FAX: 01225 425462 E-MAIL: info@apsley-house.co.uk

OWNERS: David and Annie Lanz

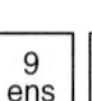

S: £55–£75
D: £70–£120

One mile from the centre of Bath, this elegant Georgian house was built in 1830 and is set in a delightful garden.

The hosts, David and Annie Lanz, greet guests with a warm welcome into their home, with its magnificently proportioned reception rooms which have been refurbished in great style and comfort including the addition of two new rooms opening onto the garden. A quite delicious breakfast is the only meal served, although drinks are available. David and Annie will recommend local restaurants and inns which visitors will enjoy.

The bedrooms are invitingly romantic with lovely drapery and delightful en suite bathrooms. Televisions almost seem to intrude in this timeless décor. Private parking available.

Places of interest nearby: There is so much to see and do in Bath, the centre of which is just a 25 minutes stroll from Apsley House. The magnificent architecture includes the Assembly Rooms, mentioned so often in Jane Austen's and in Georgette Heyer's historical novels, the Royal Crescent and the Roman Baths. Fascinating museums, the thriving theatre and excellent shopping all add to ones enjoyment of this lovely city. The Cotswolds, Mendip Hills, Stourhead, Stonehenge, Avebery and Longleat are within driving distance. **Directions: The hotel lies one mile west of the centre of Bath, on the A431 which branches off A4, the Upper Bristol Road.**

BATH LODGE HOTEL

NORTON ST PHILIP, BATH, SOMERSET BA3 6NH
TEL: 01225 723040 FAX: 01225 723737 E-MAIL: walker@bathlodge.demon.co.uk

OWNERS: Graham and Nicola Walker

8 rms | 8 ens | SMALL HOTEL

S: from £50
D: £75–£110

The Bath Lodge Hotel, originally called Castle Lodge, was built between 1806 and 1813 as one of six lodges added to a former gentleman's residence known as Farleigh House. This splendid building, with its towers, battlements, portcullis and heraldic shields, is redolent of Arthurian romance and offers guests a delightful setting in which to escape the stresses and strains of modern life.

The rooms, which are superbly decorated and furnished, are beautifully located and have many castellated features within them. Three rooms overlook the magnificent natural gardens with their cascading stream and the adjacent deer forest. The main entrance hall, lounge and conservatory all contain oak beamed ceilings, natural masonry and large log burning fireplaces. All the rooms are furnished in keeping with this unique building.

An excellent breakfast is served at the hotel. A five course dinner is available Friday and Saturday evenings. Alternatively there are many restaurants locally and in Bath. The hotel has a no-smoking policy, but guests may smoke in the conservatory area.

Places of interest nearby: Stonehenge and Longleat. Bath Lodge is an ideal location for enjoying the tourist attractions of the World Heritage City of Bath itself. Wells and Bristol are also both within easy reach. **Directions: From Bath take the A36 Warminster road. Bath Lodge is on your left after approximately seven miles.**

 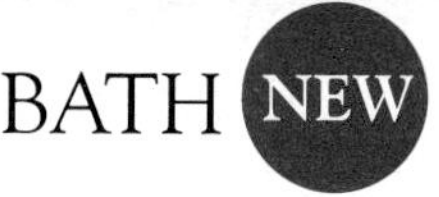

THE COUNTY HOTEL

18/19 PULTENEY ROAD, BATH, SOMERSET BA2 4EZ
TEL: 01225 425003 FAX: 01225 466493 E-MAIL: reservations@county-hotel.co.uk

OWNERS: Charles and Maureen Kent and Sandra Masson

22 rms | 22 ens | SMALL HOTEL

S: £60
D: £90–£155

The County Hotel stands tall and regal just a few minutes stroll from the city centre shops and attractions. It is an attractive stone built building with a frontage enhanced by slim, arched and sparkling white sash windows and twin balconies ornamented with open stone balustrades.

Completely refurbished in 1999, décor and sympathetic modernisation have resulted in the creation of elegant and relaxing accommodation. The 22 en suite bedrooms are exquisite and have every comfort to help guests feel at home. Some have splendid views over the Bath cricket ground. Breakfast is served in an intimate dining room which opens onto a conservatory where morning coffee, afternoon tea and light lunches can be ordered.

Dinner is not available but the hotel's hospitable owners will happily help select one of the many nearby restaurants for an evening out. Pre or after dinner drinks can be enjoyed in the hotel's cosy bar or lounge. The hotel has a non-smoking policy apart from the bar area.

Places of interest nearby: Among the many places to visit in the city are the Roman Baths, Pump Room, Royal Crescent, the thriving theatre and fascinating museums. Ample parking available. **Directions: From M4 junction 18 take the A46 and A4 towards Bath. Just before the city centre turn left onto the A36 ring road and follow signs for Exeter and Wells. The hotel is on the right after the Holburne Museum.**

THE OLD PRIORY HOTEL

CHURCH SQUARE, MIDSOMER NORTON, BATH, SOMERSET BA3 2HX
TEL: 01761 416784/410846 FAX: 01761 417851/2 E-MAIL: reservations@theoldpriory.com

OWNERS: Terri Knight
CHEF: Andy Jenner

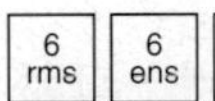

S: £60–67.50
D: £90–£110

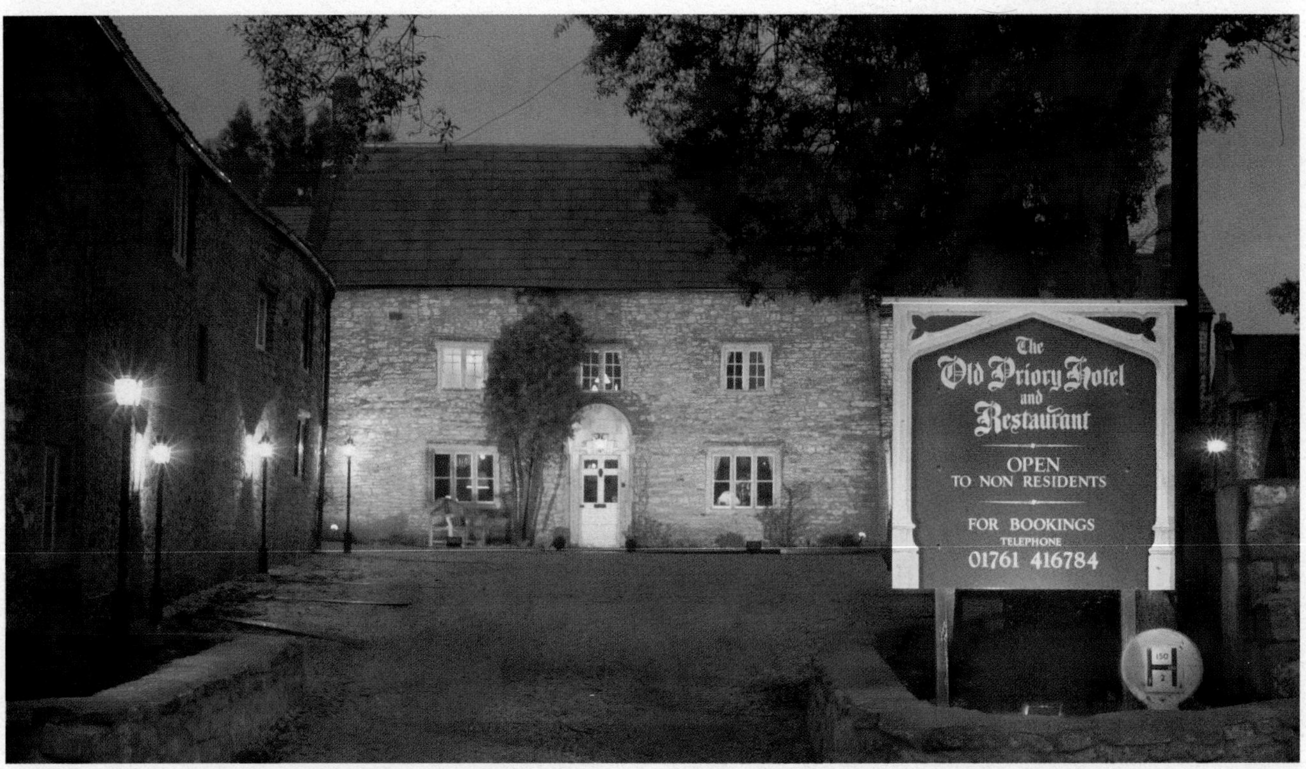

The Old Priory, circa 1152, sits in the quiet town of Midsomer Norton. The décor is Jacobean in style and the house was home to an order of monks who founded Christ College, Oxford and was owned by the college until 1712.

The charm and character of bygone times have been preserved with large Inglenook fireplaces, flagstone floors and oak beams, featured throughout the property.

The six bedrooms are all en suite and offer a range of modern comforts. Each room is individual in character, reflecting the age and uniqueness of this listed property. Fresh, local produce is used to prepare the fine cuisine, served in the attractive dining room.

Places of interest nearby: These include the Roman Baths at Bath, Cheddar Gorge and Caves, Wookey Hole and Glastonbury. The area is a delight for heritage enthusiasts as Longleat House and Safari Park, Stourhead House and Gardens, Castle Combe and Wells Cathedral are all within easy reach. **Directions: From M4, exit at junction 18 onto A46 to Bath. Join A367 towards Exeter and at Radstock turn right to Midsomer Norton. Left at roundabout into High Street then follow the brown signs.**

M 16

Paradise House

HOLLOWAY, BATH, SOMERSET BA2 4PX
TEL: 01225 317723 FAX: 01225 482005 E-MAIL: info@paradise-house.co.uk

OWNERS: David and Annie Lanz

SMALL HOTEL

S: £50–£75
D: £65–£130

In the peaceful grounds of this early 18th century mansion house, guests will forget that they are only seven minutes' walk from the Roman Baths, Pump Room and Abbey in the centre of the beautiful Georgian city of Bath.

Situated in a quiet cul-de-sac, Paradise House has been carefully modernised and restored to a high standard to enhance its classical elegance. Ornate plaster ceilings and a marble fireplace adorn the public rooms; where the décor is essentially a fusion of antique and contemporary furniture and soft pastel fabrics. The new garden room is glorious, featuring a sumptuous four-poster bed and Jacuzzi bath. The large walled garden, with its fish pond and rose covered pergola, is a delightful sun-trap affording a panoramic vista of the city and surrounding landscape, where guests may enjoy a game of boules.

The owners, David and Annie, extend a friendly welcome to their guests and are on hand to offer advice on the many nearby attractions. Although neither lunch nor dinner is served, details of over 85 local restaurants are provided. Garage parking is available.

Places of interest nearby: Wells, Glastonbury and Stonehenge are nearby. The city is also notable as a fashionable shopping centre and home of the arts. **Directions: Enter Bath on A4 London Road. Turn left onto A36. Take first left after viaduct onto A367 Exeter Road. Go left at Day and Pierce and down hill into Holloway cul-de-sac.**

Villa Magdala

HENRIETTA ROAD, BATH, SOMERSET BA2 6LX
TEL: 01225 466329 FAX: 01225 483207 E-MAIL: jsvilla@villamagdala.co.uk

OWNERS: Mr and Mrs Roy Thwaites

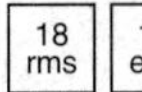
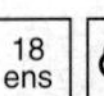

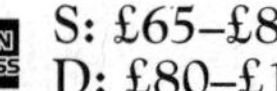

S: £65–£85
D: £80–£120

Built in 1868, the Villa Magdala is steeped in a most interesting history. The property takes its name from one of Sir Charles Napier's victories in Ethiopia as Sir Charles himself was a resident in the road at the time of construction. All the attractions of Bath are within easy reach, making the house an ideal choice for those wishing to discover the city.

The 18 bedrooms are well-appointed and feature an array of modern conveniences from colour televisions and hairdryers to refreshment trays. All are en suite. The airy dining room provides a most convivial ambience in which to enjoy a traditional English breakfast whilst at dinnertime, the attentive owners are pleased to recommend some of the many nearby restaurants and brasseries.

Places of interest nearby: Pulteney Bridge, the Roman Baths and Pump Room are only a five minute walk away whilst keen shoppers will be pleased with the variety of individual and specialist shops in the centre of Bath. The National Trust village of Lacock is worth a visit and the area abounds with many stately homes and museums. There are delightful canalside walks along the Kennet and Avon canal. **Directions: From M4, junction 18, take the A46 to Bath. Turn right into London Road, left at lights, over Cleveland Bridge and second turning right into Henrietta Road.**

Widbrook Grange

TROWBRIDGE ROAD, BRADFORD-ON-AVON, WILTSHIRE BA15 1UH
TEL: 01225 864750/863173 FAX: 01225 862890

OWNERS: John and Pauline Price

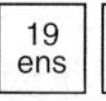    SMALL HOTEL

S: £69–£95
D: £95–£120

According to the ancient rent books, Widbrook Grange was built as a model farm in the 18th century amid eleven acres of idyllic grounds, traversed by a stream. No longer a farm, Widbrook still reflects its agricultural heritage. Together resident owners John and Pauline Price have converted the Grange with skill and care to combine contemporary comforts with a traditional ambience.

All of the bedrooms, whether a spacious four-poster room or one that is petite and cosy, are well appointed with facilities and antique furnishings. Some of the bedrooms are in the recently converted 200-year old stone barn which forms the courtyard. Evening dinner is available Monday to Thursday in the spacious antique furnished dining room and there are also many excellent restaurants locally about which your hosts can advise you. The Manvers suite, with its oak table and carver chairs has been designed for board meetings, seminars and private functions.

Widbrook boasts a superb indoor heated swimming pool and gymnasium. There is an arrangement with nearby Kingsdown Golf Club. Riding and fishing can also be arranged.

Places of interest nearby: Longleat House and Safari Park, Bath, Avebury and Stonehenge. **Directions: From Bradford-on-Avon take the A363 Trowbridge Road, the Grange is on the right after the canal bridge.**

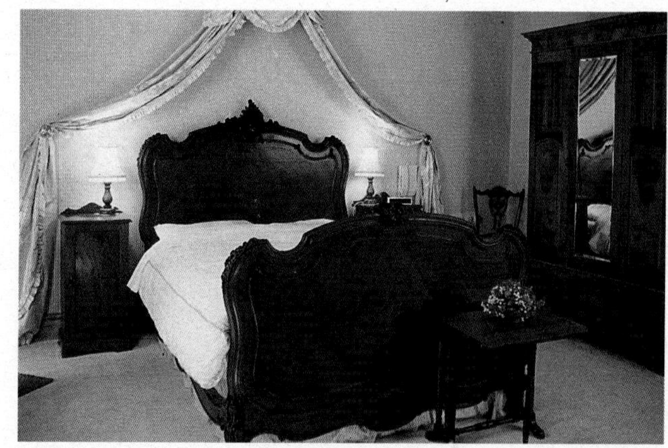

WOOLVERTON HOUSE

WOOLVERTON, NR BATH, SOMERSET BA3 6QS
TEL: 01373 830415 FAX: 01373 831243 E-MAIL: mail@bathhotel.com

OWNERS: Noel and Marina Terry

12 rms | 12 ens | SMALL HOTEL

S: £44–£55
D: £55–£90

This early 19th century house, built originally as a rectory for the 'United Parishes of Woolverton & Rode', has been sympathetically converted and restored to become an elegant English country house. It is set in over 2½ acres of grounds and commands scenic views over the 'glebe lands' on which the parson traditionally had grazing rights.

Today Woolverton House has been developed by its present-day hospitable owners into a retreat where the emphasis is on heritage, history and nature. The gardens are full of colour and also include a narrow gauge steam railway.

All the bedrooms are pleasantly decorated and furnished with private bathrooms en suite. They are fully equipped with colour television, direct dial telephone, hospitality tray, trouser press, hairdryer and minibar. Both the dining room and drawing room have log fires in the cooler months and the conservatory bar is pleasant all year.

The restaurant is beautifully furnished in excellent taste with food and wines to match and has been awarded an RAC dining award.

Places of interest nearby: There is plenty to explore in the historical and agricultural history of this area – most within a 20 mile radius. Major attractions include Bath, Longleat, East Somerset steam railway, Cheddar Caves, Wookey Hole and Rode Tropical Bird Gardens. **Directions: From M4 exit 17 take A350 and then A361 for Woolverton – or on A36 halfway between Bath and Warminster.**

The Elms

TOFT MONKS, BECCLES, SUFFOLK NR34 0EJ
TEL: 01502 677380 FAX: 01502 677362

OWNERS: Richard and Catriona Freeland

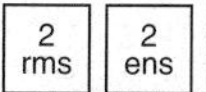
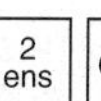

S: £35–£45
D: £70–£80

Situated on the rural Norfolk and Suffolk border, The Elms is set among rolling farmland, beautiful gardens and its very own water lily covered moat. This elegant, well-proportioned Queen Anne house offers guests comfortable rooms and open fireplaces, with an ambience of informal hospitality created by owners Richard and Teena Freeland.

Visitors to the house are treated to generous meals, prepared by Teena and stylishly served in the classically furnished dining room, or they can take advantage of a spacious, well-equipped self-catering cottage located within the grounds.

The Elms is an ideal base from which to enjoy cycling, fishing, woodland walks, and lazy boat trips on the Norfolk Broads. Whether guests choose to partake of these and other activities available such as tennis or simply unwind, they can rest assured that they will be pampered by attention to detail and lovely surroundings.

Places of interest nearby: The market town of Beccles, and Bungay, a must for keen antique hunters. Southwold, a charming seaside town is also nearby, as is the cathedral city of Norwich. **Directions: From Beccles take A146 Norwich Road. At the roundabout take the A143 towards Great Yarmouth. The village of Toft Monks is about one and a half miles. At the Toft Lion Pub turn right and proceed to t-junction ¼ mile, bear right and carry straight ahead to Elms on the right ½ mile on.**

Bibury Court

BIBURY COURT, BIBURY, GLOUCESTERSHIRE GL7 5NT
TEL: 01285 740337 FAX: 01285 740660 E-MAIL: SG@biburycourt.co.uk

OWNERS: Jane Collier, Andrew and Anne Johnston
MANAGER: Simon Gould

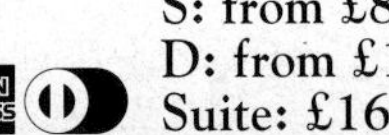

S: from £80
D: from £105
Suite: £160

Past visitors to Bibury Court are reputed to have included Charles II and during the reign of George III, the Prince Regent. This gracious mansion dates from Tudor times, but the main part was built in 1633 by Sir Thomas Sackville, an illegitimate son of the 1st Earl of Dorset. After generations of illustrious owners, it became a hotel in 1968.

The great house is set on the outskirts of Bibury, which William Morris called "the most beautiful village in England". As a hotel, it is run on country house lines with one of the main objectives being the provision of good food and wine in informal and pleasurable surroundings. Log fires during the cooler months add to the comfort of guests.

There are some lovely panelled rooms in the house, many containing antique furniture. Many of the bedrooms have four posters, all have private bathrooms and for those who like greater privacy there is the Sackville suite.

Trout fishing is available in the Coln, which forms the southern boundary of the hotel's six acres of grounds and there are golf courses at Burford and Cirencester. Water sports and riding are available nearby. The hotel is closed at Christmas.

Places of interest nearby: Bibury Court is ideally placed for touring the Cotswolds, while Stratford, Oxford, Cheltenham and Bath are all within easy reach.

Directions: Bibury is on the B4425, seven miles from Burford and seven miles from Cirencester.

Biggin Hall

BIGGIN-BY-HARTINGTON, BUXTON, DERBYSHIRE SK17 0DH
TEL: 01298 84451 FAX: 01298 84681 E-MAIL: Bigginhall@compuserve.com

OWNER: James Moffett

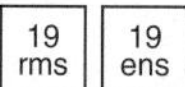   

S: £40–£55
D: £50–£75

Centrally situated in the Peak District National Park, Biggin Hall is a 17th century, Grade II* listed property set in eight acres of grounds. Situated 1,000 feet above sea level, the air may particularly benefit insomnia and asthma sufferers. Visitors come here for the peace and quiet and to enjoy the landscape with its dry-stone walling, deep wooded valleys, heather-clad moorlands and historic market towns and villages. Walkers and cyclists will appreciate the many uncrowded footpaths, trails and bridgeways nearby.

The rooms of this house feature massive oak timbers and antiques, with one containing a superb four-poster bed. One of the sitting rooms has an open log fire where guests can enjoy a convivial atmosphere. A recently converted 18th century stone building, comprising four self-contained studio apartments and two-roomed suites, each with a private bathroom, is situated 30 yards from the main house. The traditional farmhouse cooking puts emphasis on free-range produce, wholefoods and natural flavours. Dogs are accommodated in the apartments only. Horses also by prior arrangement.

Places of interest nearby: Chatsworth, Haddon Hall, Bolsover Castle, Kedleston Hall, Alton Towers, Crich Tramway Museum, Buxton, Ashbourne and Bakewell.

Directions: This country house is situated at the end of Biggin Village, which is off the A515, nine miles from Ashbourne and ten miles from Buxton.

M 20 12

BILLERICAY - GREAT BURSTEAD (Weekly Lets) ENGLAND

The Pump House Apartment

132 CHURCH STREET, GREAT BURSTEAD, ESSEX CM11 2TR
TEL: 01277 656579 FAX: 01277 631160 E-MAIL: john.bayliss@willmottdixon.co.uk

OWNERS: Edwina and John Bayliss

Prices: £400–£900 per week

Situated in picturesque rural South East England, the Pump House Apartment is an immaculately maintained two-storey apartment in the village of Great Burstead. Spacious and fully-equipped, it is an extremely comfortable home from home.

Part of a modern house, Pump House is set in its own secluded gardens, with an oriental pond and paddocks. Visitors can avail of an outdoor swimming pool heated to 80 degrees from May to September.

The house is very flexible and the air-conditioned Apartment can be let as a 1, 2 or 3 bedroomed residence. In each case two beautifully appointed lounges are available, in addition to an elegant dining room and a well designed first floor kitchen with views over the pretty gardens below.

The Pump House is the perfect place to discover the treasures of South East England. The village of Great Burstead is steeped in history, and its 14th century church has links with one of the Pilgrim Fathers and early settlers of the USA. **Places of interest nearby:** London (30 mins by train), Cambridge, Canterbury, Colchester and the Constable Country are within a 1hr drive. Country walks are a pleasure, while golf, tennis and badminton are among the many sports available nearby. **Directions: Leave M25 at jct 29 and join A127. Travel in the direction of Southend and then turn onto A176 (Noak Hill Road) towards Billericay. Church Street is on the right, with Pump House on the left before the church.**

Lower Brook House

BLOCKLEY, NR MORETON-IN-MARSH, GLOUCESTERSHIRE GL56 9DS
TEL/FAX: 01386 700286 E-MAIL: Lowerbrookhouse@compuserve.com

OWNER: Marie Mosedale–Cooper

 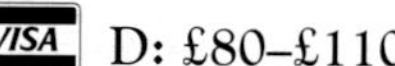 D: £80–£110

Lower Brook House has been skilfully created from a well-built detached property dating back to the 17th century and it epitomises the traditional Cotswold stone house of its period. Winner of the Times Golden Pillow Award, it is quietly situated in the village of Blockley, famous in the 1700s for its silk trade.

The hostess takes great care to ensure that guests' requirements are swiftly attended to. The five en suite bedrooms have antique furnishings and plenty of interesting bric-à-brac. One of the rooms has a four-poster bed and all have tea and coffee facilities, a colour television, hairdryer and fluffy towelling robes, fresh fruit and flowers, chocolates and mineral water are also provided.

Memorable breakfasts are enjoyed along with unlimited amounts of fresh and cooked fruits. The award-winning restaurant offers a daily-changing menu for fine dining and fresh local produce is used from the kitchen garden. A cellar of choice wines, with a selection of 36 to choose from, is available to complement your meal.

Places of interest nearby: Blockley is a short drive from Cheltenham, Oxford and Stratford-upon-Avon. As well as being a good base for exploring other picturesque local villages, Blockley is the perfect location to peruse the Moreton market every Tuesday. **Directions: As you enter the village from Moreton-in-Marsh, Lower Brook House can be found on your right.**

DIAL HOUSE

THE CHESTNUTS, HIGH STREET, BOURTON-ON-THE-WATER, GLOUCESTERSHIRE GL54 2AN
TEL: 01451 822244 FAX: 01451 810126 E-MAIL: info@dialhousehotel.com

OWNERS: Jane Howard and Adrian Campbell

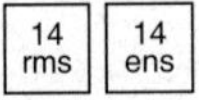

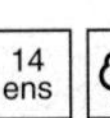

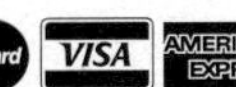

S: from £52
D: from £104

In the heart of the Cotswolds lies Dial House Hotel, a small 17th century country house which combines the charm and elegance of a bygone era with all the facilities of a modern hotel. Proprietors Lynn and Peter Boxall have many years experience in the hotel industry and extend a warm welcome to their guests. The hotel is open throughout the year and roaring log fires burn throughout the winter months.

In the summer, lunches are served in the delightful and secluded walled garden. Chef Calum Williamson creates delicious, freshly-cooked food for the à la carte restaurant, which creates an aura of old England with its inglenook fireplace and oak beams. Dial House has received 2 AA Rosettes for its cuisine and every care is taken by friendly staff to provide guests with an interesting choice of dishes and good quality wines.

An open fire in the comfortable lounge creates an ideal setting to finish off an evening with coffee and liqueurs. The décor of the bedrooms is light and cheery. Some have antique four-poster beds and overlook the garden. All are en suite, centrally-heated and equipped with tea and coffee making facilities. Bargain breaks available.

Places of interest nearby: Stratford-Upon-Avon, Bath and Cirencester, Warwick Castle, Blenheim Palace, Cheltenham, Slimbridge Wildfowl Trust and Oxford are all nearby.

Directions: Bourton-on-the-Water is 4 miles south west of Stow-on-the-Wold off A429.

THE GRANVILLE

124 KINGS ROAD, BRIGHTON BN1 2FA
TEL: 01273 326302 FAX: 01273 728294 E-MAIL: granville@brighton.co.uk

OWNERS: Mick and Sue Paskins
CHEF: Alison Lynch

24 rms | 24 ens | SMALL HOTEL

S: from £65
D: from £85

You only have to take one step through the front door to realise, and appreciate, that this Regency sea front property is a place for the style aware. Proprietor Sue Paskins believes that a hotel stay should be memorable and has furnished The Granville with flair and elegance to offer guests something unique. Situated in the heart of Brighton overlooking the sea and the splendid Edwardian West Pier, her creation is both lavish and original in its furnishings, decor and outlook and has been awarded 3 Stars by the AA and the English Tourist Board.

The majority of the 24 en suite bedrooms are not large but they are quite distinctive and have sumptuous bathrooms. Many have fabulous sea views. Among them is the romantic, pale pink and white Brighton Rock Room, the opulent Noel Coward Room with its art-deco bathroom, the huge late-Victorian four-poster bed and marble fireplaces of the Balcony Room and the Marina Room with a water bed.

Apart from breakfast, the cuisine served in Trogs Restaurant is vegetarian, comprising imaginative and substantial dishes. Meals are complemented by an excellent range of organic wines.The atmosphere is convivial with beautifully laid tables. **Places of interest nearby:** The delights of Brighton, including the Royal Pavilion, the famous Lanes, theatres and cinemas. Glyndebourne, Arundel, Chichester and Lewes are within easy reach. **Directions: The Granville is on the north side of Kings Road opposite the West Pier.**

THATCHED COTTAGE HOTEL & RESTAURANT

16 BROOKLEY ROAD, BROCKENHURST, HAMPSHIRE SO42 7RR
TEL: 01590 623090 FAX: 01590 623479 E-MAIL: ThatchedCottageHotel@email.msn.com

OWNERS: The Matysik Family

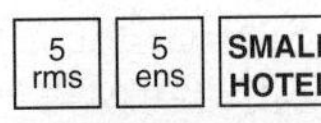

S: From £70
D: £90–£150
Suite: £150–£170

This enchanting thatched cottage was built in 1627 and only became a hotel in 1991. The Matysik family has over 120 years of hotel experience between them and this is reflected in the careful transformation that has taken place.

Set in one of the prettiest villages in the heart of the New Forest, modernisation for the comfort of guests has not detracted from its original charm. The individually decorated double bedrooms each have a special feature for example, a four-poster bed, Turkish steam shower or open hearth gas fireplace. A cosy beamed lounge is idyllic for pre/after-dinner drinks. An elegant tea garden is presented with lace table cloths and sun parasols. Memorable services include a superb late breakfast, Champagne cream tea and gourmet wicker hampers. In the evening, exquisite culinary delights are freshly prepared by the culinary team on show in their open country kitchen. The table d'hôte menu offers luxurious ingredients harmoniously combined with flair and imagination. "A dining experience difficult to surpass" set in a unique and relaxing ambience by romantic candlelight. An authentic Japanese celebration menu can be prearranged.

Places of interest nearby: Home of Lord Montagu and his National Motor Museum, Rothschild's Exbury Gardens and the yachting town of Lymington. Activities include wild mushroom hunting, riding, sailing and golf. **Directions: M27, Jct1, drive south on A337 through Lyndhurst, in Brockenhurst turn right before level crossing.**

Whitley Ridge Country House Hotel

BEAULIEU ROAD, BROCKENHURST, NEW FOREST, HAMPSHIRE SO42 7QL
TEL: 01590 622354 FAX: 01590 622856 E-MAIL: whitleyridge@brockenhurst.co.uk

OWNERS: Rennie and Sue Law
CHEF: Gary Moore

S: £70–£86
D: £98–£126
Suite: £136

Set in five acres of secluded parkland in the heart of the New Forest, this privately owned Georgian house was once a Royal hunting lodge visited by the Queen Mother. Today it has the ambience of a true country house with the accent on relaxation.

The bedrooms are individually decorated, some have a two person steam cabin and a Hydrotherapy bath, and most have lovely views over open forest. The public rooms are similarly luxurious and elegant and log fires burn on cool evenings.

Dining is always a pleasure and the two AA Rosette restaurant offers a daily changing table d'hôte menu, together with a high standard of à la carte choices and a well balanced and imaginative vegetarian menu. The wine selection includes wines from traditional areas and interesting choices from further afield.

Guests can relax in the grounds or enjoy a game of tennis. Some of the country's best woodland walks are directly accessible from the gardens. Whichever pastime you choose, Whitley Ridge guarantees a restful and enjoyable stay.

Places of interest nearby: A number of stately homes, including Broadlands and Wilton House, are within easy reach. Lord Montague's Motor Museum, Buckler's Hard and historic Stonehenge are also within driving distance.
Directions: M27 junction 1. Situated on the B3055, Brockenhurst – Beaulieu.

Grafton Manor Country House Hotel

GRAFTON LANE, BROMSGROVE, WORCESTERSHIRE B61 7HA
TEL: 01527 579007 FAX: 01527 575221 E-MAIL: steven@grafman.u-net.com

OWNERS: The Morris Family
MANAGER: Stephen Morris

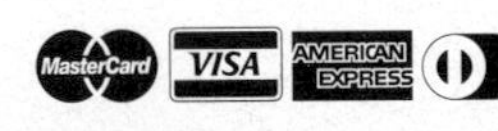

S: £85
D: from £105
Suite: £150

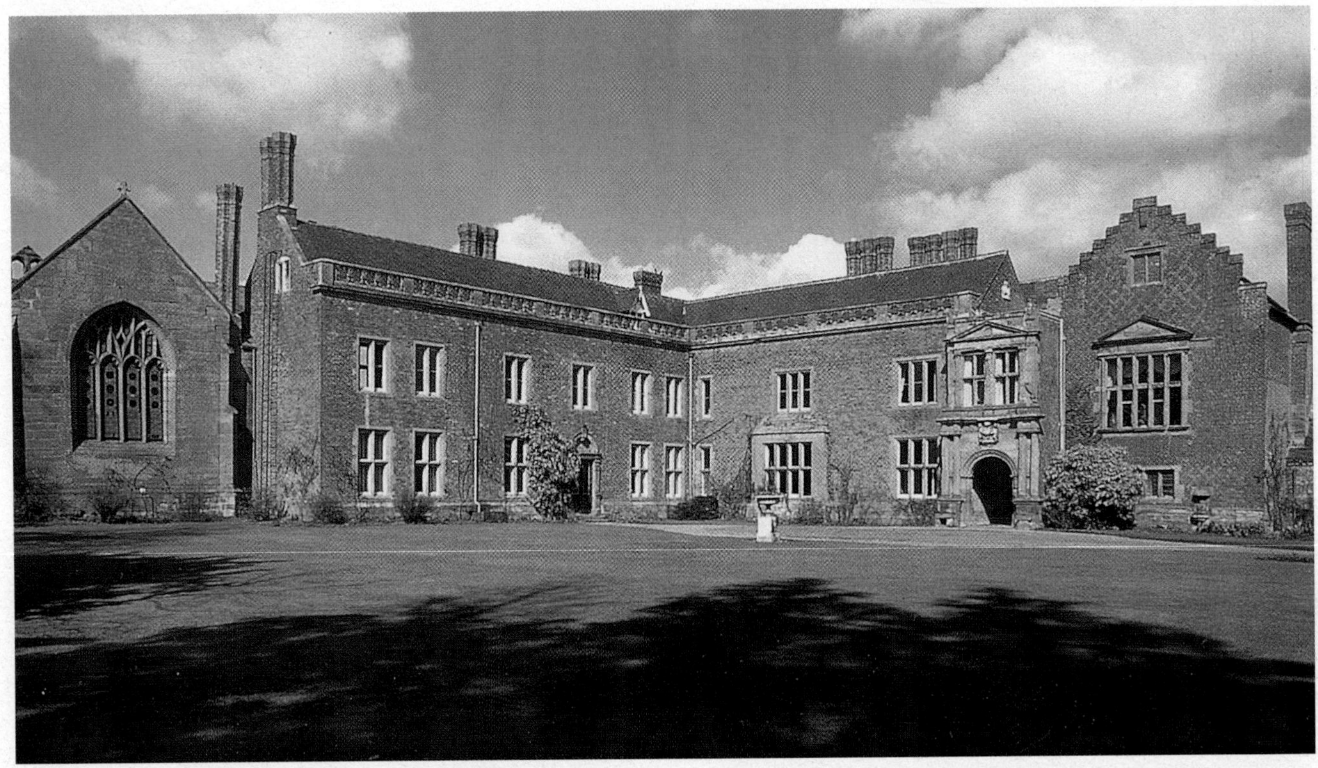

Closely associated with many of the leading events in English history, Grafton Manor's illustrious past can be traced back to Norman times. Commissioned in 1567, the present manor is set in several acres of gardens leading to a lake.

Modern comfort and style are combined with the atmosphere of an earlier age. Pot-pourri from the hotel's 19th century rose gardens scent the rooms and over 100 herbs are grown in a unique, chessboard-pattern garden. All the herbs are in regular use in the restaurant kitchen, where Simon Morris aims to 'produce only the best' for guests. Preserves made from estate produce are on sale.

Meals are served in the 18th century dining room, the focal point of Grafton Manor. Damask-rose petal and mulberry sorbets are indicative of the inspired culinary style. Indian cuisine is Simon's award-winning hobby and Asian dishes often complement the traditional English cooking.

The fully equipped bedrooms have been meticulously restored and furnished, some with open fires on cooler evenings.

Places of interest nearby: Grafton Manor is ideally placed for Birmingham, the NEC and the International Conference Centre. It is an equally good base from which to explore the Worcestershire countryside. **Directions: From M5 junction 5 proceed via A38 towards Bromsgrove. Bear left at first roundabout; Grafton Lane is first left after ½ mile.**

Melbourn Bury

MELBOURN, CAMBRIDGESHIRE, NR ROYSTON SG8 6DE
TEL: 01763 261151 FAX: 01763 262375 E-MAIL: mazecare@aol.com

OWNERS: Anthony and Sylvia Hopkinson

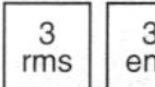

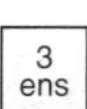

S: £65
D: £95

Set in extensive grounds with a lake and wildfowl, Melbourn Bury is an elegant manor house. It has had only two ownerships since the 1500s. The first owners were the monks of Ely and then in 1850, the property was purchased by the ancestors of Sylvia Hopkinson.

Gracious reception rooms are furnished with antiques and fine paintings, while the en suite bedrooms are comfortable and have charming views of the gardens. Fresh flowers and log fires are extra touches which guests will appreciate. Adjoining the library is a 19th century billiard room with a full-size table.

Delicious home cooking encompasses traditional English recipes and continental dishes prepared in cordon bleu style. Dinner is by prior arrangement.

Lunches and dinners for up to 22 persons seated; more can be accommodated buffet-style – small conferences, receptions and exhibitions. Closed at Christmas and Easter.

Places of interest nearby: Cambridge, Duxford Air Museum, Audley End, Ely, Wimpole Hall and Hatfield House. **Directions: Off A10, 10 miles south of Cambridge, 3rd turning on left to Melbourn; 2 miles north of Royston, 1st turning on right to Melbourn. Entrance is 300 yards on left after the turning. Look for the white gate posts and lodge cottage.**

CROSBY LODGE COUNTRY HOUSE HOTEL

HIGH CROSBY, CROSBY-ON-EDEN, CARLISLE, CUMBRIA CA6 4QZ
TEL: 01228 573618 FAX: 01228 573428 E-MAIL: info@crosbylodge.co.uk

OWNERS: Michael, Patricia and James Sedgwick
CHEF: James Sedgwick

S: £82–£95
D: £110–£150

Crosby Lodge is a romantic country mansion that has been converted into a quiet efficient hotel without spoiling any of its original charm. Grade II listed, it stands amid pastoral countryside close to the Scottish Lowlands and the Lake District.

Spacious interiors are elegantly furnished and appointed to provide the maximum of comfort. The personal attention of Michael and Patricia Sedgwick ensures that a high standard of service is maintained. All of the bedrooms are beautifully equipped, most with antique beds and half-testers. Two bedrooms are situated in the converted courtyard stables overlooking the walled garden and in these rooms guests are welcome to bring their pet dogs.

In The Lodge restaurant, extensive menus offer a wide and varied choice of dishes. Traditional English recipes are prepared along with continental cuisine complimented by an extensive international wine list. Tables are set with cut glass and gleaming silver cutlery and in keeping with the gracious surroundings. Crosby Lodge, with its spacious grounds, is a superb setting for weddings, parties, business and social events. Closed 24 December to 20 January.

Places of interest nearby: Hadrian's Wall, Carlisle Cathedral and Castle and six miles from Lanercost Priory, the Scottish Borders. **Directions: From M6 junction 44 take A689 Brampton road for three miles; turn right through Low Crosby. Crosby Lodge is on the right at High Crosby.**

Aynsome Manor Hotel

CARTMEL, GRANGE-OVER-SANDS, CUMBRIA LA11 6HH
TEL: 015395 36653 FAX: 015395 36016 E-MAIL:info@aynsomemanorhotel.co.uk

OWNERS: Tony, Margaret, Chris and Andrea Varley

S: £70
D: £93–£120
(including dinner)

In the beautiful Vale of Cartmel, with views of the priory and beyond to the village of Cartmel itself, stands Aynsome Manor, once the home of Wiliam Marshall, Earl of Pembroke. It is an ideal retreat for anyone seeking peace and quiet. Guests can stroll around the grounds or, in cooler months, relax by log fires in the lounges.

The elegant candlelit dining room is the perfect setting in which to enjoy a five-course dinner. The restaurant has an excellent reputation for its home cooking, from delicious home-made soups such as apple, celery and tomato, to main courses such as roast breast of pheasant with smoked bacon and an orange and chestnut sauce. Fresh, local produce is used wherever possible. A high tea is provided for children under five as they are regrettably not allowed in the restaurant for dinner. There are 12 bedrooms, two of which are in Aynsome Cottage, across the courtyard.

Places of interest nearby: Aynsome Manor is a perfect base for touring the Lake District. Lake Windermere is 4 miles away. In summer, Holker Hall organises ballooning and vintage car rallies. There is horseracing in Cartmel on Whitsun and August bank holidays and 5 golf courses nearby. Closed January. **Directions: Leave M6 at junction 36 and take the A590 signposted Barrow-in-Furness. At end of dual carriageway (12 miles) turn left into Cartmel. The hotel is on the right.**

DANESWOOD HOUSE HOTEL

CUCKHILL, SHIPHAM, NR WINSCOMBE, SOMERSET BS25 1RD
TEL: 01934 843145 FAX: 01934 843824 E-MAIL: info@daneswoodhotel.co.uk

OWNERS: David and Elise Hodges
CHEF: Heather Matthews

  SMALL HOTEL

S: £79.50–£95
D: £95–£110
Suite: £135

Set on elevated grounds commanding breathtaking views of the Severn Estuary and the Somerset countryside, Daneswood House offers a welcoming ambience in the most luxurious of surroundings. Originally built in the Edwardian era as a health hydro, it has been comprehensively refurbished to the highest of modern standards.

Each of the wonderfully appointed bedrooms has been individually designed with soothing fabrics and superb en suite bathrooms. Some have patios opening onto the hotel's beautifully maintained gardens. The honeymoon suite, with its frescoed ceiling and king-size bed, is particulary impressive.

The Edwardian-theme restaurant is yet another of Daneswood House's many delights. Justly awarded two AA rosettes, it offers superbly prepared meals in a combination of English and French styles, as well as a faultless selection of fine wines and liquers. During the summer, barbecue dishes are prepared and served "al fresco".

Places of interest nearby: Cheddar Hill is a mere two miles away, while Wells Cathedral, Bath, Glastonbury and Mendips are also close at hand. **Directions: Shipham is signposted from the A38 Bristol-Bridgwater road. Go through the village towards Cheddar and the hotel is on the left.**

M 40

Charlton Kings Hotel

CHARLTON KINGS, CHELTENHAM, GLOUCESTERSHIRE GL52 6UU
TEL: 01242 231061 FAX: 01242 241900

OWNER: Trevor Stuart
MANAGERS: Cassie Fuller and Aran Hayes
CHEF: Aran Hayes

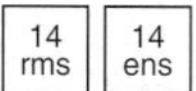

S: £53–£79.90
D: £68–£104

Surrounded by the Cotswold hills, on the outside of Cheltenham but just a few minutes by car to the heart of town stands Charlton Kings Hotel. If you seek instant peace and solitude follow the footpath running alongside the hotel into the beautiful Cotswold countryside. The famous 'Cotswold Way' escarpment walk passes just half a mile away.

The hotel is attractively furnished with an accent on light woods and pastel colouring. All rooms are en suite, some are reserved for non smokers. The Restaurant is fresh and inviting offering space and privacy for those all important business meetings or perhaps an intimate dinner for two? An à la carte menu is supplemented by a daily table d'hôte, using the finest fresh produce. The bar and conservatory are open throughout the day for snacks and refreshments. A full Sunday Roast Lunch is served 12–2. **Places of interest nearby:** Cheltenham Spa – famous for its architecture festivals and racing also has plenty to offer in the way of theatres, restaurants and a distinguished selection of shops. To the North, East and South lie charming Cotswold Villages, too numerous to mention, and to the West the Forest of Dean, Wye Valley, Malvern Hills and much more. **Directions: The hotel is the first property on the left coming into Cheltenham from Oxford on the A40 (the 'Welcome to Cheltenham' Boundary Sign is located in their front garden!).**

GREEN BOUGH HOTEL

60 HOOLE ROAD, CHESTER, CHESHIRE CH2 3NL
TEL: 01244 326241 FAX: 01244 326265 E-MAIL: greenboughhotel@cwcom.net

OWNERS: Philip and Janice Martin
CHEF: Philip Martin and Peter Howlett

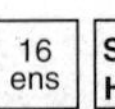  SMALL HOTEL

S: £60–£85
D: £75–£115
Suite: £125

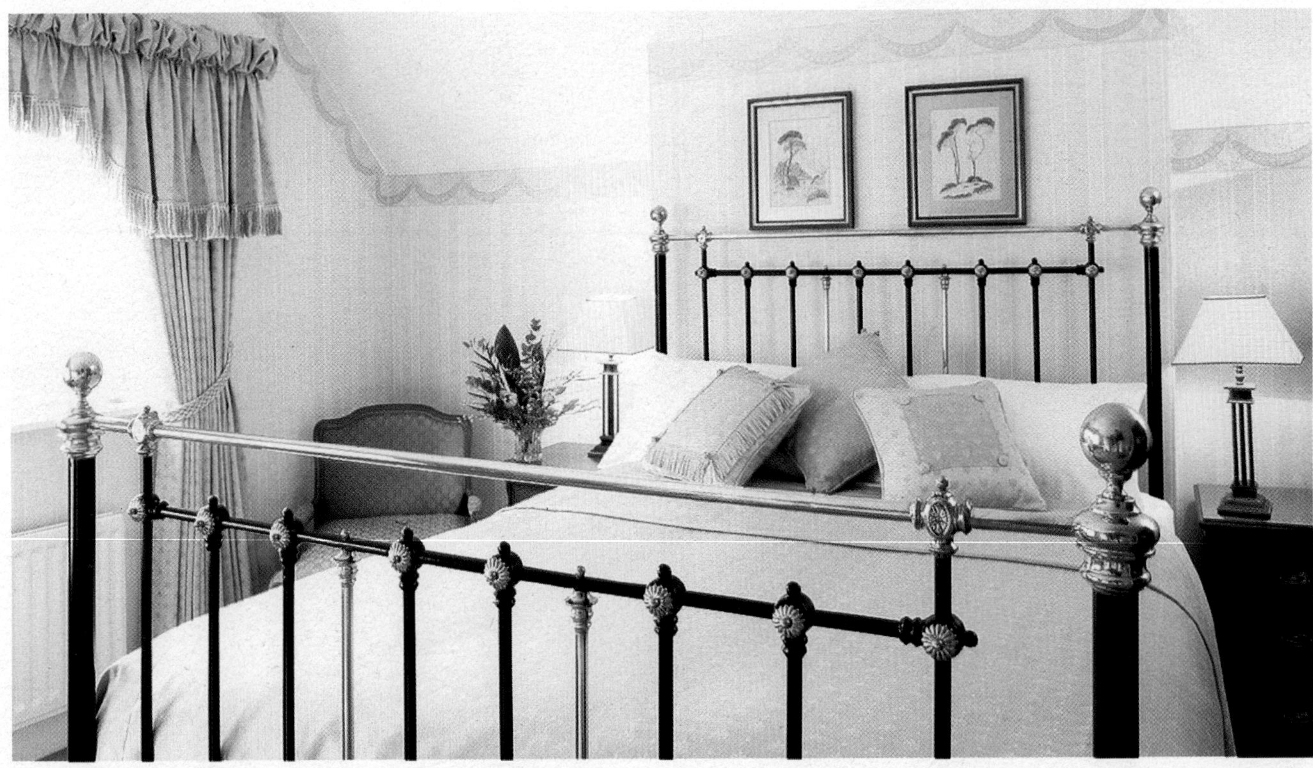

A late Victorian town house, the Green Bough Hotel is conveniently placed, as its name suggests, on a leafy route into the ancient city of Chester. Bought four years ago by Philip and Janice Martin, it has been completely refurbished and now combines the convenience of modern facilities with the charm of period features and furnishings. Of its 16 no-smoking bedrooms the majority have antique beds. Many of the original architectural features of the building and the adjoining Victorian Lodge bedroom wing remain intact.

The restaurant is presided over by Philip Martin who trained at the Savoy Hotel, working with the renowned Maitre Chef des Cuisine Silvino S Trompetto. The menu, served in the Fleur de Lys Restaurant, is complemented by a wine list of a range and quality that belies the relatively small size of the hotel.

The Green Bough provides an excellent base for exploring the city of Chester and hires bicycles for this purpose. It is also ideal for those venturing further afield into the beautiful Cheshire countryside and Snowdonia. Guests have free use of a local health and leisure club.

Places of interest nearby: The cathedral, river, racecourse and shops of the city of Chester. The Blue Planet Aquarium and the world class Chester Zoo. The castles of Cheshire. Snowdonia. **Directions: Leave the M53 at junction 12. Take the A56 into Chester for 1 mile. The Green Bough Hotel is on the right.**

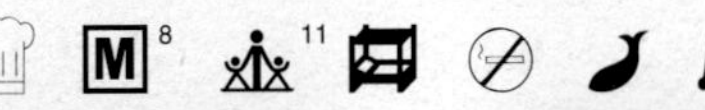

CROUCHERS BOTTOM COUNTRY HOTEL

BIRDHAM ROAD, APULDRAM, NEAR CHICHESTER, WEST SUSSEX PO20 7EH
TEL: 01243 784995 FAX: 01243 539797

GENERAL MANAGER: Lloyd Van Rooyen
CHEF: Gavin Wilson

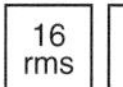

S: £45–£65
D: £65–£105

This former farmhouse, set just half a mile from the Yacht Basin and 2 miles from the centre of Chichester, has been transformed into a fine country hotel offering 16 opulent bedrooms, good food and a most attentive service.

Located in the converted coach house and barn, all the rooms are beautifully appointed with a full range of amenities, including telephone, colour television, hairdryer and tea and coffee-making facilities.

Free-range hens provide the eggs of a full English breakfast, which may be enjoyed whilst overlooking the attractive courtyard. Guests recline in the comfortable lounge or enjoy a preprandial drink in the bar before dining in the hotel restaurant, awarded three AA Stars and one Rosette. The freshly prepared dishes are the inspiration of the talented chef, Gavin Wilson, and only the finest of fresh ingredients are used. Crouchers Bottom Country Hotel will delight those wishing to merely relax and escape the pressures of a hectic lifestyle. In the summer months a tranquil ambience envelopes the courtyard as guests sip chilled drinks and laze in the sun whilst in winter the roaring log fires are truly inviting! **Places of interest nearby:** Chichester Cathedral, Marina, Museum, Art Gallery and Festival Theatre. The charming harbour village of Bosham with its Saxon church, Goodwood House and Arundel Castle. **Directions: From M27, junction 12, take A27 to Chichester and then A286 south towards The Witterings. Crouchers Bottom Hotel is on the left.**

STANTON MANOR

STANTON SAINT QUINTIN, NR CHIPPENHAM, WILTSHIRE SN14 6DQ
TEL: 01666 837552 FAX: 01666 837022 E-MAIL: reception@stantonmanor.co.uk

OWNERS: Duncan and Linda Hickling
CHEF: Roger Payne

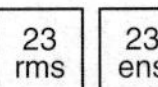 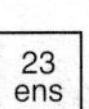  

S: £65–£95
D: £85–£135

A wide, columned entranceway welcomes visitors to this attractive stone-built hotel standing in seven acres of beautiful grounds in the delightful Wiltshire village of Stanton Saint Quintin. The original house was listed in the Domesday Book, was once owned by Lord Burghley, chief minister to Queen Elizabeth I, and was rebuilt in 1840.

Stanton Manor has recently been completely refurbished by owners Duncan and Linda Hickling, who are on hand to ensure that a friendly and attentive service is extended to guests. Modern facilities and comforts combine easily and unobtrusively with those of the past, which include magnificent Tudor fireplaces and stone flooring. The en suite bedrooms are spacious and individually designed with toning fabrics and comfortable furniture. Some have four-poster beds, antique brass beds or king-size pine beds.

Chef Roger Payne takes pride in creating traditional British cuisine of flare and quality which is immaculately served in the elegant and light Burghley restaurant, overlooking the grounds. Light snacks can be enjoyed in the cosy, copper and brass hung bar decorated with motor racing, rugby and horse racing memorabilia.

Places of interest nearby: The Roman city of Cirencester, Chippenham and plenty of pretty villages. **Directions: Exit M4 at junction 17 and join A429 towards Cirencester. After approximately 200 yards, turn left to Stanton Saint Quintin. Stanton Manor is on the left in the village.**

THE MALT HOUSE

BROAD CAMPDEN, GLOUCESTERSHIRE GL55 6UU
TEL: 01386 840295 FAX: 01386 841334 E-MAIL: nick@the–malt–house.freeserve.co.uk

OWNERS: Nick and Jean Brown
CHEF: Julian Brown

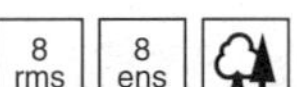

S: £59.50–£89.50
D: £85–£115
Suites: £105–£125

Nick and Jean Brown have achieved a blend of warm, relaxed and yet professional service, welcoming guests as part of an extended family. The idyllic surroundings of The Malt House, a beautiful 17th century Cotswold home in the quiet village of Broad Campden, further enhance the congenial atmosphere.

Rooms, including residents' sitting rooms, combine comfortable furnishings with antiques and displays of fresh flowers. Most bedrooms overlook the wide lawns which lead to a small stream and orchard beyond. All of the recently refurbished rooms are individually decorated and have an en suite bathroom. The Windrush Suite has an 18th century four-poster bed and a family suite is also available.

Dinner is served five days a week. The proprietors' son Julian is a highly accomplished chef who uses many ingredients from the kitchen gardens to prepare a table d'hôte menu, accompanied by a choice selection of wines. The English breakfasts are equally good.

The Malt House has earned many awards for its standard of accommodation and meals including, most deservedly, 2 Rosettes for its food and Premier Select 5Q from the AA. **Places of interest nearby:** Hidcote Manor Gardens (N.T), Chipping Camden Church, The Cotswolds, Cheltenham, Stratford-upon-Avon, Oxford and Bath. **Directions: The Malt House is in the centre of the village of Broad Campden which is just one mile from Chipping Campden.**

Tudor Farmhouse Hotel & Restaurant

HIGH STREET, CLEARWELL, NR COLEFORD, GLOUCESTERSHIRE GL16 8JS
TEL: 01594 833046 FAX: 01594 837093 E-MAIL: reservations@tudorfarmhse.u–net.com

OWNERS: Colin and Linda Gray
CHEF: Dean Wassell

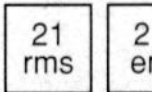
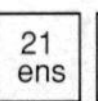

21 rms 21 ens SMALL HOTEL

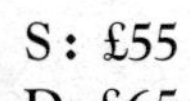

S: £55
D: £65

Tudor Farmhouse is an idyllic haven away from the hustle and bustle of everyday life. A cosy, friendly 13th century stone-built hotel in the centre of the historic village of Clearwell on the peaceful fringe of the Forest of Dean. Clearwell's history dates from Roman times and the village is dominated by the huge ramparts of a fine Neo Gothic castle.

Owners Colin and Linda Gray take pride in the standard of comfort and hospitality at Tudor Farmhouse, whose features include massive oak beams and original panelling. There is a large, roughstone inglenook fireplace in the attractive lounge providing warmth and cheer in winter. A conservatory looks onto the landscaped garden and 14 acres of fields. The bedrooms have been refurbished in traditional style. Those in the house are reached by a wide, oak spiral staircase. Others are in converted stone cider makers' cottages quietly situated in the garden and include three family suites.

The candlelit restaurant, awarded a red Rosette, with its open stonework and exposed beams is the ideal setting in which to enjoy unhurried evening meals.

Places of interest nearby: The Forest of Dean and Wye Valley, Offa's Dyke, Tintern Abbey, Monmouth and Ross on Wye, spectacular Symonds Yat, Raglan and Chepstow Castles. **Directions: From M4 join M48 taking junction 2 to Chepstow then follow A48 and B4231.**

M 20 VCR

Abbots Oak

Warren Hills Road, Near Coalville
TEL: 01530 832 328 FAX: 01530 832 328

OWNERS: Bill, Audrey and Carolyn White

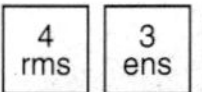

S: £50–£65
D: £60–£85

This Grade II listed building is on the edge of Charnwood Forest, with 19 acres of gardens, woodland and unusual granite outcrops where guests can stroll or play croquet and tennis.

Inside is the most spectacular carved oak panelling and stained glass – indeed the staircase goes to the top of the tower from where it is possible to look out over five counties.

The house has four bedrooms available for the use of guests, three of which are en suite. There is a gorgeous drawing room and elegant dining room. Dinner is served en famille by candlelight. The menu is therefore not extensive and the wine list short but good. After dinner enjoy a game of snooker in the superb billiard room.

Places of interest nearby: Mid-week it is ideal for businessmen with meetings in Loughborough or Leicester. There is excellent golf nearby and shooting can be arranged. Further afield are Stratford-upon-Avon, Warwick Castle and Rutland Water. 15 minutes from Donington Park race circuit. **Directions: From the M1, take the A511 towards Coalville. At the first roundabout, take the third exit to Loughborough. At the traffic lights, turn left. Abbots Oak is 1¼ miles opposite the Bulls Head pub. From the A42, take the A511 towards Coalville. At the fourth roundabout turn left and take the second right, then right at T-junction. Abbots Oak is 50 yards on the right.**

ASHELFORD

ASHELFORD, EAST DOWN, NEAR BARNSTAPLE, NORTH DEVON EX31 4LU
TEL: 01271 850469 FAX: 01271 850862 E-MAIL: tom&erica@ashelford.co.uk

OWNERS: Tom and Erica McClenaghan
CHEF: Erica McClenaghan

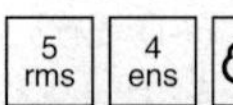

S: £83
D: £106–£141

North Devon has over 850 square miles of heritage countryside and coast that are classified as one of the last remaining tranquil areas in England. Ashelford stands in over 70 acres of superb pasture and woodland facing south at the head of its own valley with views beyond the National Trust's Arlington Court to Exmoor.

Formerly a 17th century farmhouse, Ashelford has retained its sense of history with a wealth of oak beams, slate floors and log fires. Owners Tom and Erica McClenaghan offer peace, seclusion and cosy informality where a visitor's comfort is their greatest concern.

Privacy is enhanced by enchanting, warmly decorated and well-appointed bedrooms, each having en suite facilities and extras that include a refrigerator with fresh milk, orange juice and spring water. The lounge and dining room are comfortable and welcoming with superb meals prepared from local produce.

The 8 inch reflectory telescope will delight those wishing to observe the planets and stars. Golf, fishing, riding and carriage driving can be arranged. The residence has an outside bath with hot and cold water for well-behaved dogs after they have completed one of the many nearby walks with their owners! **Places of interest nearby:** The R.H.S. Rosemoor Gardens, Dartington Glass, Arlington Court. **Directions: From Barnstaple take A39 towards Lynmouth. After Shirwell village take second turning on left and follow signs to Churchill. Ashelford is on the right.**

Coombe House Country Hotel

COLEFORD, CREDITON, DEVON EX17 5BY
TEL: 01363 84487 FAX: 01363 84722 E-MAIL: relax@coombehouse.com

OWNERS: David and Pat Jones
CHEF: Wayne Pegler

 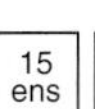   

S: £57.50–£67.50
D: £82–£102

This elegant Georgian manor is listed as a protected building of historic interest and certainly the Cellar Bar has over 700 years of history – reputedly it sheltered Cromwell's men in the Civil War. Now these elegant buildings which offer relaxation in lovely landscaped grounds are being thoughtfully refurbished and up-graded by their caring and welcoming owners.

There are 15 bedrooms in all, the spacious garden rooms at the front of the house enjoying restful views over the grounds and surrounding countryside with well-equipped bathrooms en suite; the six courtyard en suite rooms are equally pleasant but their differing quality is reflected in the price structure.

The AA 2 Rosette restaurant was once a ballroom added on in Victorian times and it provides a gracious, elegant atmosphere in which to enjoy the daily-changed cuisine and wines from the informative list. The grounds provide facilities for those who wish to play tennis, or indulge in croquet. For the more adventurous golf, shooting and riding can all be arranged. Short breaks available.

Places of interest nearby: The city of Exeter with its cathedral and university, the Taw and Torridge valleys, Dartmoor, Exmoor, RHS garden at Rosemoor and a number of National Trust properties. **Directions: From Exeter join A377 and pass through Crediton. After approximately 1½ miles further on the hotel is signposted.**

M 80

Bel Alp House

HAYTOR, NR BOVEY TRACEY, SOUTH DEVON TQ13 9XX
TEL: 01364 661217 FAX: 01364 661292

OWNERS: Jack, Mary and Rachael Twist

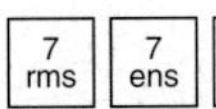

S: From £65
D: From £120
Suite: £150

Peace and seclusion are guaranteed at the Bel Alp House with its spectacular outlook from the edge of Dartmoor across a rolling patchwork of fields and woodland to the sea, 20 miles away.

Built as an Edwardian country mansion and owned in the 1920s by millionairess Dame Violet Wills, Bel Alp has been lovingly restored and the proprietors' personal attention ensures their guests' enjoyment and comfort in the atmosphere of a private home.

The set dinner is changed nightly, using only the best local produce and the meals are accompanied by a well-chosen and comprehensive wine list.

Of the seven en suite bedrooms, two still have their original Edwardian basins and baths mounted on marble plinths and all bedrooms have views over the gardens.

An abundance of house plants, open log fire and restful colours complements the family antiques and pictures to create the perfect environment in which to relax. Awarded an AA Rosette.

Places of interest nearby: Bel Alp is ideally situated for exploring Devon and parts of Cornwall. Plymouth, famed for Drake and the Pilgrim Fathers, Exeter with its Norman cathedral and National Trust properties Castle Drogo and Cotehele Manor House are all within an hour's drive. **Directions: Bel Alp House is off the B3387 Haytor road, 2½ miles from Bovey Tracey.**

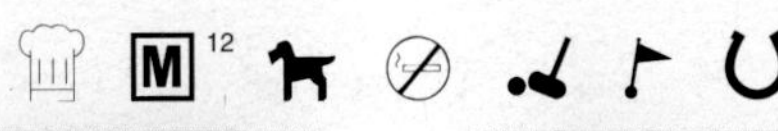

THE HOMESTEAD

SITWELL STREET, SPONDON, DERBY DE21 7FE
TEL: 01332 544300 FAX: 01332 544480 E-MAIL: enquiries@derbyshirehotel.co.uk

OWNERS: Alan and Marysia Rutherford
CHEFS: Stefan Rutherford and Christopher Smith

9 rms | 9 ens | SMALL HOTEL

S: £75
D: £95

Described as a 'country house hotel in town', The Homestead is the perfect home-away-from-home, renowned for its elegant ambience and fine cuisine.

This impressive Grade I listed Georgian house is set in the county of Derby, with its rambling countryside. Beautiful walled gardens surround the house and inside, soft fabrics and antique furnishings abound. The individually-appointed bedrooms will delight those wishing to be pampered, and the en suite bathrooms are opulent and feature many thoughtful additions.

Pre or postprandial drinks are served to guests in the elegant lounges. For private occasions, guests may enjoy the exclusive use of the oak-panelled dining room with attentive staff. Advance booking is essential and the talented chef is happy to prepare dishes upon request. Sumptuous cuisine is served in the restaurant and the inspired menu includes dishes such as loin of spring lamb pan-fried with local black pudding and horseradish mash and fresh lobster and scallops au jus with baby vegetables.

Places of interest nearby: An ideal base from which to explore the Peak District National Park and Buxton Spa Town. Other places are Derby Playhouse, Royal Crown Derby China factory and shop and Derby Football Club, home of Giorgi Kinkladze. **Directions: The Homestead is 3 miles east of Derby City Centre and 4.5 miles west of the M1/junction 25. East Midlands airport is 7 miles to the south east.**

Chippenhall Hall

FRESSINGFIELD, EYE, SUFFOLK IP21 5TD
TEL: 01379 588180/586733 FAX: 01379 586272 E-MAIL: info@chippenhall.co.uk

OWNERS: Barbara and Jakes Sargent

 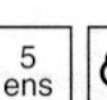 

S: £72–£78
D: £80–£84

The present manor is a listed Tudor building, although its origins date from Saxon times and is referred to in the *Domesday Book* as Cybenhalla. Secluded at the end of a long leafy drive, the hall enjoys a setting of rural tranquillity amid seven acres of lawns, trees, ponds and gardens.

Every evening, by arrangement, a superb candlelit dinner is prepared by the hostess and served in convivial surroundings. Proprietors Barbara and Jakes Sargent pride themselves in offering a fine choice of reasonably priced wines from the cellar to complement your meal. A seat beside the copper-canopied inglenook fire in the Shallow End bar room is the ideal place to enjoy pre-dinner drinks.

The house is heavily-beamed throughout, including the en suite bedrooms which are named after relevant historical associations. During the summer, guests can relax by the heated outdoor swimming pool which is set in the rose-covered courtyard. With attentive service, good food and wine, it is not surprising to learn that Chippenhall Hall won the Johansens 1998 Country Houses and Small Hotels Award and is ETB and AA 5 Diamonds rated.

Places of interest nearby: Snape Maltings, Minsmere Bird Sanctuary, the Otter Trust at Earsham and the towns of Bury St Edmunds and Norwich. **Directions: 1½ miles outside Fressingfield on the B1116 to Framlingham.**

Yalbury Cottage Hotel

LOWER BOCKHAMPTON, DORCHESTER, DORSET DT2 8PZ
TEL: 01305 262382 FAX: 01305 266412 E-MAIL: yalbury.cottage@virgin.net

OWNERS: Heather and Derek Furminger
HEAD CHEF: Russell Brown

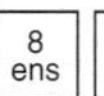

S: £53
D: £82

Yalbury Cottage Hotel is a lovely thatched property dating back about 300 years. Family run, it offers guests a warm welcome and a friendly, personal service in an atmosphere of peace, relaxation and informality.

The eight spacious en suite bedrooms (all no-smoking) are attractively decorated and furnished. Each offers a full range of desirable extras, including colour television, hairdryer and tea and coffee making facilities.

A comfortable lounge, complete with large inglenook fireplace and low, beamed ceilings, is the perfect place to relax before dinner. The proprietors pride themselves on the high standard of cuisine served in the attractive dining room. A good variety of imaginative dishes is always available, for example, seared scallops on a warm potato and caper terrine with saffron and tomato dressing; roast loin of lamb with a white bean casserole, fresh broad beans and thyme jus and raspberry shortcake crème brûlée. Yalbury cottage has been awarded 2 AA Rosettes for outstanding cuisine. A selection of carefully chosen wines is available to complement any meal. **Places of interest nearby:** Thomas Hardy's birthplace, Athelhampton House, Parnham House, Abbotsbury Swannery, Corfe Castle and Sherborne Castle. Yalbury Cottage is an excellent centre from which to explore Dorset, with its superb walking country, pretty villages and magnificent coastline. **Directions: Lower Bockhampton is a mile south of A35 between Puddletown and Dorchester.**

M 8

THE GEORGE HOTEL

HIGH STREET, DORCHESTER-ON-THAMES, OXFORD OX10 7HH
TEL: 01865 340404 FAX: 01865 341620

OWNERS: Brian Griffin
MANAGER: Michael Pinder

18 rms 18 ens

S: £65
D: £85
Four Poster: £97

In the heart of the Thames Valley lies The George. Dating from the 15th century, it is one of the oldest inns in the country. In the days of the stage coach, it provided a welcome haven for many an aristocrat including the first Duchess of Marlborough, Sarah Churchill. However, more recent times have seen famous guests of a different hue such as author DH Lawrence. The buildings of the George Hotel have changed little since their heyday as a coaching inn. It retains all the beauty and charm of those days, whilst offering every modern amenity. All the rooms are en suite and furnished with fine antiques and the owners have created a décor which suits the requirements of modern times whilst maintaining the spirit of the past. The menu changes daily allowing the chef to ensure that only the freshest and finest produce reaches your table. The imaginative cuisine, awarded 2 AA Rosettes, is beautifully presented and delicious. The beamed dining room provides a delightful setting in which to enjoy an excellent meal, served by friendly, professional staff.

Places of interest nearby: Dorchester-on-Thames provides easy access to the Cotswolds, Blenheim Palace and Oxford. Stratford-upon-Avon, Henley, Windsor and an inexhaustible source of beautiful walks and cultural and sporting activities. Excellent meeting facilities for up to 36 in the Stable Suite and two smaller rooms each for up to 8 people. **Directions: On A4074, 9 miles south of Oxford.**

WALLETT'S COURT

WEST CLIFFE, ST MARGARET'S-AT-CLIFFE, DOVER, KENT CT15 6EW
TEL: 01304 852424 FAX: 01304 853430 E-MAIL: wc@wallettscourt.com

OWNERS: Chris, Lea and Gavin Oakley
CHEF: Chris Oakley

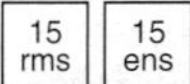

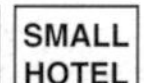

S: £70–£110
D: £80–£150

This listed Grade II house, recorded in The Doomsday Book as 'The Manor of Westcliffe', was transformed by the Oakley family who discovered it in ruins in the late 70s. The result is a charming property, enveloped in a relaxing atmosphere and set in landscaped grounds near to The White Cliffs of Dover.

The beautifully appointed bedrooms are comfortable and well-equipped with an array of modern conveniences. They are located in either the main house or barn conversion, the most recent of which also features an indoor swimming pool and leisure facilities. Fitness enthusiasts may use the steam room, sauna, spa pool, tennis courts and croquet lawn.

The attractive restaurant, awarded 3 AA Rosettes, offers imaginative lunch and dinner menus. The dishes change every month to incorporate the fresh seasonal produce. Try the St. Margaret's Bay Lobster served with pilaaf rice and roasted vegetables, Dover Sole Meuniere or Romney Marsh Lamb. The extensive wine list includes a good selection of half-bottles, all acceptably priced. Breakfast is another feast, with farm eggs, sausages made by the nearby butcher and home-made preserves.

Places of interest nearby: Enjoy cliff top walks to St Margaret's Bay, exploring the Cinque Ports and playing golf on the championship courses. The city of Canterbury and the Cruise Terminal at Dover. **Directions: From A2 roundabout immediately north of Dover take A258 signposted Deal. After 1 mile turn right and the Court is on the right.**

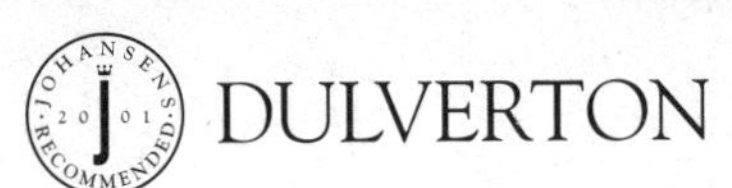

Ashwick Country House Hotel

DULVERTON, SOMERSET TA22 9QD
TEL: 01398 323868 FAX: 01398 323868 E-MAIL: ashwickhouse@talk21.com

OWNER: Richard Sherwood
CHEF: Richard Sherwood

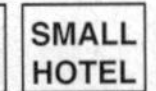

SMALL HOTEL

S: £78–£84
D: £136–£148
(including dinner)

This small, charming AA Red Star Edwardian Country House stands in six acres of beautiful grounds above the picturesque valley of the River Barle within Exmoor National Park. Sweeping lawns lead to large water gardens where guests can relax in summer shade and breathe in sweet floral scents. Ashwick House offers old world hospitality. Its atmosphere is sunny with flowers in summer and elegantly cosy with candlelight and log fires in winter.

The baronial style hall with its long, broad gallery and cheerful log fire, the restaurant opening onto a terrace where breakfast is served and the comfortably furnished lounge offer a peaceful sanctuary not easily found in today's busy world. All bedrooms are spacious and pleasantly decorated, finished with many thoughtful personal touches.

Chef-patron Richard Sherwood presents quality cuisine using fresh local produce. Shooting and riding facilities are close by. Magnificent walks on Exmoor from the hotel.

Places of interest nearby: Dunster's Norman Castle and 17th century Yarm Market, Exmoor Forest, many National Trust houses and gardens. **Directions: From the M5, exit at junction 27 onto the A361 to Tiverton. Take the A396 north until joining the B3222 to Dulverton and then the B3223 signposted Lynton and Exford. After a steep climb drive over a second cattle grid and turn left to Ashwick House.**

M 8 8

Oak Lodge Hotel

80 VILLAGE ROAD, BUSH HILL PARK, ENFIELD, MIDDLESEX EN1 2EU
TEL: 020 8360 7082

OWNERS: John and Yvonne Brown

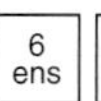

S: £79.50–£93.40
D: £89.50–£130

Oak Lodge is just nine miles from central London with excellent road and rail connections and conveniently placed for each of the capital's five airports. The hotel, awarded an ETB 2 Star Silver Award, is small but it offers a very generous welcome which encompasses charm, courtesy and old-fashioned hospitality.

Each en suite bedroom is highly individual, imaginatively furnished, and with all the facilities found in larger rooms. A superb new mini executive suite is now available.

Traditional English cuisine complemented by an exceptionally good wine list, is served in the intimate restaurant, awarded an AA Rosette, which overlooks and opens out onto a delightful evergreen garden. For after-dinner relaxation a pianist regularly entertains guests in a romantic Noel Coward style in the hotel's elegant lounge.

Enfield has excellent shopping facilities and preserves the atmosphere of the country town it once was. There are many fine old houses, particularly in Gentlemen's Row, where the 19th century author Charles Lamb lived.

Places of interest nearby: Forty Hall, built in 1632 for Sir Nicholas Raynton, Lord Mayor of London, now a cultural centre and museum, Capel Manor, St Albans cathedral and the ruins of a Roman amphitheatre. **Directions: From M25, exit at Jct25 onto A10 south. Turn right at 11th set of traffic lights into Church Street, right again at next lights into Village Road. Oak Lodge is 200 yards on the right.**

M 15

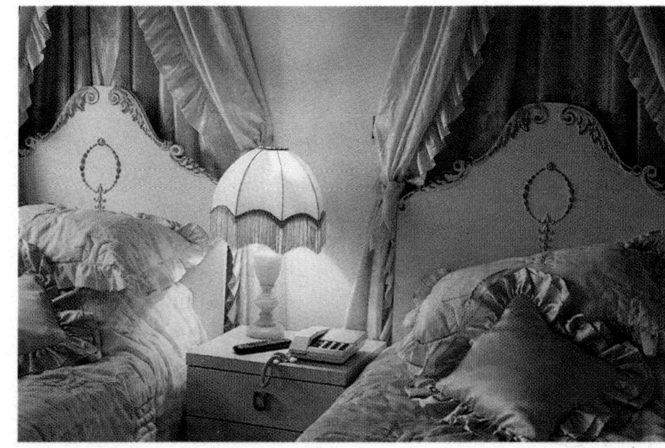

Chalk Lane Hotel

CHALK LANE, EPSOM, SURREY KT18 7BB
TEL: 01372 721179 FAX: 01372 727878 E-MAIL: chalklane@compuserve.com

OWNER: McGregor Hotels Limited

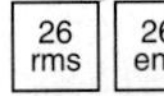  

   S: £70–£75
D: £80–£135

This delightful country house is hidden away from the hustle and bustle of modern life in the conservation area that is old Epsom. With a total refurbishment programme nearing completion in 2001, it repays handsomely any effort of locating it. The newly decorated bedrooms and bathrooms are presented to an impressive standard.

Discerning gastronomes will be delighted by the imaginative and beautifully-presented cuisine on offer. A good range of starters includes such irresistible offerings as hot roasted red pepper and goats cheese tart, Provençal-style vegetable and seared lamb fillet terrine and hot smoked Scottish salmon on a potato pancake with lemon on dill. A choice of nearly a dozen main courses includes mouth-watering dishes like Thai style monkfish curry with bok choi and jasmine rice, Scotch rib eye steak with crunchy leeks, French fries and port wine sauce and roasted salmon fillet with a red wine risotto scented with thyme and served with green asparagus. Vegetarians are also superbly catered for.

Places of interest nearby: This is an ideal location for horse-racing enthusiasts – the course at Epsom Downs is just minutes away. Wisley, Hampton Court and Richmond. **Directions: M25, junction 9 follow A24 to Ashstead and Epsom. When you reach the town centre turn right at the traffic lights by the BP garage and follow the brown signs.**

TRELAWNE HOTEL – THE HUTCHES RESTAURANT

MAWNAN SMITH, NR FALMOUTH, CORNWALL TR11 5HS
TEL: 01326 250226 FAX: 01326 250909

OWNERS: Paul and Linda Gibbons
CHEF: Rachel Dawes

12 rms | 12 ens | SMALL HOTEL

S: £65–£79
D: £135–£158
(including 4 course dinner)

A very friendly welcome awaits guests, who will be enchanted by the beautiful location of Trelawne Hotel, on the coast between the Rivers Fal and Helford. Large picture windows in the public rooms, including the attractively decorated, spacious lounge/bar, ensure that guests take full advantage of the panoramic vistas of the ever-changing coastline.

The bedrooms are charming, many with views of the sea. The soft colours of the décor, the discreet lighting and attention to detail provide a restful atmosphere, in harmony with the Wedgwood, fresh flowers and sparkling crystal in The Hutches Restaurant, which has been awarded 2 AA Rosettes.

The menu changes daily and offers a variety of inspired dishes, including local seafood, game and fresh vegetables.

Ideally located for coastal walks along Rosemullion Head and the picturesque Helford Estuary. There are also a wealth of famous gardens within the area. 'Slip Away Anyday' spring, autumn and winter breaks. Closed January. **Places of interest nearby:** The Royal Duchy of Cornwall is an area of outstanding beauty, with many National Trust and English Heritage properties to visit and a range of leisure pursuits to enjoy. **Directions: From Truro follow A39 towards Falmouth, turn right at Hillhead roundabout, take exit signposted Maenporth. Carry on for 3 miles and Trelawne is at the top overlooking Falmouth bay.**

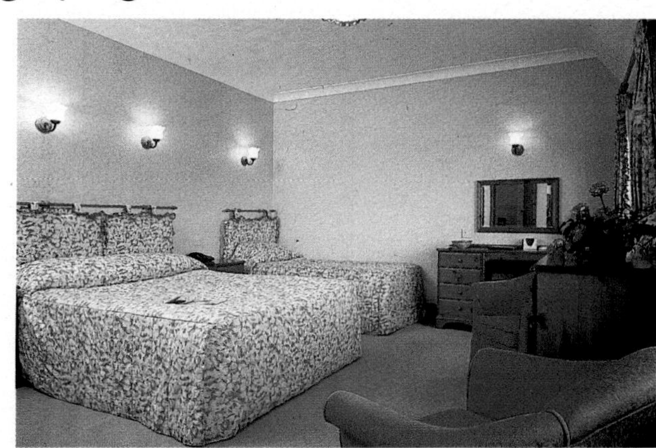

NEW FOLKESTONE (Sandgate) ENGLAND

SANDGATE HOTEL ET RESTAURANT LA TERRASSE

WELLINGTON TERRACE, THE ESPLANADE, SANDGATE, FOLKESTONE, KENT CT20 3DY
TEL: 01303 220444 FAX: 01303 220496

OWNERS: Zara and Samuel Gicqueau
RESTAURANT MANAGER: Joel Fricoteaux
CHEF: Samuel Gicqueau

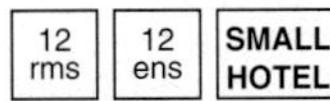

S: from £53
D: £58–£76

This is an enchanting bit of France on the English coast where Samuel and Zara Gicqueau welcome guests to their home with English hospitality and unmistakable French flair. Essentially it is a very fine restaurant with rooms. In Samuel's sea view restaurant, amid cast-iron fireplaces and paintings of his Loire Valley homeland, diners enjoy the innovative cooking of this talented chef who trained at Raymond Blanc's Le Manoir Aux Quat'Saisons.

Fresh fish and lobster are a speciality and artistically presented, and there are superb and exciting modern interpretations of traditional French cuisine and classical dishes. Drinks can be enjoyed in the intimate lounge or, on warmer days, on the long, sun-catching balcony overlooking the Channel.

The seafront terrace hotel was built in the mid 19th century and although retaining many features of its past, such as an elegant lounge, floor to ceiling windows, antique gilt mirrors and open fires, also offers every modern amenity. The bedrooms are cosy and decorated in warm pastel colours. Some have small balconies on which to take a full English or French breakfast while enjoying the beach and sea vistas.

Places of interest nearby: Sandgate antique shops, numerous historic little churches of the Romney Marsh, Dover Castle, Rye, Hythe, France by day excursion. **Directions: Sandgate is on the A259 between Folkestone and Hythe after exiting the M20 at junctions 11 or 12.**

Stanhill Court Hotel

STAN HILL ROAD, CHARLWOOD, NR HORLEY, SURREY RH6 0EP
TEL: 01293 862166 FAX: 01293 862773 FREEPHONE: 0800 594 3619 E-MAIL: enquiries@stanhillcourthotel.co.uk

OWNERS: Antonio and Kathryn Colas

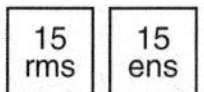   

S: from £110
D: £125–£200

Built in 1881 in the Scottish Baronial style, Stanhill Court Hotel is set in 35 acres of ancient wooded countryside and offers spectacular views over the North Downs. It boasts an original Victorian walled garden and amphitheatre available for concerts or corporate presentations and events.

The hotel is traditionally furnished to provide an intimate, warm and comfortable atmosphere, with rich pitch pine panelling evident throughout the hall, minstrels gallery and barrel roof. There is a wide choice of bedrooms, all decorated and furnished to the same high standards and offering a full range of facilities. A superb à la carte restaurant offers a menu which is international in flavour and complemented by an excellent range of regional and vintage wines. A choice of vegetarian dishes is always included and old style, personal service is guaranteed.

Versatile conference facilities include small meetings rooms and five function rooms. Stanhill Court is also a fine venue for wedding receptions, family celebrations and social gatherings and was voted Hotel of the Year 1998 by the South East England Tourist Board and Most Romantic Hotel by the AA. **Places of interest nearby:** Leonardslee, High Beeches, Nymans and Wakehurst Place. **Directions: Charlwood is north west of the airport and reached off the M23/A23 via Hookwood or Lowfield Heath. Go through Charlwood and follow signs towards Newdigate.**

M 180

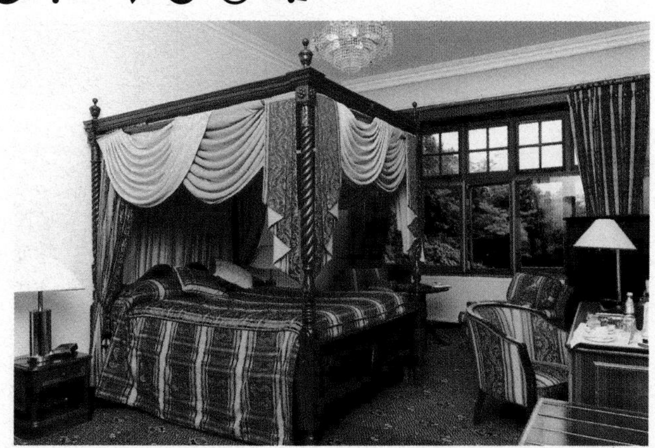

THE WIND IN THE WILLOWS

DERBYSHIRE LEVEL, GLOSSOP, DERBYSHIRE SK13 7PT
TEL: 01457 868001 FAX: 01457 853354 E-MAIL: info@windinthewillows.co.uk

OWNERS: Ian and Alison Wilkinson
CHEF: Hilary Barton

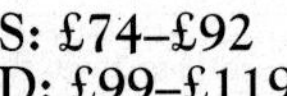

S: £74–£92
D: £99–£119

"Not so much a hotel, more a delightful experience" wrote a guest of this charming, small, family-run hotel on the edge of the Peak District. It won the AA Greatest Courtesy and Care in the North of England award 1996/97.

Antiques add to the delightful Victorian charm that is characteristic of The Wind in the Willows. If you don't know how it gets its name, stay there and read your bedside book!

The marvellous scenery of the National Park is, literally, at the doorstep. All of the twelve, en suite bedrooms enjoy superb views and all are full of character, even the newer ones, opened in 1995, having their share of antique furniture and traditional décor that embellishes the whole house. There are some very special features, too – huge antique mahogany beds, a Victorian style bath and individual touches in various rooms.

Hilary Barton presides in the kitchen from where delicious home-cooking is served to both the private dining room and the purpose-built meeting room. Many activities can be arranged locally, including pot-holing, horse-riding, gliding and para/hang gliding. Adjacent 9 hole golf course. **Places of interest nearby:** Chatsworth, Haddon Hall, Castleton and Bakewell are all within easy reach. **Directions: One mile east of Glossop on the A57, 400 yards down the road opposite the Royal Oak.**

The Cormorant Hotel

GOLANT BY FOWEY, CORNWALL PL23 1LL
TEL: 01726 833426 FAX: 01726 833426

OWNERS: Carrie and Colin King

11 rms 11 ens    SMALL HOTEL

S: £40–£62.50
D: £76–£98

The Cormorant Hotel stands high above the beautiful Fowey Estuary with magnificent views over the shimmering waters and the Cornish countryside. A warm, friendly and inviting atmosphere pervades the hotel which is enjoying gradual artistic refurbishment.

All the 11 entirely individual bedrooms, are en suite, with colour television, radio, direct dial telephone and extensive views over the estuary and creeks. Guests can relax in an extremely comfortable lounge which has full length picture windows and a log fire in winter. The bar is small and welcoming. Guests can also enjoy lounging on the terrace near the hotel's heated swimming pool which has a sliding roof for opening on hot summer days.

This corner of Cornwall is a living larder of wholesome produce all made use of by enthusiastic chef and served in a pretty candlelit restaurant. A choice of good and imaginative menus is offered.

Places of interest nearby: Miles of walking along the coastline, fishing villages, Lanhydrock House and gardens, Eden project and many National Trust properties. Fishing, riding and golf can be arranged locally. **Directions: From Exeter, take A30 towards Bodmin and then B3269 towards Fowey. After six miles turn left at a staggered junction to Golant. Bear right as you approach the estuary and continue along the water's edge. The hotel is on the right.**

WHITE MOSS HOUSE

RYDAL WATER, GRASMERE, CUMBRIA LA22 9SE
TEL: 015394 35295 FAX: 015394 35516 E-MAIL: dixon@whitemoss.com

OWNERS: Peter and Susan Dixon

8 rms | 8 ens | SMALL HOTEL

S: £80–£95
D: £130–£190
(including 5-course dinner)

Set in a fragrant garden of roses and lavender, White Moss House was once owned by Wordsworth, who often rested in the porch here between his wanderings. Built in 1730, it overlooks beautiful Rydal Water. Many famous and interesting walks through fells and lakeland start from the front door. Guests have free use of the local leisure club and swimming pool and free fishing on local rivers and lakes.

It has been described by a German gourmet magazine as 'probably the smallest, most splendid hotel in the world'. Proprietors Peter and Susan Dixon have created an intimate family atmosphere with a marvellous degree of comfort and attention to detail.

The seven bedrooms in the main house and the two in the Brockstone Cottage Suite are individually furnished, and most have lake views. Chef Peter Dixon has won international acclaim for his culinary skills including 2 AA Rosettes and a Red Star. The restaurant is deservedly famous for food prepared with imagination and style – 'the best English food in Britain', said *The Times* – and offers an extensive wine list of over 300 bins. Special breaks available. Closed December, January and February.

Places of interest nearby: Dove Cottage and Rydal Mount (Wordsworth's houses) are both one mile away. **Directions: White Moss House is off the A591 between Rydal Water and Grasmere, on the right as you drive north to Grasmere.**

THE OLD RECTORY

BARSHAM ROAD, GREAT SNORING, NORFOLK NR21 OHP
TEL: 01328 820597 FAX: 01328 820048 E-MAIL: greatsnoringoldrectory@compuserve.com

OWNERS: Rosamund and William Scoles

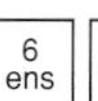

S: £71–£78
D: £93–£101

The Old Rectory, a former manor house, stands in $1^1/_2$ acres of walled gardens amid the unspoilt countryside of North Norfolk. The house, believed to date back to 1490, when it was the seat of Sir Ralph Shelton, was originally hexagonal. Two towers now remain with an intricate south east façade showing stone mullion windows bordered with frieze designs in terracotta tiles. The timeless tradition of the decor and furnishings creates an ambiance of bygone days. This secluded haven promises the discerning traveller old fashioned charm with a homely warmth and friendliness. The ideal base from which to explore this special part of Norfolk.

Established since 1978, The Old Rectory has also become a popular venue for group entertaining where 10–12 guests can enjoy the exclusive use of the house.

For those who like to be cosseted, but who relish the idea of independence, The Sheltons, self contained cottages in the grounds, are available. These are serviced daily and provide complete privacy in delightful surroundings. The house is closed from 24–27 December. **Places of interest nearby:** Heritage coast, nature reserves, Sandringham and Walsingham. **Directions: Great Snoring is 3 miles north-east of Fakenham from the A148. The Old Rectory is on the Barsham Road, behind the church.**

EDGE HALL HOTEL

2 HIGH STREET, HADLEIGH, IPSWICH, SUFFOLK IP7 5AP
TEL: 01473 822458 FAX: 01473 827751

OWNERS: Rod and Angela Rolfe

8 rms | 8 ens | SMALL HOTEL

S: £38–£50
D: £55–£85

Hadleigh is a small country town bustling with character. Located in Suffolk, central to East Anglia, it is the ideal base for business and for exploring the pretty coastal towns and villages in the Norfolk and Essex regions.

Built in 1590, the hotel is one of the oldest houses standing in Hadleigh High Street. The warm and friendly hosts welcome guests to their extremely comfortable hotel, which is perfect for those who feel like a relaxing break.

Great effort has been made to restore and retain the original features of the house and guests can admire the stunning staircase enhancing the flagstone hallway. Each bedroom is individually decorated and some enjoy views of the attractive gardens.

The hotel produces its own vegetables and a varied set dinner menu serves a wonderfully traditional English meal. Guests are invited to choose their own wines from the large selection in the cellar.

Places of interest nearby: Visitors can admire the many impressive buildings in the town, the magnificent wool church and guildhall or feed the ducks from the ancient Toppesfield Bridge, which is only a short walk away. There is boating and bird watching along the Essex coasts or antique shopping in Long Melford, and the more energetic can hire bicycles to explore the interesting villages nearby. **Directions: From A14 at Bury St Edmunds take A134 then A1141; from Ipswich take A1071; from A12 take B1070.**

Chase Lodge

10 PARK ROAD, HAMPTON WICK, KINGSTON-UPON-THAMES, SURREY KT1 4AS
TEL: 020 8943 1862 FAX: 020 8943 9363

OWNERS: Nigel and Denise Stafford-Haworth

11 rms | 11 ens | SMALL HOTEL

   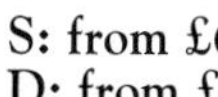

S: from £65
D: from £75

Chase Lodge is situated in a conservation area of architectural merit adjacent to Bushy Park. Originally built in 1870, the Lodge is now a very successful small hotel, run with great style and personality by proprietors Nigel and Denise Stafford-Haworth. The interiors have been designed with particular regard to the bijou nature of the building, to an extremely high standard with well-chosen items of furniture and striking décor and fabrics. The bedrooms are beautifully appointed; great care has been taken with lighting, and the most recently refurbished bathrooms all feature either a Jacuzzi bath or a steamroom/shower facility. The delightful restaurant looks onto an attractive courtyard garden.

Its proximity to many major events in the English social season makes Chase Lodge an outstanding choice for value. Wimbledon tennis; the Oxford and Cambridge Boat Race; horse racing at Kempton Park, Epsom Downs, Sandown Park and Royal Ascot; rugby at Twickenham; and the now annual flower show at Hampton Court. Central London with its shops and theatres is a short train ride away.

Other places of interest nearby: Richmond Park, Windsor Castle, Syon Park, Ham House, Kew Gardens. **Directions: From the M3 (junction 1) or Kingston take the A308. At western end of Kingston Bridge is the Hampton Wick roundabout; take White Hart exit into High Street (A310), then left at The Forresters into Park Road.**

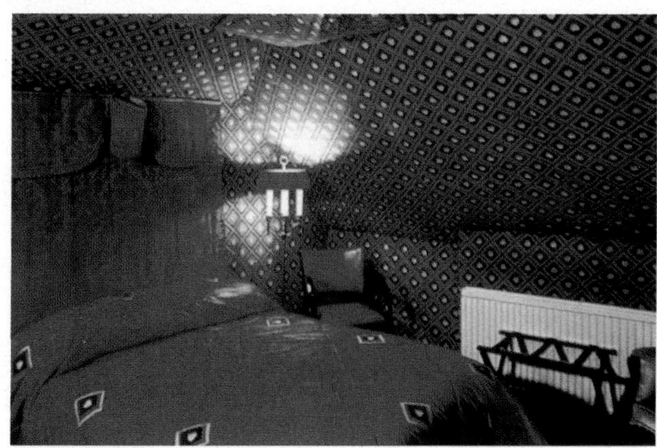

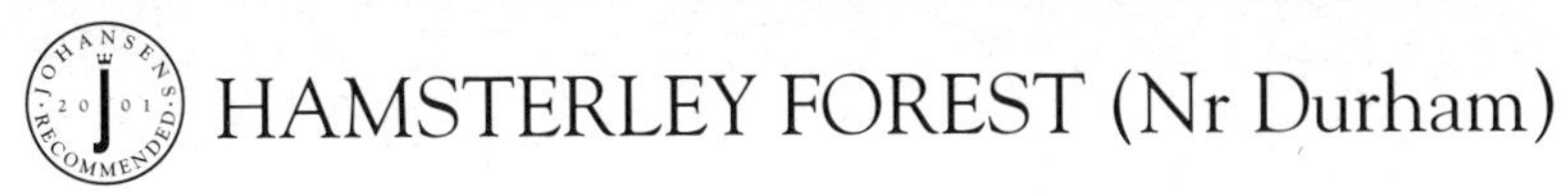

Grove House

HAMSTERLEY FOREST, NR BISHOP AUCKLAND, CO DURHAM DL13 3NL
TEL: 01388 488203 FAX: 01388 488174 E-MAIL: X0V47@dial.pipex.com

OWNERS: Helene Close

S: £47–£60
D: £94–£100
(including 5 course dinner)

Grove House nestles at the heart of a beautiful garden in the middle of glorious Hamsterley Forest. Two small rivers run, on each side of the property, through 5,000 acres of old oaks and moors. It is an idyllic situation. Peaceful, quiet and historical, the house was built in 1830 as an aristocrat's shooting box and it exudes grandeur. There are fine furnishings and fabrics, stylish décor and open fires. The bedrooms, two doubles with en suite bathroom, a twin with en suite shower and toilet – have full facilities and are extremely comfortable. This is a non smoking house.

Helene prepares five-course evening meals from the best fresh ingredients. Often on the set menu are venison and pheasant direct from the forest. Grove House is unlicensed so guests are invited to take their own wine.

Those requiring total seclusion can stay at the adjoining, fully fitted, three-bedroomed Grove Cottage which has a large patio and a hillside rock garden.

Places of interest nearby: Bowes Museum, Raby Castle, High Force waterfall, Killhope Wheel, Beamish Open Air Museum and Durham Cathedral. **Directions: From A1(M) turn off onto A68 and just over two miles after Toft Hill turn left, through Hamsterley Village until the sign for "The Grove". Follow road to right, then left and after ½ a mile turn right to Hamsterley Forest and Grove House. Grove House is three miles further on.**

The White House

10 PARK PARADE, HARROGATE, NORTH YORKSHIRE HG1 5AH
TEL: 01423 501388 FAX: 01423 527973 E-MAIL: info@whitehouse–hotel.demon.co.uk

OWNER: Jennie Forster

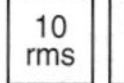

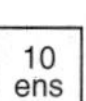

S: £70–£95
D: £90–£140

The White House enjoys a splendid location overlooking the Stray, 200 acres of parkland just a few minutes from the town centre. You will discover a unique residence in which luxury and comfort have blended with informality creating a relaxed atmosphere. The en suite bedrooms are individually furnished with designer fabrics and antiques together with full facilities.

The Venetian Room Restaurant offers a wide variety of exquisite and original dishes, with a very fine wine list and has held two AA Rosettes for many years.

Some of the many awards the hotel has achieved recently are 'Which?' County Hotel of the Year, A.C.E. Best Small Hotel, RAC Restaurant and Hospitality awards.

A perfect hotel for a private house party or wedding, where attention to detail is a foregone conclusion. Special mini breaks, available all year round.

Places of interest nearby: Harrogate is a spa town with its own Turkish bath, beautiful parks and gardens and numerous shops including antiques. Other attractions include Fountains Abbey, Harewood House and the Yorkshire Dales. **Directions: The White House is situated on The Stray and is set back from the A59. Request a map when booking for detailed directions.**

ROOKHURST COUNTRY HOUSE HOTEL

WEST END, GAYLE, HAWES, NORTH YORKSHIRE DL8 3RT
TEL: 01969 667454 FAX: 01969 667128 E-MAIL: rookhurst@lineone.net

OWNER: Richard and Judith Hynds

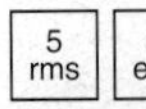

S: £70
D: £100–£140
(including dinner)

Nestling in the midst of Wensleydale, the front gate of this part-Georgian, part-Victorian country house opens onto the 250 mile-long Pennine Way. The cosy oak-beamed Georgian bedrooms are well-appointed and the more spacious Victorian bedrooms are furnished with four-poster beds whilst the rustic attic is particularly ornate, featuring a half-tester bed. This is a non smoking house.

Judith specialises in traditional home-cooked English dishes, made with fresh mostly locally produced ingredients and bakes the bread for Breakfast. An open fire creates a cosy atmosphere in the sitting room, where guests can relax with a drink and enjoy the views over the landscaped garden and fields to the fells. Special break rates available.

Places of interest nearby: Rookhurst makes an ideal base for exploring Herriot country – the Yorkshire Dales are a delight for both serious walkers and strollers. Nearby is the Carlisle to Settle railway and you can be collected from Garsdale Station. Just round the corner is the Wensleydale Creamery, and in Hawes the Upper Dales folk museum. **Directions: Take A684 Sedbergh–Bedale road. At Hawes take Gayle Lane to Gayle. At the top of the lane turn right and the hotel is 300 yards further on the right.**

SAWREY HOUSE COUNTRY HOTEL

NR SAWREY, HAWKSHEAD, AMBLESIDE, CUMBRIA LA22 0LF
TEL: 015394 36387 FAX: 015394 36010 E-MAIL: enquiries@sawrey–house.com

OWNERS: Shirley and Colin Whiteside

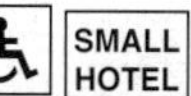
10 rms 10 ens SMALL HOTEL

S: £45–£65
D: £90–£120

Marooned in three acres of sculpted gardens designed for lazy indolence, Sawrey House Country Hotel is a quintessentially English rural hideaway. Built in the 1830s with slate from the local quarry, it is one of the prettiest buildings in the pristine conservation hamlet of Near Sawrey. Next door is 'Hilltop' once the home of Beatrix Potter, and visitors to Near Sawrey cannot fail to be captivated by the village's quaint tranquillity which so inspired her writings.

Owners Shirley and Colin are justifiably proud of their Chef's dinners which have received 2 AA Rossettes and their comfortable dining room, which has spectacular views over Esthwaite water and the lush forests beyond. Guests can take afternoon tea in the spacious lounge, while the bar offers guests some of the finest locally-brewed ales. The whole area is surrounded by National Trust land and is idyllic for walking. The hotel is centrally situated with the Windermere ferry only minutes from the House and Hawkshead, Ambleside and Coniston only a few minutes drive away. For the more energetic, Sawrey House will organise horse riding, fishing, sailing and even hot-air ballooning.

Places of interest nearby: Langdale and the Grizedale Forest are amongst the many natural attractions in the near vicinity.

Directions: Take junction 36 off M6, and follow A591 in the direction of Windermere, and continue to Ambleside. Take sign B5286, then the B5285 to Near Sawrey. Sawrey House is on the right.

M 25

THE PHEASANT

HAROME, HELMSLEY, NORTH YORKSHIRE YO62 5JG
TEL: 01439 771241/770416 FAX: 01439 771744

OWNERS: Kenneth and Tricia Binks

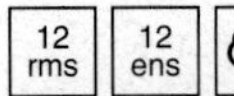
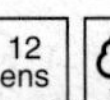

S: £65.50–£72
D: £131–£142
(including dinner)

The Pheasant, rich in oak beams and open log fires, offers two types of accommodation, some in the hotel and some in a charming, 16th century thatched cottage. The Binks family, who built the hotel and now own and manage it, have created a friendly atmosphere which is part of the warm Yorkshire welcome all guests receive.

The bedrooms and suites are brightly decorated in an attractive, cottage style and all are complete with en suite facilities. Traditional English cooking is the speciality of the restaurant, many of the dishes prepared using fresh fruit and vegetables grown in the hotel gardens.

During the summer, guests may chat or relax on the terrace overlooking the pond. The opening of a new indoor heated swimming pool is an added attraction. Other sporting activities available locally include swimming, riding, golf and fishing.

Places of interest nearby: York is a short drive away, as are a host of historic landmarks including Byland and Rievaulx Abbeys and Castle Howard of Brideshead Revisited fame. Also nearby is the magnificent North York Moors National Park. Dogs by arrangement. Closed Christmas, January and February. **Directions: From Helmsley, take the A170 towards Scarborough; after ¼ mile turn right for Harome. Hotel is near the church in the village.**

NANSLOE MANOR

HELSTON, CORNWALL TR13 0SB
TEL: 01326 574691 FAX: 01326 564680 E-MAIL: info@nansloe-manor.co.uk

OWNERS: The Ridden Family

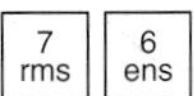

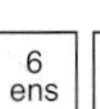

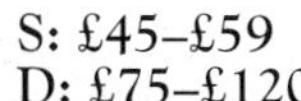

S: £45–£59
D: £75–£120

This enchanting Georgian manor stands in romantic Daphne du Maurier country and guests are instantly aware they are coming to somewhere very special, as they approach the house along the tree lined drive.

Discovering Nansloe is serendipity – peaceful, surrounded by verdant, rural countryside, the hotel is owned (and managed) by the Ridden family, who have personally added so much to its warm ambience.

The bedrooms have lovely views across the Loe Valley. Each differs from the next, all are spacious and luxurious, with curtains and covers in gorgeous fabrics.

The drawing room has a fine Victorian fireplace, a welcome sight on cool evenings. It is charmingly furnished, big bowls of fresh flowers adding colour; the overall effect is relaxing – the ideal spot for a traditional Cornish tea or apéritif, in summer enjoyed alfresco on the croquet lawn.

The two AA Rosette and 3 RAC Dining Seals restaurant is famed for its inspired menus, featuring local specialities including fish fresh from the sea, and the cellar contains excellent wines.

Places of interest nearby: Helston, Falmouth, St Ives and many gardens. Golf and sailing. Special breaks are available. **Directions: The Manor is situated the end of a well signed drive some 800 yards from junction of A394 from Falmouth and A3083 to the Lizard.**

The Steppes

ULLINGSWICK, NR HEREFORD, HEREFORDSHIRE HR1 3JG
TEL: 01432 820424 FAX: 01432 820042 E-MAIL: bookings@steppeshotel.fabusiness.co.uk

OWNERS: Henry and Tricia Howland

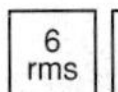
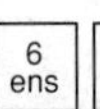

S: from £45
D: from £80

A Grade II listed 14th century yeoman's house, The Steppes is located in Ullingswick, a *Domesday Book* hamlet set in the Wye Valley. The gleaming whitewashed exterior conceals a host of original features. Cobble and flag-flooring, massive oak timbers and an inglenook fireplace were part of the ancient dairy and cider-making cellars, which form the splendid cellar bar and lounge.

Winner of the Johansens 1996 "Value for Money Award", the ambience of this non–smoking house has been applauded by *The Sunday Telegraph*, *The Guardian* and *The Independent* newspapers – all of which praise the enthusiasm and hospitality of owners Henry and Tricia Howland and, in particular, Tricia's cooking. The candlelit dinners are compiled from medieval recipes, revived local dishes, Mediterranean delicacies and French cuisine. The interesting breakfast menu is complemented by generous service. Exceptionally high standard en suite accommodation is provided in either the Tudor Barn or Courtyard Cottage, both located within the grounds. Closed December and January.
Places of interest nearby: River Wye (salmon fishing), Black Mountains, Malvern Hills (Elgar's birthplace), Welsh Marches, Gloucester and Worcester. Riding can be arranged. **Directions: A mile off A417 Gloucester–Leominster, signed Ullingswick.**

Santo's Higham Farm

MAIN ROAD, HIGHAM, DERBYSHIRE DE55 6EH
TEL: 01773 833812/3/4 FAX: 01773 520525 E-MAIL: reception@santoshighamfarm.demon.co.uk

MANAGER: Santo Cusimano
CHEF: Craig Beastall

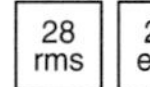   

S: £52–£83
D: £62–£93
Suite: £103

This delightful and rambling former 15th century farmhouse stands in the heart of the beautiful Derbyshire countryside overlooking the Amber Valley. The hotel has been tastefully refurbished and extended over the past four years to an excellent standard and offers visitors every modern amenity to make a stay comfortable and memorable. Old character and atmosphere are immediately evident and many of its original and unique features are still on view.

The bedrooms are superbly furnished and equipped, and each has a stylish and luxurious en suite bathroom. Two offer Jacuzzi air baths, two have four-poster beds and three boast waterbeds. A new Italian wing comprises eight bedrooms and there is an internationally themed wing of seven bedrooms.

The hotel has a reputation for fine dining with excellent à la carte and table d'hôte cuisine being attentively served in Guiseppe's restaurant, whilst less formal Italian and Continental meals are offered in the Sports Bar.

Guests can go for interesting walks in the surrounding area and there is lake fishing, golf, riding and a leisure centre with indoor and outdoor swimming pools nearby. Conference facilities for up to 34 delegates.

Places of interest nearby: The stately homes of Chatsworth House, Hardwick Hall, Haddon Hall and the Crich Tram Museum. **Directions: Exit M1 at junction 28 and take A38 to Alfreton. Then join A61 towards Chesterfield. Higham is reached after approximately 4 miles.**

M 100

FELBRIGG LODGE

AYLMERTON, NORTH NORFOLK NR11 8RA
TEL: 01263 837588 FAX: 01263 838012 E-MAIL: info@felbrigglodge.co.uk

OWNERS: Jill and Ian Gillam

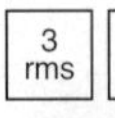 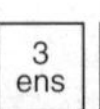  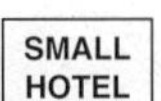

S: £82
D: £110
Suite: £130

Jill and Ian Gillam have created this charming Lodge with the aim of providing the highest possible standards of accommodation in North Norfolk in a setting of total quiet and relaxation. Evoking an informal and welcoming ambience, the Lodge provides complete freedom for guests to mix with others or to seek solitude. Here time has stood still. Nothing disturbs over 50 different species of birds and other wildlife amongst rolling lawns and specimen trees and shrubs.

Felbrigg Lodge enjoys an unrivalled position just outside the Felbrigg Hall estate, a 17th century house owned by the National Trust. Approached by a long drive, the eight acres of grounds are totally secluded. The rooms, which are all at ground level, are situated around the gardens to take the greatest advantage of the view and landscape. All are sumptuously decorated with flair and imagination and have luxurious en suite bathrooms. Full English breakfasts and candlelit dinners are served in the converted stables. Jill is an enthusiastic cook and uses the best local produce.

Guests may relax in the privacy of their own rooms, wander at leisure through the gardens, play croquet, take afternoon tea in the summer house or swim in the heated indoor pool. A small, well-equipped gym is provided for the more energetic. **Places of interest nearby:** Felbrigg Hall, Blickling Hall and Holkham Hall. The cathedral city of Norwich is worth a visit whilst the North Norfolk coast is just 2km away. **Directions: Please ring the Lodge for detailed directions and brochure.**

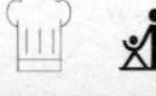   

The Old Rectory

CRICKET MALHERBIE, ILMINSTER, SOMERSET TA19 0PW
TEL: 01460 54364 FAX: 01460 57374 E-MAIL: TheOldRectory@malherbie.freeserve.co.uk

OWNERS: Michael and Patricia Fry-Foley, Ruth Parker

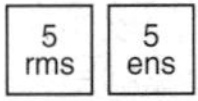   

 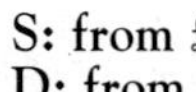 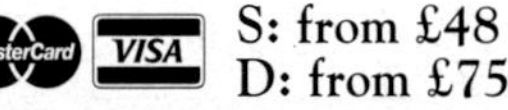

S: from £48
D: from £75

Set in the tiny hamlet of Cricket Malherbie, The Old Rectory is a delightful country house with Strawberry Hill Gothic windows, a thatched roof and weathered hamstone walls. The flagstoned hall leads guests through to the enchanting sitting room, adorned with exquisite carved oak beams and exuding a tranquil atmosphere.

The five bedrooms are peaceful and furnished in a very tasteful manner, some with Gothic windows and all overlooking the gardens. Well-equipped and offering every possible comfort, the rooms include en suite bathrooms and showers. This is a totally non-smoking property.

The dining room is beautifully presented with large shuttered windows affording views of the lawns on both sides of the house. Guests sit at the grand table in dinner-party fashion and indulge in the daily-changing four-course menu. Produce from the vegetable garden and local fish and game feature highly in the inspired dishes.

Places of interest: Those with an interest in architecture will be pleased with the location as Bath, Stonehenge, Wells and Glastonbury are ideal destinations for day trips. Montacute House, Barrington Court and Yeovilton Air Museum are all close by. **Directions: The nearest motorway is M5. Exit at junction 25, join A358 towards Chard at A303 roundabout take the Chard exit again onto A358. Drive through the village of Donyatt, turn left for Ilminster and then right for Cricket Malherbie.**

Ilsington Country Hotel

ILSINGTON, NEWTON ABBOT, DEVON TQ13 9RR
TEL: 01364 661452 FAX: 01364 661307 E-MAIL: hotel@ilsington.co.uk

OWNERS: Tim and Maura Hassell
CHEF: Mike O'Donnell

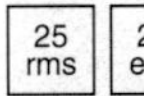

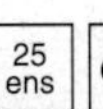

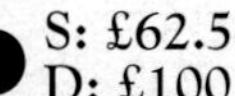

S: £62.50
D: £100

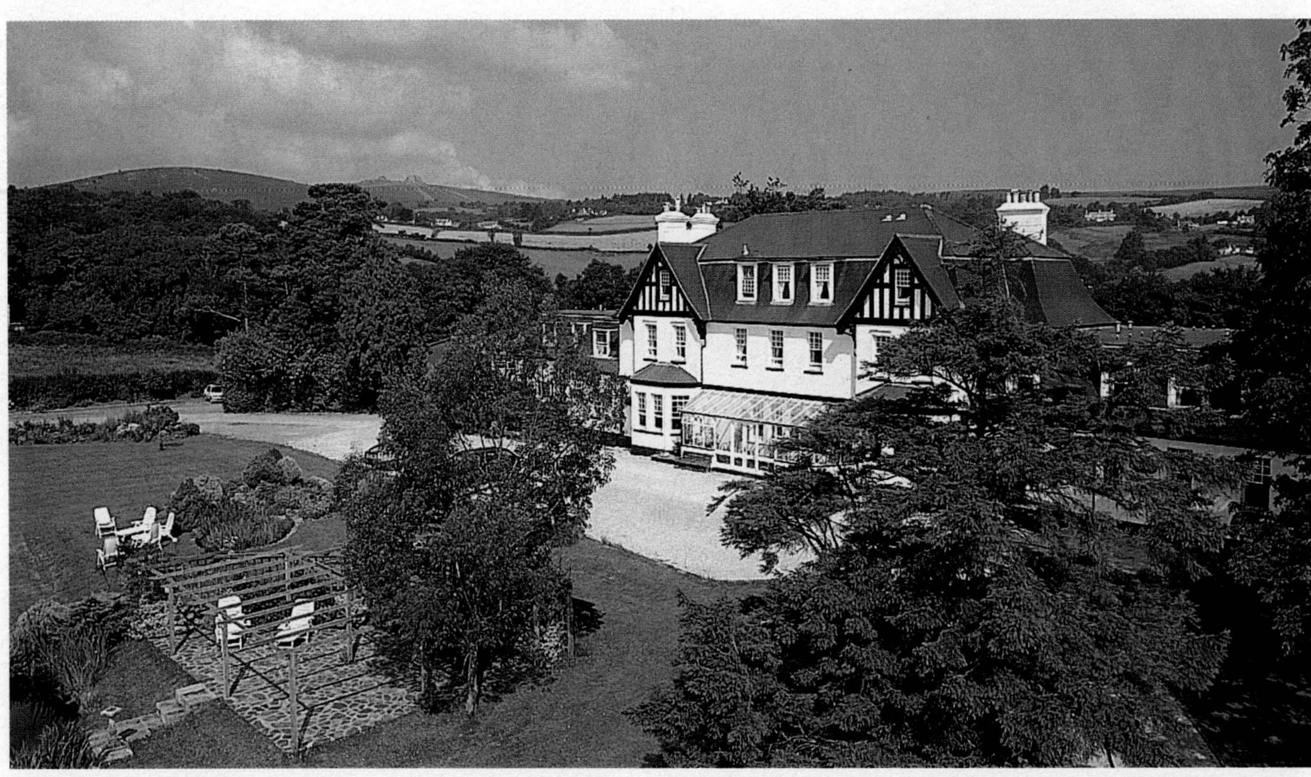

The Ilsington Hotel stands in ten acres of beautiful private grounds within the Dartmoor National Park. Run by friendly proprietors, Tim and Maura Hassell, the delightful furnishings and ambience offer a most comfortable environment in which to relax. Stylish bedrooms and suites all boast outstanding views across the rolling pastoral countryside and every comfort and convenience to make guests feel at home, including English toiletries. The distinctive candle-lit dining room is perfect for savouring the superb cuisine, awarded an AA rosette, created by talented chefs from fresh local produce. The library is ideal for an intimate dining party or celebration whilst the Victorian conservatory is the place for morning coffee or a Devon cream tea. There is a fully equipped purpose built gymnasium, heated indoor pool, sauna and spa – also experienced masseurs.

Places of interest nearby: Some of England's most idyllic and unspoilt scenery surrounds Ilsington, with the picturesque villages of Lustleigh and Widecombe-in-the-Moor close by. Footpaths lead from the hotel on to Dartmoor. Riding, fishing and many other country pursuits can be arranged. **Directions: From M5 join A38 at Exeter following Plymouth signs. After approximately 12 miles exit for Moretonhampstead and Newton Abbot. At roundabout follow signs for Ilsington.**

Rylstone Manor

RYLSTONE GARDENS, SHANKLIN, ISLE OF WIGHT PO37 6RE
TEL: 01983 862806 FAX: 01983 862806 E-MAIL: rylestone@dialstart.net

OWNERS: Neil Graham and Alan Priddle
CHEF: Neil Graham

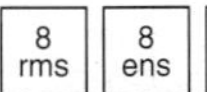   

   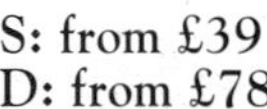

S: from £39
D: from £78

Neil Graham and Alan Priddle are the proud owners of this hidden gem uniquely located in 4½ acres of tranquil gardens on the fringe of Shanklin. Just two minutes' walk away through the gardens are the promenade and beach and the manor gardens enjoy stunning views out across Shanklin Bay.

An atmosphere of comfort and relaxation is engendered in the stylish day rooms where afternoon tea and a good book are just the thing on inclement days.

In the restaurant, Neil prepares a nightly table d'hôte menu with an eagle eye on the best available produce and an expert's touch in its preparation. Poached fillet of salmon, roast loin of lamb and breast of duck are served with imaginative, simple sauces.

Both the restaurant and bedrooms are designated non-smoking; no children under 16 are taken; and dogs are not permitted. Rylstone Manor is truly a haven of peace, in a delightfully protected environment.

Places of interest nearby: For the more active, water sports, fishing, riding and golf can all be arranged. In addition to being a walkers' paradise, the island has many other manor houses and gardens to visit. Nearby are the thatched cottages of Shanklin Old Village, Queen Victoria's Osborne House, Carisbrook Castle and Rylstone Gardens Countryside Centre.

Directions: Just off the A3055 Sandown to Ventnor road in Shanklin Old Village, follow signs directly into Rylstone Gardens.

Dale Head Hall Lakeside Hotel

THIRLMERE, KESWICK, CUMBRIA CA12 4TN
TEL: 017687 72478 FAX: 017687 71070 E-MAIL: onthelakeside@dale–head–hall.co.uk

OWNERS: Alan and Shirley Lowe and family

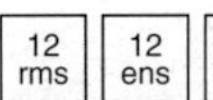

S: £88–£105
D: £125–£180
(including 5 course dinner)

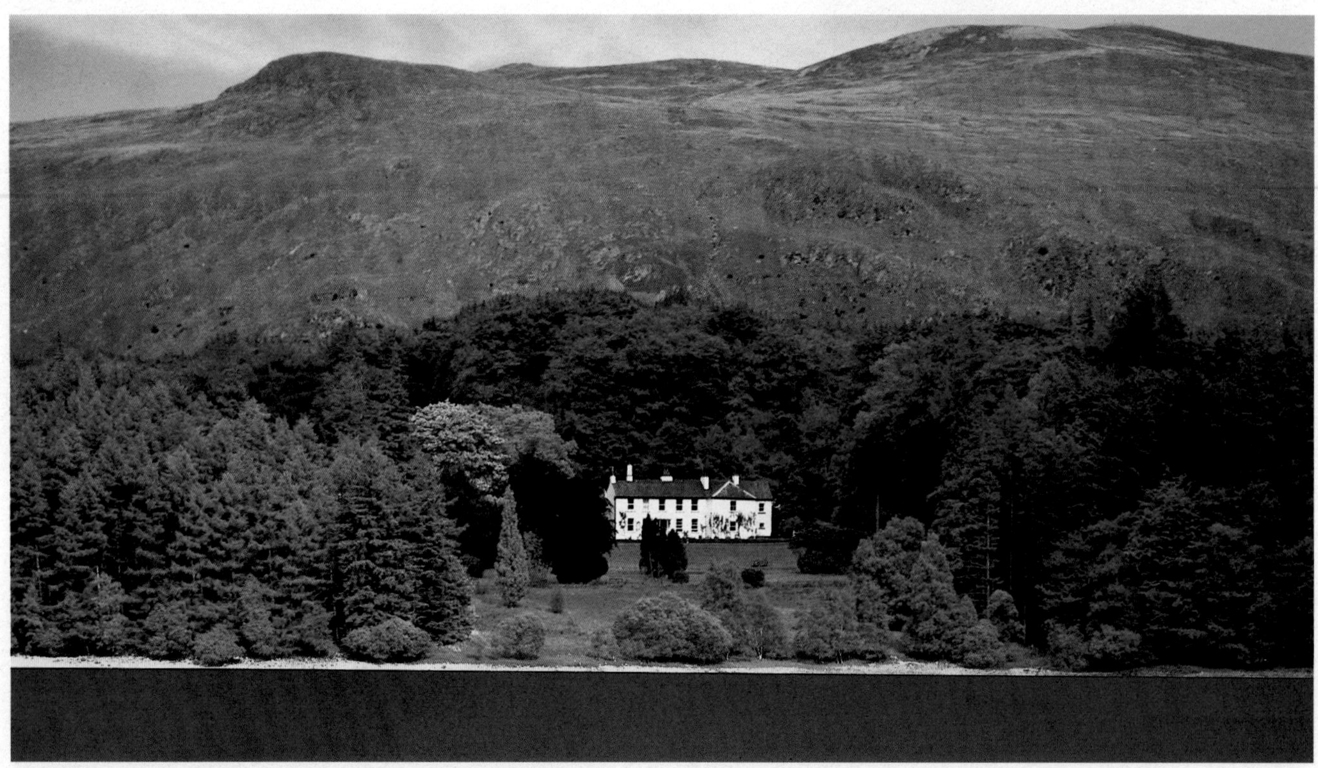

On the edge of Thirlmere, Cumbria's most central lake, with only the sound of the birds breaking the silence stands Dale Head Hall. It is a truly scenic gem. At the foot of Helvellyn, almost completely surrounded by lush woodlands, this glorious 16th century house reigns alone on the shores of the lake and must surely command one of the most tranquil settings in the Lake District. Hosts Alan and Shirley Lowe and family, having restored the 16th century authenticity of the house, now offer exceptional accommodation and service. The hotel was deservedly runner-up for the Johansens 1995 Most Excellent Country House Hotel.

Bar and lounge are both delightful, sharing views over lake and mountains. The oak panelled dining room is the ideal place to enjoy the hotel's superb cuisine (Michelin; Good Food Guide; AA Red Rosettes; RAC Restaurant Award). The bedrooms are extremely welcoming, warm and spacious and have all the things that you will expect to find, plus those little extras that make your stay so very special. Dale Head is one of those wonderful secrets which you would like to keep for yourself.

Places of interest nearby: All the splendours of the Lake District: Helvellyn is on the doorstep and Borrowdale is close by. **Directions: On the A591, halfway between Keswick and Grasmere. The hotel is situated along a private driveway overlooking Lake Thirlmere.**

Swinside Lodge Hotel

GRANGE ROAD, NEWLANDS, KESWICK, CUMBRIA CA12 5UE
TEL/FAX: 017687 72948 E-MAIL: info@swinsidelodge-hotel.co.uk

OWNER: Kevin and Susan Kniveton
CHEF: Chris Astley

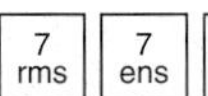
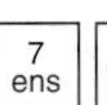

S: £72–£95
D: £136–£175
(including dinner)

Swinside Lodge, situated at the foot of Catbells, is a Victorian lakeland house, surrounded by hills, valleys and woodland, and close to the shores of Derwentwater.

The house has seven attractive en suite bedrooms, each offering a high degree of comfort and equipped with colour TV, radio, hairdryer, tea making facilities plus a wealth of extras. Begin your day with a hearty Cumbrian breakfast and later return to the comfort of the charming sitting rooms before enjoying your four-course dinner in the intimate candle-lit dining room. Menus change daily and a typical meal could include wild mushroom souffle on a dressed salad with red pepper vinaigrette, a delicious soup with home-baked rolls followed by pan-fried breast and stuffed leg of guinea fowl with a red wine and shallot sauce with freshly cooked vegetables. A choice of puddings or a variety of British farmhouse cheeses is followed by coffee and home-made petit fours. Vegetarian and specialist diets can be provided.

An AA Red Star hotel with 2 Rosettes for food, RAC Blue Ribbon Award and ETB Gold Award, Swinside Lodge is a non-smoking house and is licensed.

Places of interest nearby: Keswick Pencil Museum, Castlerigg Stone Circle, Wordsworth's birthplace, excellent walks from the house. **Directions: M6 junction 40 take the A66 bypassing Keswick – over main roundabout – take second left. Go through Portinscale towards Grange; hotel is two miles further on the right.**

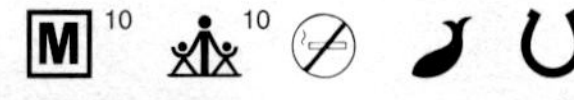

THE WHITE HOUSE

CHILLINGTON, KINGSBRIDGE, DEVON TQ7 2JX
TEL: 01548 580580 FAX: 01548 581124

OWNERS: Robin and Tina Kerswell

7 rms | 7 ens | SMALL HOTEL

MasterCard VISA S: £52–£75
D: £80–£112

Standing in lawned and terraced gardens in rural South Devon, The White House has an atmosphere reminiscent of a quieter and less hurried age. A period Grade II listed building of great charm, the hotel is an ideal base for exploring the countryside and coastline.

To the west is the busy market town of Kingsbridge and the Salcombe Estuary famous for its sailing. To the north are Totnes, Dartington and the wild expanses of Dartmoor. Historic Dartmouth, Torquay and the English Riviera are to the east and south is the spectacular South Hams coastline with its rugged cliffs, sandy beaches and quiet coves.

The White House offers the utmost comfort with well-proportioned bedrooms, two of which are spacious suites. Guests can relax in the elegant Brockington Room and Doctor Smalley's Drawing Room which opens onto the south-facing terrace and garden. The Bar Lounge is another comfortable meeting place.

The Copper Beech Restaurant makes a delightful setting for enjoying appetising cuisine prepared by the chef who makes the maximum use of local and seasonal produce. **Places of interest nearby:** Kingsbridge, Totnes, Salcombe, Dartmouth, numerous picturesque villages and several National Trust properties. **Directions: Leave Totnes on the A381 to Kingsbridge and then turn left onto the A379 Dartmouth road to Chillington.**

HIPPING HALL

COWAN BRIDGE, KIRKBY LONSDALE, CUMBRIA LA6 2JJ
TEL: 015242 71187 FAX: 015242 72452 E-MAIL: hippinghal@aol.com

OWNERS: Richard and Jean Skelton

6 rms | 6 ens | PRIVATE HOUSE

S: £74
D: £92–£110

Hipping Hall is a 17th century country house set in three acres of walled gardens on the Cumbria/North Yorkshire borders, so an ideal centre from which to tour both the Lake District and Yorkshire Dales. Having just four double rooms and two cottage suites, this is an especially suitable venue for small groups wanting a place to themselves – families or friends celebrating an anniversary, golfing parties, corporate entertaining etc – and these house parties (available throughout the year) are a feature of Hipping Hall's success.

But from March to November it is mostly individual guests who enjoy the comfort and informality of staying with Jean and Richard. The well-equipped bedrooms are largely furnished with antiques and all have attractive bathrooms.

Guests help themselves to drinks from an honesty bar in the conservatory before feasting on the delights of the à la carte menu created by Jean. A typical dinner may start with baked brie and toasted almond butter, followed by shank of lamb with a mint and rosemary jus and crispy potato rosti, and rounded off with rhubarb and white chocolate chip crumble or a classic cheese board with bread and biscuits.

Places of interest nearby: The Lake District, The Yorkshire Dales, The Settle to Carlisle Railway, Brontë country, Sizergh Castle. **Directions: Hipping Hall lies on the A65, two miles east of Kirkby Lonsdale towards Settle & Skipton, eight miles from M6 junction 36.**

Penhallow Manor Country House Hotel

ALTARNUN, LAUNCESTON, CORNWALL PL15 7SJ
TEL: 01566 86206 FAX: 01566 86179

OWNERS: Valerie and Peter Russell
CHEF: Valerie Russell

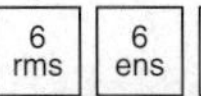   

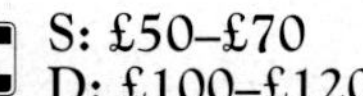

S: £50–£70
D: £100–£120

A grade II listed building dating from the 1840s, Penhallow Manor is a Georgian style country house offering peace, tranquillity and every conceivable creature comfort. Visitors are immediately struck by the beautifully presented interior which abounds with wonderful antiques, prints and pictures. The six bedrooms have all been individually decorated with charming fabrics and benefit from en suite bathrooms.

Penhallow prides itself on its succulent cuisine. Served in magnificent, yet informal surroundings it utilises only the finest of local produce, and is cooked to order. Eclectic in its inspiration, a typical meal may include parsnip, lemon and ginger soup, followed by shoulder of Devon lamb, with tarte aux pommes Normande to finish. The wine list is no less impressive, especially for a small hotel. Personally chosen by the hotel's owner, the selection is a mixture of the familiar and the unusual, and thus accommodates the taste of the adventurous and less adventurous alike.

Places of interest nearby: With the North and South Cornish coasts a short drive away, Penhallow is ideally located for those visitors wishing to explore Cornwall. Padstow with its windsurfing and sailing facilities is nearby. The numerous National Trust Houses and Gardens are all easily accessible and the championship golf courses are a short drive away. **Directions: M5 exit Junction 31, join A30 signposted Okehampton and carry on past Launceston; leave A30 at slip signed for Five Lanes, Trewint and Alternun.**

LOWER BACHE HOUSE

KIMBOLTON, NR LEOMINSTER, HEREFORDSHIRE HR6 OER
TEL & FAX: 01568 750304 E-MAIL: leslie.wiles@care4free.net

OWNERS: Rose and Leslie Wiles

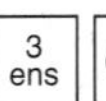

S: £39
D: £59

A Johansens award winner 4 miles from historic Leominster, Lower Bache is an oasis for nature lovers in 14 acres of a gentle Herefordshire valley. This substantial 17th century stone farmhouse has been restored by Rose and Leslie Wiles. While retaining its exposed stone walls, wealth of oak beams and flagstone flooring, it incorporates all the comforts of modern living. An annexe of three en suite bedrooms is furnished in a charming cottage style. Each bedroom has its own private sitting room. Water colours, original prints, plants, books and ornaments create an atmosphere of quality and comfort. With its vaulted ceiling and original cider mill, the dining room is unique. Rose and Leslie are acclaimed gourmet cooks: their set menus are superb value. Bread, ice-cream and preserves are all home-made; fish, game and poultry are smoked on the premises and most of the vegetables are grown organically in the garden. The breakfast menu offers an exceptional choice including laverbread, kedgeree, sautie bannocks, floddies and scrambled eggs with smoked salmon. Organic wines are also available.

Places of interest nearby: The Marches, Ludlow, Hereford, Worcester and Hay-on-Wye. 13 golf courses and 3 race courses are situated within 25 miles. **Directions: Kimbolton village is 2 miles north-east of Leominster (which is off the A49). Lower Bache is signposted at the top of the hill on the Leysters road A4112.**

WASHINGBOROUGH HALL

CHURCH HILL, WASHINGBOROUGH, LINCOLN LN4 1BE
TEL: 01522 790340 FAX: 01522 792936 E-MAIL: washingborough.hall@btinternet.com

OWNER: Margaret Broddle
EXECUTIVE CHEF: Mike Richardson

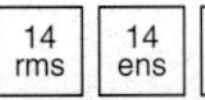

S: £65–£80
D: £85–£99.50

This listed Georgian Manor House is set in four acres of secluded grounds, containing many mature trees and wonderful colourful borders. During the summer months, its main lawns are an ideal place for relaxing with a drink or playing croquet whilst in winter, guests can recline in the lounge in front of a roaring fire. The bedrooms are individually styled and furnished to a very high standard with en suite bathrooms, tea and coffee making facilities, hairdryer, trouser press and many other amenities. There is also a Computer Lounge with a high specification computer with complimentary Internet access and other software.

Overlooking the gardens, the Lounge Bar and Restaurant offer the highest quality of fresh local produce, prepared to the highest standards, complemented by an extensive wine list and well-stocked bar. The Wedgwood Dining Rooms were awarded two AA Rosettes yet again for their outstanding cuisine and are now aiming for a third. The Washingborough is happy to arrange golf at Blakeney and Canwick Golf Clubs as well as a host of other activities including tennis and riding. **Places of interest nearby:** The city of Lincoln with its magnificent 11th century cathedral and castle. Aircraft buffs should visit The Battle of Britain Memorial Flight and The Aviation Heritage Centre. **Directions: From Lincoln take B1188 towards Branston and turn left onto B1190 towards Bardney. Turn right (approx 2 miles) opposite telephone box. The Hall is 200 yards on the left.**

Winder Hall Country House

LOW LORTON, NR COCKERMOUTH, CUMBRIA CA13 9UP
TEL: 01900 85107 FAX: 01900 85107 E-MAIL: stay@winderhall.co.uk

OWNERS: Derek & Mary Denman

 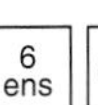  

S: £55–£65
D: £95–£110
(including dinner)

With its grey-stone walls, tall chimneys, stone-mullioned windows and diamond patterned leaded-lights this historic old manor house is one of the most attractive hotels in Lakeland. It stands majestically on the River Cocker in a peaceful little village surrounded by the rugged charm of the Lake District National Park and close to Loweswater, Crummock and Buttermere Lakes. Grade II listed, the Hall is named after the Winder family who owned the estate and built the Hall between 1397 and 1699.

Despite renovations and refurbishments over the years Winder Hall retains many original features which combine gracefully with the comforts required by today's discerning guests. Six en suite bedrooms are luxurious and charmingly decorated and furnished with antiques in keeping with the elegance of the Hall. All offer panoramic views over Lorton Fells and welcoming fresh flowers and Cumbrian handmade chocolates on arrival. Chef proprietor Derek Denman provides superb, full Cumbrian breakfasts and four-course dinners in the oak panelled dining room which overlooks the formal walled garden.

Places of interest nearby: William Wordsworth's birthplace at Cockermouth, the market town's ruined 12th century castle. **Directions: From Keswick take A66 west to Braithwaite and then follow B5292 to the T-junction with B5289. Turn left through Low Lorton and Winder Hall is on the right.**

The Old Manor Hotel

11-14 SPARROW HILL, LOUGHBOROUGH, LEICESTERSHIRE LE11 1BT
TEL: 01509 211228 FAX: 01509 211128 E-MAIL: bookings@oldmanor.com

OWNER: Roger Burdell

7 rms | 7 ens | SMALL HOTEL

MasterCard VISA S: £65–£87.50 D: £75–£140

Overlooking the ancient churchyard of All Saints parish church at the heart of old Loughborough, the Old Manor Hotel is a treasure trove of history. It was rebuilt in the 1480s and later remodelled by Edward, First Lord Hastings of Loughborough, Lord Chamberlain to Queen Mary Tudor. Today it is a lovely hotel, full of interesting furnishings and superb fabrics. Alongside many antiques, some of the fine furniture has been beautifully made by the owner.

The Old Manor has undergone many alterations and renovations over the centuries. Today it has all modern comforts but retains a number of original features. These include extensive exposed beams and timberwork. The décor is individual, rich and earthy throughout with an emphasis on comfort and an atmosphere of total friendliness. The Old Manor is an entirely non-smoking house.

Although recently developed into a hotel the building has been a restaurant in the ownership of Roger Burdell for more than 15 years. His menus are thoughtfully planned. The food is simple but innovative with an Italian influenced style.

Places of interest nearby: Charnwood Forest, Donnington Park Motor Racing Circuit, Rutland Water, Nottingham Castle, National Watersports Centre at Holme. **Directions: From A6 South. At traffic lights past Jarvis Hotel, (Kings Head), turn right onto Baxter Gate. At traffic lights by Flan O'Brien pub turn left onto Sparrow Hill. The Old Manor Hotel is the first main building on the right hand side.**

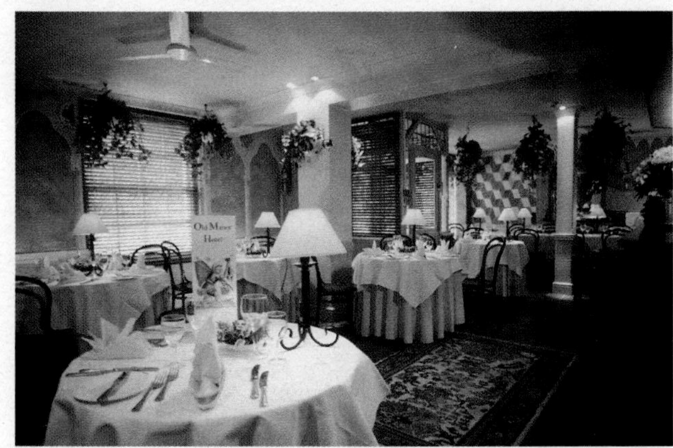

Overton Grange Hotel

OVERTON, LUDLOW, SHROPSHIRE SY8 4AD
TEL: 01584 873500 FAX: 01584 873524

OWNERS: Christine Ward
MANAGER: Ignacio Gonzalez
CHEF: Wayne Vickerage

14 rms | 14 ens

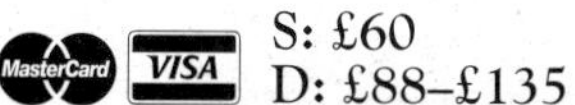

S: £60
D: £88–£135

The setting of Overton Grange Hotel, which stands in 2½ acres of peaceful gardens overlooking the scenic Shropshire countryside, would be hard to rival for guests seeking to relax and refresh their spirits. A genuinely friendly and courteous staff delivers a first class personal service.

Most of the generously sized and elegant bedrooms offer excellent views over the landscape and have been individually designed with the highest standards of comfort in mind. Similar attention to detail has been paid in the spacious and attractive public rooms. For a quiet drink there is a choice of location – the cosy cocktail bar or the conservatory, which opens out onto the gardens and patio.

A comfortable oak-panelled restaurant is the setting in which to enjoy the gastronomic delights of chef Wayne Vickerage – his dishes might include braised cornish lobster, saffron bouillon and red pepper. pineapple frangipan, blackpepper caramel with coconut ice cream.

Sporting facilities such as tennis, swimming, fishing, golf and riding are all available within the local area.

Places of interest nearby: The hotel is only 1½ miles from the centre of the country town of Ludlow with its impressive castle and interesting museum. Stokesay Castle and Berrington Hall are also within easy reach. **Directions: From A49, exit 2 miles South of Ludlow, take B4361 Ludlow-Richard Castle road. The hotel is about ¼ mile along this road.**

Little Offley

HITCHIN, HERTFORDSHIRE SG5 3BU
TEL: 01462 768243 FAX: 01462 768243

OWNERS: Martin and Lady Rosemary French

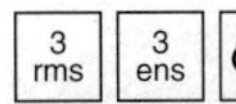

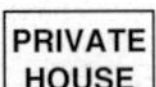

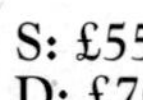

Set in 650 acres of farmland in the Chiltern Hills, Little Offley, not a hotel but a beautiful 17th century country house, affords wonderful views over the garden and surrounding countryside. One complete wing of the house has been set aside for guests and it provides a quiet haven comprising a large drawing room with a listed carved fireplace, dining room and 3 double bedrooms with bathrooms. The rooms are spacious and comfortable and there is an outdoor swimming pool available for guests' use in summer.

Accommodation is offered on a bed-and-breakfast basis. Lunch and dinner for larger groups can be provided, as can exclusive house parties, meetings, small exhibitions and receptions.

Alternatively, there are pubs – with restaurants – in the nearby village of Great Offley, 1½ miles away. Guests may leave their car at the house when flying from Luton Airport. No children under 12.

Places of interest nearby: Little Offley is an ideal touring base from which to visit Hatfield House, Luton Hoo, Whipsnade Zoo, Woburn Abbey and Cambridge. The nearest town is Hitchin, which has large open-air markets on Tuesdays and Saturdays. London is 30 minutes by train. **Directions: Take A505 Luton–Hitchin road. At Great Offley, turn off for Little Offley.**

Moor View House

VALE DOWN, LYDFORD, DEVON EX20 4BB
TEL: 01822 820220 FAX: 01822 820220

OWNERS: David and Wendy Sharples
CHEF: Wendy Sharples

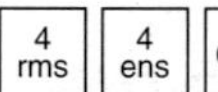

SMALL HOTEL

S: from £65
D: from £110
(including dinner)

This small Victorian country house has offered hospitality to the traveller throughout its life. The four double bedrooms make it ideal for small groups who want exclusive use of a house for special occasions or simply to relax with friends and enjoy good food and friendly service. Christmas and New Year parties are very popular and from spring to autumn, it is mainly individual guests who stay with the charming owners. The property faces Dartmoor from the front, while to the west are wonderful vistas of the landscape are lit by the setting sun.

Always putting their guests' comfort first, David and Wendy Sharples have created a friendly hotel with a genuinely relaxing ambience. Awarded AA and RAC 5 Diamonds. The reception rooms reflect the cheery glow of open fires and tasteful furnishings are a feature throughout. A Victorian decorative theme characterises the well-appointed bedrooms.

Sparkling crystal, bone china and gleaming silver in the dining room ensure that each meal is a special occasion. The daily four-course dinner menu embodies traditional country-style recipes using the finest local seasonal meat, fish and game, complemented by sound, sensibly priced wines. Awarded the RAC Dining Award.

Places of interest nearby: Lydford Gorge and Castle, Tavistock, Clovelly and Exeter. **Directions: From Exeter take A30 Okehampton bypass to Sourton Cross. Then take A386 signposted to Tavistock; Moor View's drive is situated four miles along on the right.**

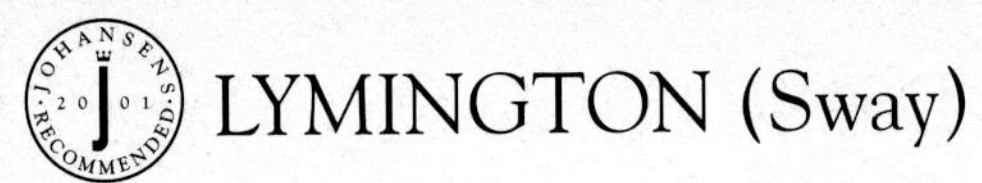

The Nurse's Cottage

STATION ROAD, SWAY, LYMINGTON, HAMPSHIRE SO41 6BA
TEL/FAX: 01590 683402 E-MAIL: nurses.cottage@lineone.net

OWNER: Tony Barnfield
CHEF: Tony Barnfield

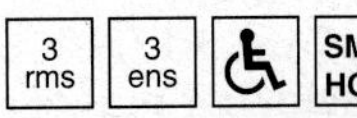

S: £55–£65
D: £95

This remarkable little house is centrally situated in a quiet, thriving village on the southern edge of the magnificent New Forest, which is rich in history and famed for its free-roaming ponies and deer. Dating from the early 1900s, The Nurse's Cottage was for nearly 70 years home to Sway's successive District Nurses, from whom the bedrooms are named.

The delightful cottage exudes character and charm with chef patron Tony Barnfield placing great emphasis on attention to detail and value for money. His dinner menus are served with imagination and flair in an intimate dining room overlooking the attractive garden. A balanced choice of delicious dishes is offered, including house specialities such as avocado, orange and prawn salad and breast of guinea fowl. The wine list contains over 60 selections.

All three en suite ground floor bedrooms are immaculately and tastefully furnished. Thoughtful extras include video player, refrigerator, complimentary fruit juices, fresh milk, biscuits and Beaulieu chocolates. No smoking throughout. Closed 3 weeks in November and 2 weeks in March.

Places of interest nearby: A number of stately homes, including Broadlands and Wilton House, the National Motor Museum at Beaulieu, Rothschild's Exbury Gardens, the yachting town of Lymington and historic Stonehenge.

Directions: From M27, junction 1 take A337 to Brockenhurst and then B3055 signed to New Milton. The Nurse's Cottage is next door to Sway Post Office.

Eleven Didsbury Park

DIDSBURY VILLAGE, MANCHESTER M20 5LH
TEL: 0161 448 7711 FAX: 0161 448 8282 E-MAIL: enquiries@elevendidsburypark.com

OWNER: Eamon O'Loughlin

S: £67–£140
D: £85–£155

Built in 1858 as a wealthy Victorian gentleman's family residence this quite modernistic establishment was opened to guests in November 1999 after having been totally refurbished and transformed into a contemporary townhouse hotel. Décor and furnishings are elegant, simplistic and individual, and quality and comfort abound. Within walking distance of Didsbury village and just four miles from the centre of Manchester, Eleven Didsbury Park offers total relaxation in a contemporary country atmosphere encompassing a secluded walled garden and a verandah where guests can just sit back and enjoy their privacy. The 14 en suite bedrooms are delightfully furnished and have every facility to satisfy the most discerning visitor. Breakfast is served in an intimate and attractive breakfast room and although dinner is not available, guests can enjoy light snacks in their bedroom or the hotel's lounge, which features an honesty bar. More than 30 excellent restaurants are within close proximity to which the hotel will provide courtesy transport.

Places of interest nearby: The Lowry Centre, Old Trafford, the Trafford Centre, the Opera House and Bridgewater Hall are nearby. **Directions: Exit M56 at junction 1 and take A34 towards Manchester. At traffic lights turn left onto A5145 towards Didsbury. At second set of traffic lights turn right into Didsbury Park. The hotel is on the left after about 100 yards.**

OXENWAYS

MEMBURY, DEVON EX13 7JR
TEL: 01404 881785 FAX: 01404 881778 E-MAIL: oxenways@aol.com

OWNERS: Ken and Sheila Beecham

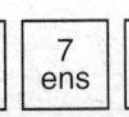

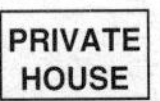

3 cotts | 4 rms | 7 ens | PRIVATE HOUSE

S: from £75
D: from £100

Totally secluded and breathtakingly beautiful, Oxenways is an Edwardian country house and former hunting lodge nestled in its own valley in East Devon, just ten miles from the sea. Ken and Sheila have created a beautiful home, luxurious and elegant, yet warm, intimate and friendly.

70 acres of its own gardens, lake and woodlands provide excellent walks, with mountain bikes to venture further afield. Why not try Western riding? Gentle Quarter horses and big Western saddles make this comfortable and fun for beginners and experienced riders alike.

Oxenways also offers a unique house party experience, hosted by Ken and Sheila. Guests are invited to arrive on a Friday afternoon and spend the weekend enjoying this lovely estate. A massage or facial followed by a soak in the hot tub helps guests unwind after the day's activities and the stunning oak-panelled dining room is a wonderful setting in which to enjoy traditional English fare.

There are four luxurious en suite double bedrooms in Oxenways House, each exquisitely decorated in period style, and three luxury holiday rental properties, each elegantly furnished and equipped with every modern comfort.

Places of interest nearby: Lyme Regis, Sidmouth, Beer, Branscombe, Forde Abbey, Montacute, Parnham, Honiton for antiques and Dartmoor are nearby. **Directions: M3/A303 or M5/J25, then A358 to Chard and Axminster; right through Smallridge towards Membury, Oxenways is on the right.**

PERITON PARK HOTEL

MIDDLECOMBE, NR MINEHEAD, SOMERSET TA24 8SN
TEL: 01643 706885 FAX: 01643 706885

OWNERS: Richard and Angela Hunt

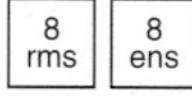   

  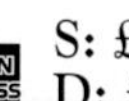 

S: £65
D: £99

As you climb the winding drive through the woods, rhododendrons and azaleas to this Victorian country house hotel on the edge of the Exmoor National Park, it is not hard to see why Periton Park is described as a place "where time stands still". Richard and Angela Hunt run the hotel in an efficient and friendly way ensuring that, while their guests are staying with them, they will be carefully looked after. All the rooms are spacious and well proportioned, enlivened with warm autumn colours to create a restful atmosphere.

The wood panelled restaurant, with its double aspect views over the grounds, is the perfect place to enjoy some of the finest food on Exmoor. Menus change with the seasons to reflect the best of West Country produce – fresh fish, local game, delicately cooked vegetables, local cheeses and Somerset wine.

Exmoor is for country lovers with miles of varied, unspoilt, breathtaking landscape. A perfect retreat from the trials of everyday life. Riding is available from stables next to the hotel. Website: http://www.smoothhound.co.uk/hotels/periton.html

Places of interest nearby: Dunster Castle and Gardens, Knightshayes, Rosemoor, Selworthy, Arlington Court and Exmoor. **Directions: Exit M5 junction 24. Take the A39 towards Minehead. Follow signs to Porlock and Lynmouth. Hotel is on the left hand side.**

WATERFORD HOUSE

19 KIRKGATE, MIDDLEHAM, NORTH YORKSHIRE DL8 4PG
TEL: 01969 622090 FAX: 01969 624020

OWNERS: Everyl and Brian Madell

4 rms | 4 ens | PRIVATE HOUSE

S: £50–£60
D: £75–£90

Overlooking the main square of Middleham, an unsullied village typical of the county, the Waterford House is an enchanting Georgian style small private hotel that styles itself as a 'restaurant with rooms'. On entering, visitors are struck by the charming décor and friendly ambience.

However, it is the award-winning restaurant, holder of two AA Rosettes and listed in the Good Food Guide, that attracts visitors from afar with its eclectic cuisine and outstanding collection of wines. Crafted by the inspired chef, Everyl Madell, the menus comprise English-style dishes with European influences such as fresh asparagus, parma ham and parmesan and gambas a la plancha. Those with a more traditional palate will favour the roast duck served with a spiced plum and fig sauce. Featuring nearly 1000 bins, the impressive wine list is one of the best in the country and recently won the Wine by the Glass Award. With over 200 Burgundies, vintages dating back to the 50's and 60's and a superb Spanish list, the restaurant is an oenologist's delight! After dinner guests can relax by a log fire in the drawing room, which is crammed with antiques and other memorabilia.

Places of interest nearby: Dating from the 12th century Middleham Castle was once considered the court of England. Fountains Abbey is one of the most archaeologically significant ruins in Europe. **Directions: From the north, take A1 south, turn right onto A684 to Leyburn. Take A6108 to Middleham. From the south, take B6267 via Masham.**

BURLEIGH COURT

MINCHINHAMPTON, GLOUCESTERSHIRE GL5 2PF
TEL: 01453 883804 FAX: 01453 886870 E-MAIL: burleighcourthotel@talk21.com

OWNERS: Ian and Fiona Hall

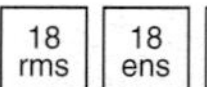 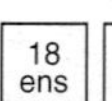   

S: from £90
D: from £130
(including dinner)

Burleigh Court is a very special hotel, where a warmth reminiscence of an era long forgotten greets all guests from the moment they arrive at this beautiful 18th century Gentleman's Manor House. Situated amidst 3.5 acres of lovingly restored landscape gardens with terrace, pool and hidden pathways, every visitor is beguiled into enjoying all the pleasures of a tranquil Cotswold life.

All of the 18 individually decorated bedrooms are full of character and recreate the atmosphere of staying in a family home with friends. Indeed the house is still owned and operated by a close-knit family. In the dining room the thoughtfully prepared dishes offer an ideal blend of traditional cooking, with simplicity, freshness and purity. Many of the herbs and salad vegetables are home-grown.

Places of interest nearby: Burleigh Court's setting in an area of outstanding natural beauty near Minchinhampton and Rodborough Commons affords the ideal location for touring the Southern Cotswolds, the Regency Spa towns of Bath and Cheltenham a short distance away and the picture postcard Cotswold villages on the doorstep.

Directions: Leave Stroud on the A419, heading towards Cirencester. 2½ miles outside Stroud take a right turn, signposted Burleigh and Minchinhampton, about 500 yards along this road there is a sharp left turn signposted Burleigh Court, the house will be on your right after a further 400 yards.

WIGHAM

MORCHARD BISHOP, NR CREDITON, DEVON EX17 6RJ
TEL: 01363 877350 FAX: 01363 877350 E-MAIL: info@wigham.co.uk
FROM USA TOLL FREE: 1 800 805 8210

OWNERS: Stephen and Dawn Chilcott

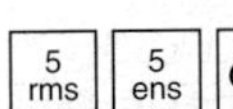   

S: £65.50–£100
D: £118–£150
(including dinner)

Wigham is set within its own 30 acre organic farm in a delightful secluded valley, Soil Association approved this year. The picturesque 16th century thatched longhouse has been restored, providing a high standard of accommodation.

Wigham uses all its own lamb, pork, beef and poultry and dairy produce: smoked bacon and sausages and vibrant yellow yolked eggs are a feature at breakfast time. Dinner is served en famille at the large table and comprises mostly organic and local produce. The cuisine is home-cooked freshly each day and complements the excellent wine list, creating a very enjoyable atmosphere. 5 Diamond rated.

Proprietors Stephen and Dawn Chilcott have created a warm and welcoming atmosphere at this charming retreat. The interiors are characterised by low ceilings, exposed beams, massive fireplaces and original wall panelling. The bedrooms are individually furnished in cottage style and have pretty, co-ordinated fabrics. In the honeymoon suite there is a rustic four-poster bed. All the bedrooms are en suite and have a television and direct dial telephone. For further entertainment there is a snooker lounge with a 7-foot table, a heated outdoor pool with a barbecue and a well-equipped 'honour' bar.

Places of interest nearby: Exmoor, Dartmoor, Exeter, Tiverton and Barnstable. **Directions: From Morchard Bishop, take the road marked Chawleigh–Chumleigh, fork right after ¾ mile, and ¾ mile further on, on the right, is a small private road marked Wigham.**

Romney Bay House

COAST ROAD, LITTLESTONE, NEW ROMNEY, KENT TN28 8QY
TEL: 01797 364747 FAX: 01797 367156

OWNERS: Jennifer and Helmut Gorlich

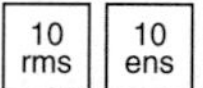 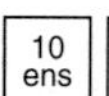  

S: from £55
D: £75–£130

This spectacular house was built in the 1920s for the American actress and journalist, Hedda Hopper, by the distinguished architect, Sir Clough Williams-Ellis.

The gracious drawing room overlooks the English Channel, panoramically surveyed through the telescope in the first floor library. There is access to the beach, a tennis court, croquet lawn and golf course. A 5 minute drive to Lydd airport and you can fly to Le Touquet for lunch.

The owners have completed an impressive refurbishing programme. Upstairs, designated non-smoking, the charming en suite bedrooms are furnished with antiques.

Wonderful cream teas can be enjoyed on the terrace in the sun-lit sea air, a traditional four-course dinner is served most nights and guests will strongly approve of the short but excellent wine list. Less than 20 minutes drive from the Channel Tunnel Terminal

Places of interest nearby: There is so much history in Romney Marsh, renowned years ago for its smuggling. Caesar landed here in 55BC at Port Lympne and the famous Cinque Ports stretch along the coast. Canterbury Cathedral is a reasonable drive inland. Littlestone Golf Courses adjoin the hotel and windsurfing is popular.

Directions: From New Romney head for the coast by Station Road leading to Littlestone Road – pass the miniature railway station – at the sea, turn left and follow signs for Romney Bay House for about a mile.

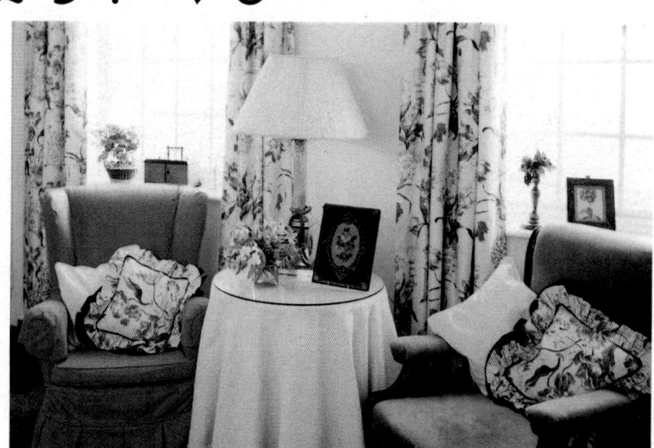

THREE CHOIRS

NEWENT, GLOUCESTERSHIRE GL18 1LS
TEL: 01531 890223 FAX: 01531 890877 E-MAIL: ts@threechoirs.com

OWNERS: Three Choirs Vineyards Ltd
DIRECTOR: Thomas Shaw
CHEF: Anthony Warburton

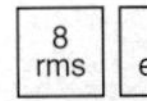    

  D: £65

Three choirs is a 70 acre vineyard in the heart of the Gloucestershire countryside, and a rising star in English wine making. New this year are eight beautifully appointed bedrooms in an idyllic location perched high on the vine terraces overlooking the estate below. Each has a private patio that catches the evening sun, and a perfect spot to sip a chilled glass of wine chosen from the day's tasting.

Comfortable beds and invigorating power showers will ensure a good night's sleep and refreshing start to the next day's lesson in vine cultivation! The emphasis at Three Choirs is on informality and the local staff offer the warmest of welcomes and cater for your every need during your stay.

A wide-ranging menu of delicious and beautifully presented food accompanies the wines with tempting dishes like "Tartlet of avocado pear, tomato and cured ham with Single Gloucester cheese" and "Spiced fillets of Black Bream with marinated vegetables and Coriander cream", and there is a good choice of vegetarian dishes.

Places of interest nearby: In addition to the wine tasting tour and exhibition on site, there is the Three Choirs Music Festival and Eastnor Castle to visit, and golf and riding can all be arranged nearby. **Directions: from the A40 take B4125 to Newent. Follow brown heritage signs to vineyard.**

NORTH BOVEY (Nr Moretonhampstead) NEW

BLACKALLER

NORTH BOVEY, DEVON TQ13 8QY
TEL: 01647 440322 FAX: 01647 441131 E-MAIL: peter@blackaller.fsbusiness.co.uk

OWNERS: Peter Hunt and Hazel Phillips
CHEF: Hazel Phillips

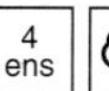

4 rms 4 ens

S: £32–£48
D: £80

Peace and hospitality are guaranteed at this former 17th century woollen mill situated on the banks of the Bovey River close to Chagford and Moretonhampstead. A truly delightful house full of character and ambience, it stands in three acres of garden surrounded by moorland and woods.

All four en suite rooms are beautifully furnished and have every home-from-home comfort from central heating and TV to tea and coffee making tray.

Owners Peter Hunt and Hazel Phillips offer unrivalled hospitality. Peter, a wool-spinning, sitar-playing host Hazel takes pride in producing superb four-course dinners using finest local produce, including organic Jacob's Lamb and fresh fish from Brixham or the rivers Teign and Dart. For breakfast guests can savour freshly baked bread, home produced honey, yoghurt and muesli.

For outdoor enthusiasts there are many fine walks, excellent birdwatching, fungi hunting, riding, fly-fishing on the River Teign and golf at the testing Manor House course. Dinner is unavailable on Sundays and Mondays. Special midweek breaks.

Places of interest nearby: Dartmoor National Park, Devon and parts of Cornwall; The South Hams, Torbay, Castle Drogo, Killerton Gardens and Fingle Bridge are nearby.

Directions: At the newsagent turn left into Pound Street and onwards to north Bovey, at village turn right. Blackaller is at bottom of the hill.

The Great Escape Holiday Company

DOCKING, KINGS LYNN, NORFOLK PE31 8LY
TEL: 01485 518717 FAX: 01485 518937 E-MAIL: holidays@greatescapes.demon.co.uk

CONTACT: Marian Rose-Cartwright

  WEEKLY LETS

  **Prices from: £295–£7000**

The north-west Norfolk coast, sweeping towards the Wash consists mainly of a long stretch of sand and low cliffs, exposed saltings and tidal inlets. There are picturesque little harbours and villages, an abundance of birdlife and marshland stretching from King's Lynn westwards into Lincolnshire. It is a place of peace where one can believe that time stands still.

Scattered along the coastline are a variety of unique and charming Great Escape holiday homes, all of which can help the visitor unwind from the pressures of everyday life. There are grand country houses, particularly attractive for corporate gatherings, charming and secluded little cottages, fascinating period houses and airy barn conversions. Some have large gardens leading down to the marshes, and boats are available for use. Others have a sunny patio, a studio or stables waiting for riding guests. The common denominator is the quality and style of décor, furnishings and service.

After a personal welcome guests are provided with wine and the ingredients for a simple meal. White bed and bath linen together with first-class maid service ensure a perfect home-from-home environment. Daily staffing can be arranged.
Places on interest nearby: Apart from enjoying the sea and the marshes, the many attractions in the area include nature reserves, 18th century Holkham Hall and Sandringham. The Company has other homes which have not been inspected by Johansens. **Directions: All properties are within easy reach of A149 coast road. Short breaks are available.**

Beechwood Hotel

CROMER ROAD, NORTH WALSHAM, NORFOLK NR28 0HD
TEL: 01692 403231 FAX: 01692 407284

OWNERS: Don Birch and Lindsay Spalding
CHEF: Steven Norgate

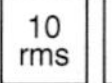   

S: £50–£65
D: £70–£90

The combination of an elegant, spacious, ivy-clad house, surrounded by well laid-out gardens, dating back to 1800, with a lovely ambience generated by the proprietors' warm welcome and the attentive staff has created a very special country house hotel in East Anglia.

For many years residents in North Walsham knew it as the doctor's house, then it was extended and transformed to accommodate guests, including Agatha Christie, who visited regularly until the mid-60s when it was a private house.

The bedrooms are delightful, with big windows, individually decorated and filled with traditional and antique furniture. The comfortable drawing room is well supplied with books and magazines and residents enjoy the intimate bar. The atmosphere in the Dining Room reflects the contentment of diners appreciating a menu that includes classic English dishes and the Chef's personal suggestions, incorporating the excellent local produce available, together with fine wines, many from the New World, selected by the owners. Winner of the 1999 Johansens Most Excellent Value for Money Award. **Places of interest nearby:** Sandringham, Blickling Hall and Holkham Hall. Bird-watchers head for Cley Marches and the Nature Reserves; others enjoy the Norfolk Broads or explore Norwich Cathedral. **Directions: Leave Norwich on B1150, driving 13 miles to North Walsham. Pass under the railway bridge, then left at the first traffic lights and right at the next set, finding the hotel 150m on the left.**

NORTH WALSHAM (Thorpe Market)

ELDERTON LODGE

GUNTON PARK, THORPE MARKET, NR NORTH WALSHAM, NORFOLK NR11 8TZ
TEL: 01263 833547 FAX: 01263 834673 E-MAIL: elderton@mistral.co.uk

OWNERS: Martin and Christine Worby
CHEF: Robert Richardson

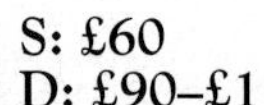

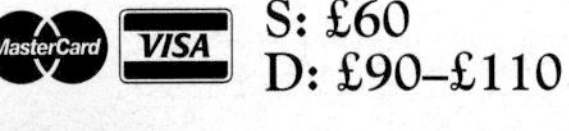

S: £60
D: £90–£110

Quietly grazing red deer, proudly strutting pheasants and cooing wood pigeons provide memorable awakening viewing to guests gazing from their bedroom windows over the vast and tranquil Gunton Park that is the scene of this 18th century, Grade II listed hotel. Standing in the heart of unspoiled countryside yet only four miles from the coast, the impressive Elderton Lodge Hotel and Restaurant, with its own six acres of mature gardens, was once the Shooting Lodge and Dower House to Gunton Hall Estate. Gunton Hall, home of the Barons of Suffield, was a favoured retreat for Lillie Langtry, the celebrated Victorian beauty, who according to legend entertained Edward VII here when he was Prince of Wales. Owners Christine and Martin Worby are restoring the hotel to its original country house splendour, complete with gun cupboards and elegant panelling. Bedrooms are attractive and comfortable, the bar informal and welcoming and the excellent cuisine featuring local game and seafood specialities – fit for a King, not only the Prince of Wales. This is an ideal venue for small meetings and conferences. **Places of interest nearby:** The cathedral city of Norwich, National Trust properties including Blickling Hall, Felbrigg Hall, Sheringham Park and the Heritage Coast and Norfolk Broads National Park are nearby. **Directions: Leave Norwich on A1151. Join A149 towards Cromer and the hotel is on the left prior to entering Thorpe Market. Price guide: Single £60; double £90–£110.**

The Beeches Hotel and Victorian Gardens

2–6 EARLHAM ROAD, NORWICH, NORFOLK NR2 3DB
TEL: 01603 621167 FAX: 01603 620151 E-MAIL: reception@beeches.co.uk

OWNERS: Keith and Elisabeth Hill
CHEF: Simon Woodward

S: £54–£74
D: £70–£88

With three acres of English Heritage Victorian Gardens, this hotel offers a warm welcome and an exceptionally high standard of comfort in a relaxed and informal atmosphere. The 3 separate Grade II listed Victorian mansions have been beautifully restored, extended and attractively decorated and are collectively known as the Beeches.

When the houses were built in the mid-1800s, an idyllic Italianate garden was created in the deep hollow it overlooks. In 1980, this 'secret' garden, now known as The Plantation Garden, was rediscovered. It is being restored to its former glory and guests are free to wander through this enchanting and extraordinary reminder of our Victorian heritage with its ornate Gothic fountain and amazing terraces. All bedrooms feature charming individual décor, separate modern facilities and are non smoking.

A varied selection of tempting dishes, which have won an AA Rosette for their quality, daily table d'hôte and seasonal à la carte is cooked to order and served in the airy Restaurant overlooking a delightful patio garden. Residents and diners can enjoy pre-dinner drinks in the comfortable lounge bar.

Places of interest nearby: The city of Norwich, with its cathedral and castle containing a famous collection of the Norwich school of painting, and the Norfolk coast and Broads. **Directions: From the A11 take the ring road west, turn onto the B1108 (Earlham Road) to city centre. The hotel is next to Roman Catholic cathedral.**

CATTON OLD HALL

LODGE LANE, CATTON, NORWICH, NORFOLK NR6 7HG
TEL: 01603 419379 FAX: 01603 400339 E-MAIL: enquires@catton–hall.co.uk

OWNERS: Roger and Anthea Cawdron

5 rms | 5 ens | SMALL HOTEL

S: £55
D: from £155

Catton Old Hall was built in 1632 and has been sympathetically restored to its former glory. It lies just 2½ miles north east of Norwich city centre and within easy reach of the airport. The Hall, once a farmhouse, retains a wealth of oak beams and one of the largest inglenooks in Norwich. Now the family home of Roger and Anthea Cawdron, it provides luxurious accommodation for its guests. The en suite bedrooms are spacious, tastefully decorated and furnished to the highest standards. The dining room and lounge have a homely atmosphere and are ideal places in which to enjoy quiet comfort.

Full English breakfast is served at the Hall and evening meals are available if booked in advance. A typical evening meal might be a choice between breast of Barbary duck, cooked in blackberry and blueberry sauce laced with Crème de Mûre, or fillet of beef Wellington, a steak with a mushroom and onion farce wrapped in crisp pastry served with a rich port and thyme jus.

A full range of office facilities is available and arrangements can be made to visit local sporting events.

Places of interest nearby: The ancient cathedral city of Norwich, with its 12th century castle, fine museums and many other historic buildings. Also the Norfolk Broads and the long sandy beaches on the Norfolk coastline.

Directions: 2½ miles north east of Norwich centre. Lodge Lane is just off Spixworth Road.

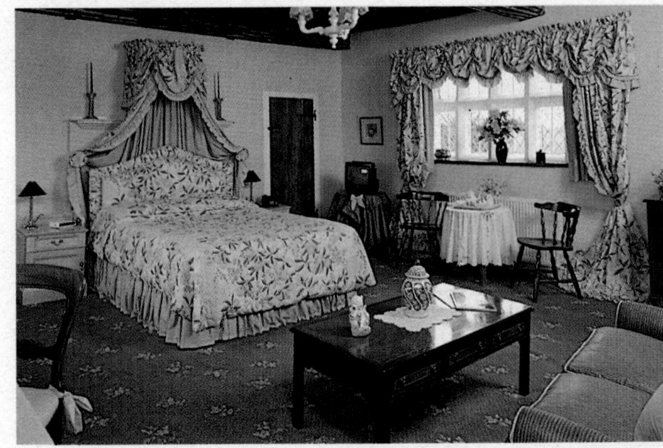

THE NORFOLK MEAD HOTEL

COLTISHALL, NORWICH, NORFOLK NR12 7DN
TEL: 01603 737531 FAX: 01603 737521

OWNERS: Don and Jill Fleming
RESIDENT BEAUTY THERAPIST: Nicki Fleming
CHEF: Mark Sayers

S: £65–£85
D: £75–£110

This elegant Georgian manor house, dating back to 1740, sits on a quiet edge of the Norfolk Broads, standing in 12 acres of lovely gardens and rolling lawns which sweep down to the River Bure. Guests can stroll down to the water to catch a glimpse of a kingfisher or heron and enjoy the variety of birdlife. The owners Don and Jill Fleming have added a host of personal touches to create a homely atmosphere, the fragrance of fresh flowers pervades the hotel.

The delightful restaurant, overlooking the gardens and the river, offers a constantly changing menu thoughtfully selected by the chef to utilise the abundance of local produce, which includes fish caught off the Norfolk coast, game from the local estates, vegetables and herbs from the gardens. An extensive wine list has been carefully selected. Relax with a drink before dinner in the bar, where a log fire burns in winter and French windows open onto the old walled garden in the summer. Those wishing to be pampered will enjoy 'Nicki's Beauty Spot', the hotel's own salon offering a range of health and beauty treatments. Sport facilities include a well-stocked fishing lake, off-river mooring and a 60ft pool. Situated only 7 miles from the centre of Norwich and 12 miles from the coast, the Norfolk Mead is well-situated for both business and leisure. **Directions: On reaching Norwich take outer ring road to B1150 signposted North Walsham. After Horstead/ Coltishall bridge, bear right on the B1354, signposted Wroxham. Entrance signposted on right just before church.**

The Old Rectory

103 YARMOUTH ROAD, NORWICH, NORFOLK NR7 OHF
TEL: 01603 700772 FAX: 01603 300772 E-MAIL: RectoryH@aol.com

OWNERS: Chris and Sally Entwistle

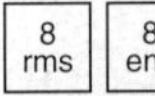
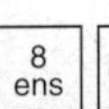

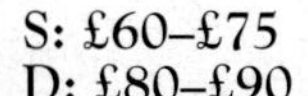

S: £60–£75
D: £80–£90

Chris and Sally Entwistle extend a warm and hospitable welcome and the promise of fine personal service to guests at the Old Rectory. Dating back to 1754, their delightful Grade II listed Georgian home, clad with Wisteria and Virginia Creeper, stands in an acre of mature gardens on the outskirts of Norwich overlooking the River Yare.

The spacious and well-furnished bedrooms, both in the hotel and the adjacent Coach House, offer quality, comfort and every modern amenity. After a busy day, guests may unwind over a pre-dinner drink in the elegant Drawing Room, enhanced by a roaring log fire during the winter and choose from a table d'hôte menu. The tempting dishes are changed daily and are freshly prepared to order.

The Wellingtonia Room and the Conservatory, overlooking the sun terrace and gardens, are excellent venues for business meetings and private luncheons or dinners.

Places of interest nearby: Within easy reach of the city centre and the Norfolk Broads, The Old Rectory is an ideal base from which to explore the historic city of Norwich, the beautiful Broadland countryside and the Norfolk coast.

Directions: Follow the A47 Norwich bypass towards Great Yarmouth. Take the A1042 exit and follow the road into Thorpe St Andrew. Bear left onto the A1242 and the hotel is approximately 50 yards on the right after the first set of traffic lights.

THE STOWER GRANGE

SCHOOL ROAD, DRAYTON, NORFOLK NR8 6EF
TEL: 01603 860210 FAX: 01603 860464

OWNERS: The McCoy Family
CHEF PATRON: Mark Smith

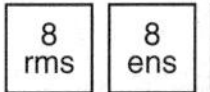

S: £57.50–£62.50
D: £72.50–£75
Four Poster: £92.50

The Stower Grange, built of mellow Norfolk bricks under Dutch pantiles, dates back to the 17th century. In former times it was a gracious rectory. Today it offers travellers a peaceful retreat – the gardens have fine lawns with inviting shade provided by the mature trees – yet the property is only 4½ miles from the commercial and historic centre of Norwich. Stower is owned by the McCoy family; the atmosphere is friendly and informal. In cooler months open fires add to the welcome. There are eight spacious individually-decorated bedrooms with en suite facilities, including one with a pine four-poster bed for those in a romantic mood. The Blue Restaurant, locally renowned as a 'special place' to dine, is supervised by the owners' daughter Kate and looks directly on to the gardens. The imaginative cooking of their son-in-law Mark ensures good eating from the individually priced menus. The restaurant closes on Sunday evenings, however, residents can enjoy a steak and salad in the Lounge Bar.

Places of interest nearby: Norwich, Norfolk Broads, Holkham Hall, Houghton Hall, Blickling Hall, Sandringham and the Norfolk Coast are all nearby.

Directions: From A11, turn left on to inner ring road and proceed to the ASDA junction with A1067 Norwich–Fakenham Road. Approximately two miles to Drayton turn right at the Red Lion public house. After 80 yards bear left. The Stower Grange is on the right.

Cockliffe Country House Hotel

BURNT STUMP COUNTRY PARK, BURNT STUMP HILL, NOTTINGHAMSHIRE NG5 8PQ
TEL: 01159 680179 FAX: 01159 680623 E-MAIL: enquiries@cockliffehouse.co.uk

OWNERS: Dane and Jane Clarke
CHEF: Nathan Measurers

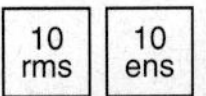

S: from £95
D: from £105

This is Robin Hood country and Cockliffe is situated in the heart of it, six miles north of Nottingham. A lovely, unusually designed 17th century house with turreted-style corners it stands in two acres of colourful, mature gardens adjacent to the open spaces of Burnt Stump Country Park.

Dane and Jane Clarke rescued the house from disrepair five years ago and are proud of their renovations and refurbishments, many of which are in keeping with original features. Décor and furnishings throughout are elegant and tasteful and most rooms afford splendid views over the garden. The ten bedrooms are individually designed and comfortably appointed to reflect the needs of discerning guests. All are en suite, with thoughtful touches, period furniture and adorned with beautiful curtain fabrics carefully chosen by Jane Clarke.

Chef Nathan Measurers produces an excellent and imaginative menu using local fish and game when in season served in the attractive restaurant, adjoining the cocktail bar which is popular with guests for pre-meal drinks and after dinner coffee. A conference room with high-tech facilities is available. Golf, fishing, riding and fitness and leisure can be arranged locally.

Places of interest nearby: Nottingham and its castle, Sherwood Forest, 12th century Newstead Abbey and Southwell Minster with its medieval carvings, the earliest of their kind in England. **Directions: Exit M1 at junction 26 and take the A60 north from Nottingham.**

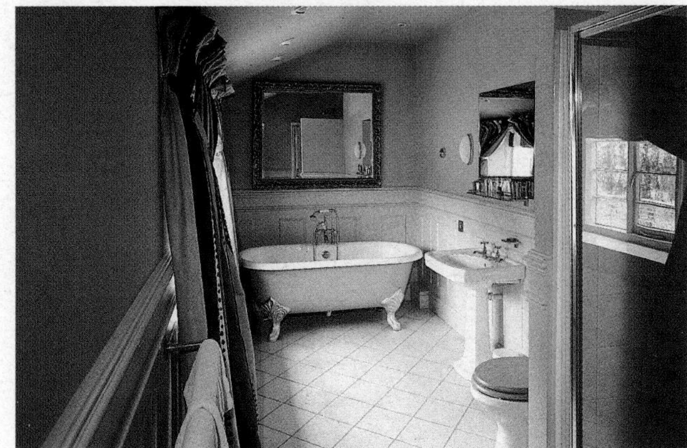

The Cottage Country House Hotel

EASTHORPE STREET, RUDDINGTON, NOTTINGHAM NG11 6LA
TEL: 01159 846882 FAX: 01159 214721

OWNERS: Christina and Tim Ruffell
CHEF: Christina Ruffell

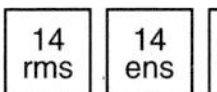

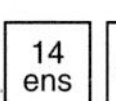

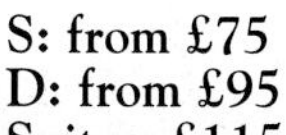

S: from £75
D: from £95
Suites: £115

Roses and honeysuckle ramble over the walls of The Cottage Country House Hotel, a unique restoration of 17th century cottages; it lies tucked away in the village of Ruddington, yet only a few minutes drive from the bustling city of Nottingham. It is the imaginative concept of the designer proprietors and with its private, gated courtyard and delightful walled garden it has won three major awards, including the Conservation Award for the best restoration of an old building in a village setting.

Christina and Tim Ruffell are proud of their attention to detail and they engaged local leading craftsmen to renovate and refurbish the hotel in keeping with its original features. Their aim was to provide quality, style and comfort in tranquil surroundings. They have succeeded in every way.

All the hotel's rooms are individually designed and furnished to reflect the needs of discerning guests. The bedrooms are all en suite, with thoughtful extra touches, and each room is individually named. The hotel offers two superb honeymoon suites. The excellent restaurant serves contemporary international cuisine and fine wines, there are two guest sitting rooms, one with an original inglenook fireplace. The terrace bar overlooks the enclosed courtyard and fountain, and there is a second terrace leading into the garden. Golf, tennis and water sports are within easy reach. **Directions: Ruddington is three miles south of Nottingham on the A60 Loughborough road. The hotel is situated at the heart of the village.**

Langar Hall

LANGAR, NOTTINGHAMSHIRE NG13 9HG
TEL: 01949 860559 FAX: 01949 861045 E-MAIL: langarhall–hotel@ndirect.co.uk

OWNER: Imogen Skirving

S: £65–£97.50
D: £90–£150
Suite: £175

Set in the Vale of Belvoir, mid-way between Nottingham and Grantham, Langar Hall is the family home of Imogen Skirving. Epitomising "excellence and diversity" it combines the standards of good hotel-keeping with the hospitality and style of country house living. Having received a warm welcome, guests can enjoy the atmosphere of a private home that is much loved and cared for.

The en suite bedrooms are individually designed and comfortably appointed. The public rooms feature fine furnishings and most rooms afford beautiful views of the garden, park and moat. Imogen and her kitchen team collaborate to produce an excellent, varied menu of modern British food. This is an ideal venue for exclusive 'House party' bookings and private dinner parties. The new children's adventure playground area will please younger visitors. Dogs can be accommodated by arrangement.

Places of interest nearby: Langar Hall is an ideal venue for small boardroom meetings. It is also an ideal base from which to visit Belvoir Castle, to see cricket at Trent Bridge, to visit students at Nottingham University and to see Robin Hood's Sherwood Forest. **Directions: Langar is accessible via Bingham on the A52, or via Cropwell Bishop from the A46 (both signposted). The house adjoins the church and is hidden behind it.**

Sutton Bonington Hall

MAIN STREET, SUTTON BONINGTON, LOUGHBOROUGH, LEICESTERSHIRE LE12 5PF
TEL: 01509 672355 FAX: 01509 674357 E-MAIL: aweldon@uk.packardbell.org

OWNERS: Henry and Ali Weldon

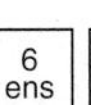

S: £80–£110
D: £120–£150

Large, green wrought-iron gates open onto a long drive which leads visitors through expansive landscaped gardens to this elegant, red brick hotel just four miles from the M1. Sutton Bonington Hall is of the Queen Anne period and abounds in character and charm. Despite renovations and refurbishment over the years, it retains many original features which combine gracefully with modern comforts. The emphasis is on country house style and homeliness with owners Henry and Ali Weldon offering a friendly welcome and attentive service.

Guests may relax in three superb reception rooms, which include a large conservatory. In keeping with the Hall's history the bedrooms have retained their original names: Lady Elton's Room with a comfortable seating area, The Dressing Room, The Round Room and The Oriental Room all with four-poster beds, and The Garden Room with twin beds. The Attic, with twin beds, sink, but no bathroom, is ideal for children. Breakfast is served in an intimate dining room; dinner can be had by arrangement.

Places of interest nearby: Charnwood Forest, Donington Park Motor Racing Circuit, Rutland Water, Nottingham Castle, Belvoir Castle, National Watersports Centre at Holme Pierpont. **Directions: Exit M1 at junction 24 and follow A6 towards Loughborough, Kegworth and then Sutton Bonington. Pass village church and the Hall is on your left.**

M 60

The Hautboy

OCKHAM LANE, OCKHAM, SURREY
TEL: 01483 225355 FAX: 01483 211176

CHEF: Darren Tidd

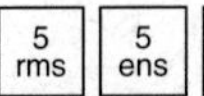 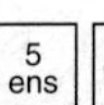  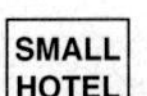

S: £98
D: £115–£125

More than 150 years of history, character and atmosphere are absorbed into the lovely interior of this warm, redbrick Gothic hotel ideally situated in the heart of the Surrey countryside midway between Heathrow and Gatwick airports. Family managed, The Hautboy is a magnificent hotel sympathetically refurbished and modernised but with many original features such as mullioned windows, steam bent wooden beams, vaulted ceilings and intimate corners.

The bedrooms are sumptuous, offering the grace and charisma of the past with the comfort and facilities of today. Each has its own fascinating architectural character, elegant furnishings and views over the garden, fields and woodlands.

Award winning chef Darren Tidd provides à la carte delights and six-course gastronomic menus to please every taste in the The Chapel restaurant, an opulent room of high vaulted ceilings and wonderful murals inspired by the owners' love of Tuscany. Less formal meals are served in the lively Oboe Bistro with its framed curios and garden access.

Places of interest nearby: Guildford cathedral, The Royal Horticultural Society's Wisley Gardens, Clandon Park, Loseley House, horse racing at Sandown Park, Esher. Epsom, Windsor and Ascot are within easy reach.

Directions: Exit M25 at Jct10 and join A3 towards Guildford. Turn left onto B2039 Ockham road, then left again at the war memorial. The Hautboy is 400 yards ahead.

Pen-Y-Dyffryn Country Hotel

RHYDYCROESAU, NR OSWESTRY, SHROPSHIRE SY10 7JD
TEL: 01691 653700 FAX: 01691 650066 E-MAIL: stay@peny.co.uk

OWNERS: Miles and Audrey Hunter
CHEF: David Morris

S: £59–£65
D: £80–£100

Pen-y-Dyffryn Country Hotel is an oasis of peace and quiet, set in five acres of grounds in the unspoilt Shropshire hills, midway between Shrewsbury and Chester. And while civilisation is close at hand, buzzards, peregrine falcons, badgers and foxes regularly delight the guests with their unscheduled appearances. The stream in front of the hotel marks the border with neighbouring Wales.

All the bedrooms have modern amenities and overlook the attractively terraced hotel gardens. In the cooler months, log fires burning in the two homely lounges help to create a cosy and informal atmosphere in which to relax and forget the pressures of everyday life. The best of British cuisine is served in the hotel's renowned restaurant which has been awarded two rosettes by the AA. Adventurous menus offer dishes using the finest local and increasingly organic ingredients. The bar, an antique sideboard, and even the wine list also incorporate a range of organic beers and wines.

Although Pen-y-Dyffryn provides the perfect setting for total relaxation, for more active guests there are facilities for hill-walking and riding on the doorstep, six 18-hole golf courses within 15 miles and a trout pool just yards away.

Places of interest nearby: Powys and Chirk Castles, Erddig and Attingham. Historic towns of Shrewsbury and Chester. Excursions to Snowdonia. **Directions: From Oswestry town centre take B4580 Llansilin road for 3m due West. After sharp bend turn left in village.**

THE OTTERBURN TOWER

OTTERBURN, NORTHUMBERLAND, NE19 1NS
TEL: 01830 520620 FAX: 01830 521504 E-MAIL: reservations@otterburntower.co.uk

OWNERS: John Goodfellow
MANAGER: Charles Weeks

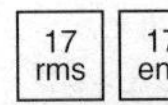

S: £49–£79
D: £70–£130
suite: £130

The Otterburn Tower is a magnificent sight. A thick, stone walled fortress, tall and solid with shoulder high ramparts and arrow-slit windows that look out over beautiful Northumberland and National Park countryside. Standing in 32 acres of formal terraced gardens and lush woodland The Otterburn Tower has witnessed centuries of history. It was built in 1076 as a defence against marauding Scots by a cousin of William the Conqueror.

Reminders of its turbulent past remain but once guests have strolled through its imposing, arched entranceway topped by a carved heraldic shield they find comfortable and relaxing surroundings with the warmth of a family home. Elegant public rooms have luxurious furnishings and blazing log fires in winter. Seventeen spacious, en suite guest rooms, some with four-poster beds and large open fireplaces, are individually designed and offer superb comfort and views over the grounds. One of the fireplaces is listed and depicts scenes from the Battle of Otterburn in 1388 when Scots forces lost their leader while defeating the English. Dining at The Otterburn Tower is a delight creating imaginative and tasty lunch and dinner menus using the finest local produce.

Places of interest nearby: Hadrian's Wall, Holy Island and Bamburgh Castle are within easy reach. **Directions: From Newcastle take A696 to Otterburn.**

Sea Marge Hotel

HIGH STREET, OVERSTAND, NORFOLK NR27 0AB
TEL: 01263 579579 FAX: 01263 579524 E-MAIL: seamarge.hotel@virgin.net

OWNERS: Mr and Mrs M MacKenzie
MANAGER: Maria Cooper
CHEF: Laurie Malabar

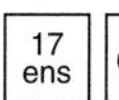

S: £59–£64
D: £78–£92

In spectacular setting amidst perfectly laid gardens with views over the Norfolk coast, the Sea Marge Hotel is a delightful Grade II listed building steeped in history. Commissioned by Sir Edgar Speyer, a wealthy banker in 1908, the Sea Marge remains one of the best examples of an Elizabethan-styled house on the Norfolk coast.

The hotel is set in the peaceful fishing village of Overstrand, a short distance from Cromer, where the Norfolk school of painters were inspired by the wealth of idyllic pastoral scenery. Norwich city centre is just 25 miles away, making the Sea Marge an ideal small conference venue.

The large Speyers bar typifies the character to be found in the hotel, exuding Edwardian style with a long gallery, elegant wood panelling and large open fireplace. The relaxed and informal Galleon restaurant is where chef Laurie Malabar serves a wide variety of English and continental cuisine as well as some wonderful local dishes such as "Poachers Pocket" and "Sea Marge Crab and Prawn Fishcakes". There is plenty of choice for the vegetarian and light dishes for lunch or supper.

Places of interest nearby: Blickling Hall, Felbrigg Hall, Holkham Hall and The Muckleburgh Military Collection. Mannington Hall Gardens and North Norfolk Steam Railway. **Directions: From Norwich take A140 to Cromer and follow signs to Overstrand.**

OWLPEN MANOR

NR ULEY, GLOUCESTERSHIRE GL11 5BZ
TEL: 01453 860261 FAX: 01453 860819 E-MAIL: sales@owlpen.com

OWNERS: Nicholas and Karin Mander
CHEF: Karin Mander

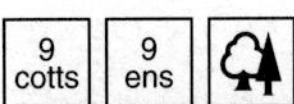

From:
£50-£150
(minimum stay conditions may apply)

Set in its own remote and picturesque wooded valley in the heart of the South Cotswolds, Owlpen Manor is one of the country's most romantic Tudor manor houses. It is steeped in peace and timeless English beauty with the surrounding estate leading the wildlife lover through miles of private woodland paths. Scattered along the valley are distinctive historic cottages, sleeping from two to eight and managed in the style of a country house hotel. There are snug medieval barns and byres, a watermill first restored in 1464, the Court House of the 1620s, weavers' and keepers' cottages and even a modern farmhouse.

All are equipped with every home-from-home comfort, from antiques and chintzes to prints and plants. They are individually furnished in traditional English style and stand in their own secluded gardens. Some have open fireplaces or four-poster beds. An atmospheric restaurant in the medieval cyder house serves seasonal produce from the estate. For sporting visitors fly-fishing and shooting can be arranged. Riding, gliding and golf are nearby. **Places of interest nearby:** Owlpen Manor, Uley Tumulus, Westonbirt Arboretum, Berkeley Castle and the Wildfowl Trust at Slimbridge. **Directions: From the M4, exit at junction 18, or M5 junctions 13 or 14, and head for the B4066 to Uley. Owlpen is signposted from the Old Crown opposite the church, or follow the brown signs.**

Fallowfields

KINGSTON BAGPUIZE WITH SOUTHMOOR, OXON OX13 5BH
TEL: 01865 820416 FAX: 01865 821275 E-MAIL: stay@fallowfields.com

OWNERS: Peta and Anthony Lloyd

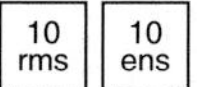

S: £115–£125
D: £122–£155

Fallowfields, once the home of Begum Aga Khan, dates back more than 300 years. It has been updated and extended over past decades and today boasts a lovely early Victorian Gothic southern aspect. The house is set in two acres of gardens, surrounded by ten acres of grassland.

The guests' bedrooms, which offer a choice of four poster or coroneted beds, are large and well appointed and offer every modern amenity to ensure maximum comfort and convenience. The house is centrally heated throughout and during the winter months, there are welcoming log fires in the elegant main reception rooms.

The cuisine is mainly British, imaginative in style and presentation and there is a good choice of menus available. The walled kitchen garden provides most of the vegetables and salads for the table and locally grown and organic produce is otherwise used wherever possible. **Places of interest nearby:** Fallowfields is close to Stratford, the Cotswolds, Stonehenge, Bath and Bristol to the west, Oxford, Henley on Thames, the Chilterns and Windsor to the east. Heathrow airport is under an hour away. **Directions: Take the Kingston Bagpuize exit on the A420 Oxford to Swindon. Fallowfields is at the west end of Southmoor, just after the Longworth sign.**

Westwood Country Hotel

HINKSEY HILL, NR. BOARS HILL, OXFORD OX1 5BG
TEL: 01865 735 408 FAX: 01865 736 536 E-MAIL: reservations@westwoodhotel.co.uk

OWNER: Anthony Healy

S: £65
D: £85
4 Poster: £ 95

This delightful Edwardian Country House Hotel is set in four acres of landscaped gardens surrounded by an area of outstanding natural beauty. The Westwood Country Hotel is located in the salubrious area of Boars Hill only 2½ miles from Oxford city centre. The gardens, officially opened by the world-renowned botanist, David Bellamy, several years ago, provide a natural habitat for a large variety of wildlife. Owner Anthony Healy, himself a keen gardener, has created a vegetable and fruit garden which, together with his chickens, provides produce for the hotel's kitchen.

The hotel has been tastefully and elegantly refurbished retaining and enhancing many of its original features. It provides 24 comfortable en suite bedrooms, including two beautiful four-poster rooms and a self-contained suite.

The menu is imaginative and varied, and the wine list boasts selections from around the world. Dining is enjoyed in the comfortable Oaks restaurant overlooking the gardens.

Places of interest nearby: Blenheim Palace and the many sights of Oxford are close by. The ancient city of Bath, Stratford-on-Avon and the Cotswolds Route are all within a comfortable one hour drive, as is London Heathrow airport.

Directions: The hotel is located south west of Oxford. Take Oxford Ring Road, and where A34 meets the ring road at the roundabout, follow signs for Wootton and Boars Hill. At the top of the hill the road bears to the left. The hotel is on the right.

Cross House Hotel

CHURCH STREET, PADSTOW, CORNWALL PL28 8BG
TEL: 01841 532391 FAX: 01841 533633 E-MAIL: info@crosshouse.co.uk

OWNERS: Cross House Hotel Limited
MANAGER: Nichola Gidlow

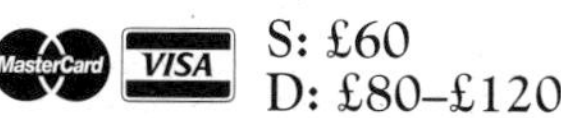

S: £60
D: £80–£120

Tucked away in the quiet and serene area of Padstow, the Cross House Hotel is a delightful Georgian Grade II listed house. Luxury and comfort are important criteria and the décor is distinctly elegant with beautiful fabrics and tasteful paintings. The bedrooms, four of which are in their house adjacent to the hotel, are individually furnished and offer every modern amenity as well as extra touches such as air-conditioning and videos. With large fluffy towels, soft bathrobes and fine toiletries, the en suite facilities are both stylish and well-equipped.

Guests often frequent the lounge during the afternoon and enjoy reading or playing a board game in front of the cosy, glowing fire, with its comfortable furnishings and elegant chandeliers, it is also the ideal place to recline during the evening and enjoy an apéritif. There is a choice of either Full English or Continental breakfast and the fresh pastries are delicious. Many fine restaurants are recommended nearby.

Beautiful walks along the Cornish coast, sea-fishing, cycling and trying the various water sports offered at the Estuary are some of the many pastimes available nearby. Golf enthusiasts will be delighted with the challenging courses.

Places of interest nearby: Prideaux House and Deer Park, the Camel Estuary and the picturesque town of Wadebridge are all within easy reach. **Directions: On approaching Padstow from A30, take 3rd turn on the right, following signs to the parish church. The hotel is 50 yards on the left.**

Temple Sowerby House Hotel

TEMPLE SOWERBY, PENRITH, CUMBRIA CA10 1RZ
TEL: 017683 61578 FAX: 017683 61958 FREE PHONE: 0800 146157 E-MAIL: stay@temple–sowerby.com

OWNERS: Paul and Julie Evans

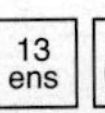

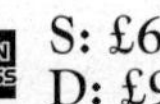

S: £68–£78
D: £96–£116

Temple Sowerby House looks over at Cross Fell, the highest peak in the Pennines, noted for its spectacular ridge walk. This old Cumbrian farmhouse is set in two acres of gardens and guests are assured of peace and quiet. Paul and Julie Evans offer a warm, hospitable and friendly family service upon which the hotel prides itself.

Awarded an AA Rosette, the hotel has two dining rooms – the cosy Restaurant and The Garden Room, a lovely setting for private entertaining. The seasonally inspired à la carte menu might include a starter of Terrine of Pigeon, Duck & Chicken layered with Pistachio Nuts served with Redcurrant Sauce, followed by Turbot with a Parsley & Parmesan Crust with Saffron Rice and Lime Beurre Blanc, rounded off with Chocolate & Raspberry Tart with marinated Figs.

The individually furnished bedrooms all have private bathrooms. Four of the rooms are situated in the Coach House, just yards from the main house. During the winter, apéritifs are taken by the fireside, while in the summer, guests can sip drinks on the terrace and enjoy views across the fells. Private fishing, with tuition if required, takes place on the River Eden, two miles away. Fishing breaks available.

Places of interest nearby: Lakes Ullswater and Derwentwater, the Scottish Borders, Hadrian's Wall, Yorkshire Dales and the Pennines are within easy reach by car. **Directions: On A66, 7 miles from exit 40 of M6, between Penrith and Appleby. (Special breaks available).**

M 30

Langrish House

LANGRISH, NR PETERSFIELD, HAMPSHIRE GU32 1RN
TEL: 01730 266941 FAX: 01730 260543

OWNERS: Nigel and Robina Talbot-Ponsonby
CHEF: Alex Stock

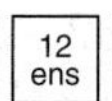

S: £63–£72
D: £96–£104
Suite: £120

Standing in 12 acres of beautiful mature grounds including a picturesque lake, Langrish House combines the welcoming ambience of a traditional country house with the facilities expected from a modern hotel. Extended by the present owners' forbears in 1842, it opened as a hotel in 1979 and remains very much a family home. Today, new life is being breathed into the house by Nigel and Robina Talbot-Ponsonby whose family portraits and heirlooms once again adorn the rooms.

Each of the bedrooms overlooks the grounds, giving guests ample opportunity to savour Langrish's peace and tranquillity. All are fully equipped with en suite bathrooms, direct dial telephones, colour televisions and many thoughtful touches.

The recently refurbished Cellar Restaurant and Dungeon Bar are now complemented by the addition of the Garden Room Restaurant, which affords glorious views of the lawns. Fresh regional produce features in the fine cuisine. Langrish House is an ideal venue for wedding receptions and business conferences and offers dining facilities for up to 120 people.

Places of interest nearby: This is an excellent base for touring the Hampshire countryside and the New Forest. Gilbert White's Selbourne, Jane Austen's Chawton, Goodwood and Cowdray Park are also close by. **Directions: Follow A272 from the M3/A31 at Winchester (16 miles) or from A3 at Petersfield (3 miles). Langrish House is signposted from the village on the road to East Meon.**

Andrew's On The Weir

PORLOCK WEIR, PORLOCK, SOMERSET TA24 8PB
TEL: 01643 863300 FAX: 01643 863311 E-MAIL: information@andrewsontheweir.co.uk

OWNERS: Andrew Dixon and Sarah Baudains

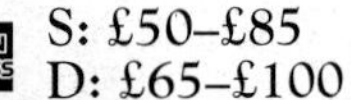

S: £50–£85
D: £65–£100

A haven of peace and tranquillity, guests staying at Andrew's On The Weir are offered a quite exceptional experience. In an idyllic location overlooking the picturesque Porlock Weir, and with views reaching to Wales, this Georgian Manor house has been recently taken over by Chef Patron Andrew Dixon and its fine cuisine is already attracting considerable interest.

Recommended for 3 AA Rosettes after just seven months of business, the restaurant is really putting Andrew's On The Weir on the map, and with a strong patronage of local farmers and suppliers, guests are assured of true West Country fayre! A delight to the eye as well as the palate, the cuisine is imaginative and unusual with such tempting dishes as "Warm goats cheese pithivier with plum tomatoes and basil" or "Fillets of seabass with saffron mash, olive puree and fennel veloute".

The bedrooms are delightful, and will provide a restful night's sleep, prior to sampling the stunning breakfast menu, and any dietary requirements are met with maximum creativity. The restaurant is closed Sunday night and all day Monday, but bed and breakfast is available.

Places of interest nearby: Dunster's Norman castle, the smallest church in England at Culborne, Lynmouth's picturesque harbour and cove, and the beautiful walking country of Exmoor. **Directions: Exit M5 at junction 25 and join A358 to Minehead. Then take A39 to Porlock and onto Porlock Weir.**

Porlock Vale House

PORLOCK WEIR, SOMERSET TA24 8NY
TEL: 01643 862338 FAX: 01643 863338 E-MAIL: info@porlockvale.co.uk

OWNERS: Helen and Kim Youd
CHEFS: Nick Robinson and Christine Collins

 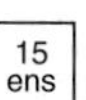 

S: £45–£65
D: £75–£100

This former hunting lodge positioned in a truly spectacular setting pinioned by the sea and lush forest, offers a welcome friendly, informal and comforting atmosphere to visitors tired of the formality of traditional hotel accommodation.

Porlock Vale's extensive gardens are a sight to behold, visitors always cherish fond memories of the lazy summer afternoons spent there in quiet repose. Winter season also sticks in the mind, with the coast and the Bristol channel viewed from the tranquillity of the lounge with its crackling log fire. Visitors dine in a beautiful dining room, where top-notch local fare is served within mouth-watering menus. The delightful bedrooms are all individually styled, commanding views of the ocean, the tastefully laid out gardens or the wooded combe that flanks the hotel.

Places of interest nearby: At the heart of the Exmoor National Park, the Porlock Vale House is the ideal base for a walking tour around this region of dramatic beauty. The area is literally awash with quaint traditional villages dotted along the awe-inspiring coast. Famous landmarks, such as the Dunkery Beacon and the Doone Valley, are also close at hand. **Directions: Join the A39 and follow the signs to Minehead. When in Porlock Village, pick up the signs for Porlock Weir.**

Tye Rock Country House and Apartments

LOE BAR ROAD, PORTHLEVEN, NR HELSTON, SOUTH CORNWALL TR13 9EW
TEL/FAX: 01326 572695 RESIDENTS NO: 01326 563087 E-MAIL: tyerockhotel@compuserve.com

OWNERS: Richard and Pat Palmer

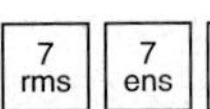   

S: £65–£75
D: £84–£100

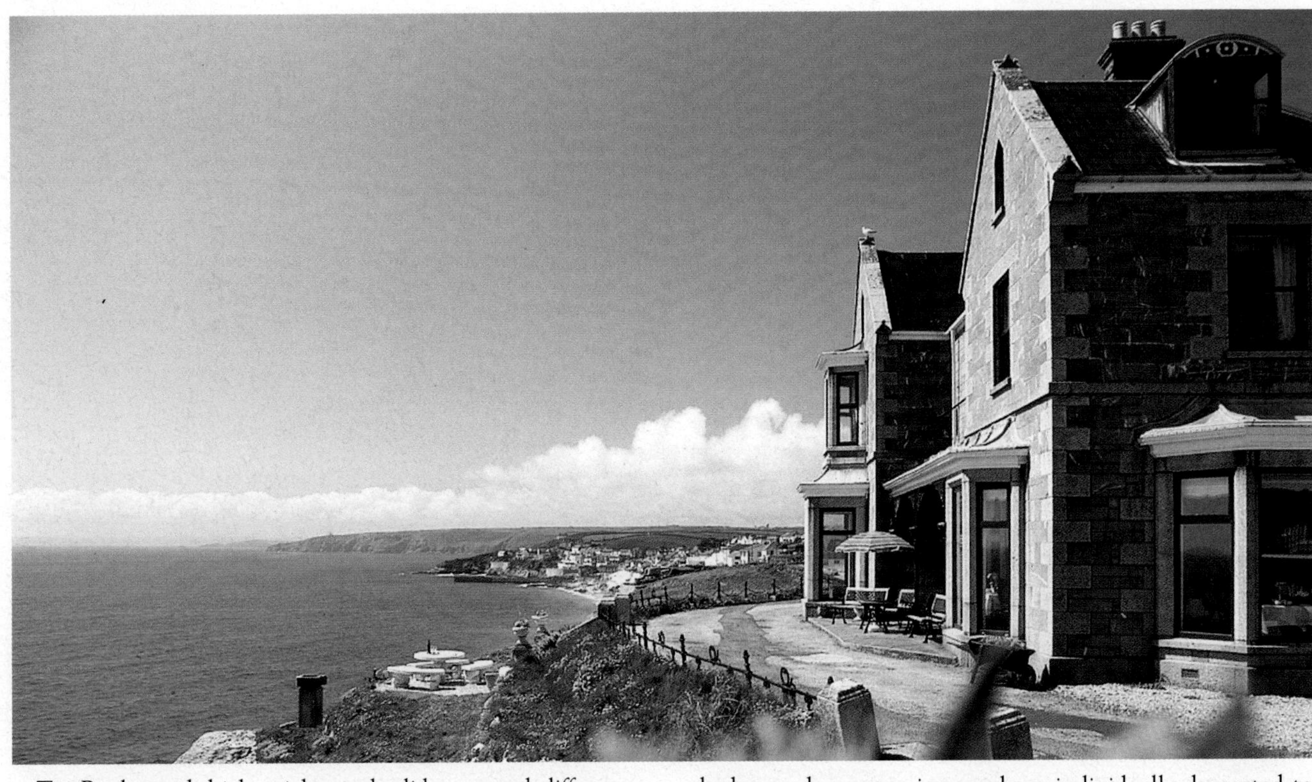

Tye Rock stands high, mighty and solid on rugged cliff tops overlooking Mounts Bay with magnificent views extending from The Lizard to Land's End. Surrounded by 3½ acres of terraced gardens and the wild expanse of National Trust land, this former 19th century manor house offers a relaxing and welcoming atmosphere.

It has a stylish air of quiet seclusion yet is only a short walk from the pretty fishing harbour of Portleven and within two miles of the market town of Helston, famed for its annual Furry Dance through the streets on Flora Day, May 8.

Richard and Pat Palmer have created a delightful, friendly country house hotel with dramatically fashioned rooms encompassing various themes. All seven, comfortable en suite bedrooms have sea views and are individually decorated to high standards. There are also eight self catering apartments in the grounds which offer guests the independence of their own front door.

Delicious, traditional English cuisine is served in the elegant Victorian restaurant which opens onto a terrace from which guests can enjoy the views while sipping pre- and after-dinner drinks. Winter breaks and activity weekends are also available. **Places of interest nearby:** St Michael's Mount, Goonhilly Earth Satellite Station, Mullion Cove, Land's End and many Cornish gardens. **Directions: From Helston take the Portleven road, then follow signs for Loe Bar. Take first left, first right and left at the T-junction.**

The Beaufort Hotel

71 FESTING ROAD, SOUTHSEA, PORTSMOUTH, HAMPSHIRE PO4 ONQ
TEL: 023 9282 3707 FAX: 023 9287 0270 E-MAIL: enquiries@beauforthotel.co.uk

OWNERS Anthony and Penelope Freemantle
CHEF: Michael Freyne

18 rms

AMERICAN EXPRESS

S: from £60
D: from £80

Conveniently located in the heart of Southsea, just one minute's walk from the sea, lies The Beaufort Hotel. A relaxed and friendly atmosphere pervades this comfortable and spotless hotel, creating an ideal setting for relaxation. Owners Penny and Tony Freemantle and their staff pride themselves on providing guests with a personal service that is second to none.

The 18 bedrooms have all been designed to give them individual character, from the magnificent Oxford Room, decorated in royal blue and gold, to the bright and sunny Cambridge Room which is tastefully decorated in Burgundy and overlooks the Canoe lake. All the attractive bathrooms feature porcelain and gold fittings and include a selection of luxurious toiletries.

A comfortable cocktail bar is the ideal place to enjoy a pre-dinner drink before moving on to the charming restaurant. The Beaufort is proud to hold the highest percentage rating by the AA of any hotel in Portsmouth. **Places of interest nearby:** The Mary Rose, H.M.S Warrior, H.M.S Victory and the Royal Naval Museum provide a fascinating insight into life on board Britain's most famous warships. The Isle of Wight and Le Havre and Cherbourg in France are all within easy cruising distance. **Directions: Festing Road is off St Helen's Parade at the eastern end of the seafront.**

Chequers Hotel

CHURCH PLACE, PULBOROUGH, WEST SUSSEX RH20 1AD
TEL: 01798 872486 FAX: 01798 872715 E-Mail: chequershotel@btinternet.com

OWNERS: Pandora and Martin Pellett
MASTER CHEF: Geoffrey Welch

11 rms | 10 ens | SMALL HOTEL

S: £49.50–£59.50
D: £85–£100

A warm welcome awaits visitors to this historic hotel built in 1548 and Grade II listed. Situated in the heart of West Sussex and in a local conservation area, Chequers stands high on a sandstone ridge facing south with spectacular views across the Arun Valley to the South Downs beyond.

Pandora and Martin Pellett have brought fresh ideas and set new high standards for this delightful small hotel. Chequers Restaurant enjoys an excellent reputation locally and has been awarded two AA Rosettes for high standards of food quality. Master Chef, Geoffrey Welch, produces the finest food on a daily changing menu using local produce whenever possible.

Breakfast, morning coffee, lunches and cream teas are served every day of the week in the conservatory. It is also popular for an informal dinner under the stars.

Places of interest nearby: The Roman City of Chichester, Goodwood Horse and Motor Racing, Arundel Castle, Petworth House with its collection of paintings by Turner and the classic Sussex seaside. **Directions: 100 metres north of the junction of A29 and A283 at the top of the hill opposite the church.**

Moortown Lodge

244 CHRISTCHURCH ROAD, RINGWOOD, HAMPSHIRE BH24 3AS
TEL: 01425 471404 FAX: 01425 476052 E-MAIL: hotel@burrows–jones.freeserve.co.uk

OWNERS: Bob and Jilly Burrows-Jones
CHEF: Jilly Burrows-Jones

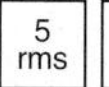
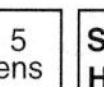

S: from £50
D: from £75

The busy market town of Ringwood stands on the edge of the vast and beautiful New Forest with its abundance of woodland, wildlife and enchanting walks. Moortown Lodge is a perfect base from which to explore this rolling and historic countryside. Dating back to the 1760s this charming, family-run hotel stands just outside the town on the main road to Christchurch and is renowned for its warm and welcoming ambiance. Owners Bob and Jilly Burrows-Jones are justly proud to have been one of the first recipients of an AA Courtesy and Care Award for hospitality.

All the hotel's rooms are well-proportioned and enlivened with furnishing, fabrics and colourings to create a restful atmosphere. There are five en suite double and twin-bedded rooms, including one with a luxury four-poster. All have every amenity and facility to make visitors feel at home.

The intimate restaurant is the ideal place to enjoy some of the finest food in the area. Jilly's menus are varied and she uses local produce whenever possible. Her high standard of cuisine has won an AA Rosette and has been acclaimed as excellent yet delightfully uncomplicated.

Places of interest nearby: Broadlands, the old home of Lord Mountbatten, Beaulieu, Breamore House and the New Forest. Bournemouth, Poole, Southampton and Salisbury are within easy reach. **Directions: Enter Ringwood from the A31 and follow the signs for the B3347. Moortown Lodge is approximately 1½ miles south of the town.**

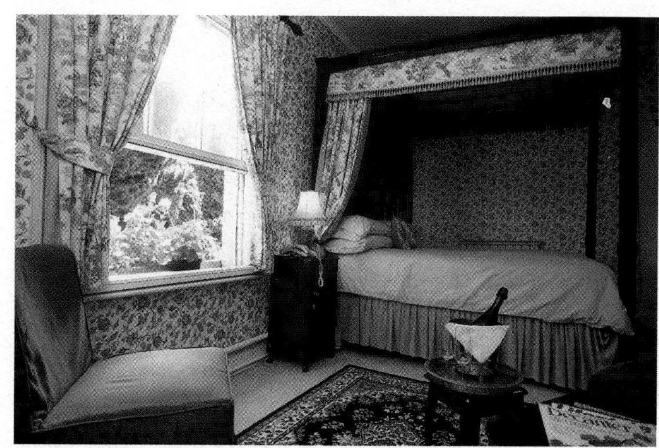

GLEWSTONE COURT

NR ROSS-ON-WYE, HEREFORDSHIRE HR9 6AW
TEL: 01989 770367 FAX: 01989 770282 E-MAIL: glewstone@aol.com

OWNERS: Bill and Christine Reeve-Tucker

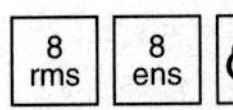

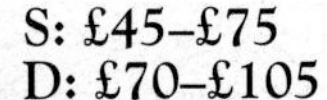

S: £45–£75
D: £70–£105

Glewstone Court is set in three acres of fruit orchards, lawns and flower-beds. It is a refreshingly un-stuffy establishment, although secluded, it is only three miles from Ross-on-Wye. Furnishings and an eclectic collection of antiques, bric a brac and books reflect the relaxed, hospitable personality of the owners. Most country pursuits can be arranged, including canoeing, fishing and riding. This is marvellous walking country, alternatively guests may wish to simply laze around in front of the log fires or on fine days, recline out in the garden.

Christine's food is always innovative and whilst reflecting a love of good fresh local ingredients; organic and free-range products are used as much as possible on both the restaurant and bistro menus. Featuring both modern and traditional British dishes, the cuisine is always prepared and served with care and attention to detail. Now in their 15th year, accolades awarded include an AA Rosette for good food and the AA Courtesy & Care award

The bedrooms are comfortable and individually decorated. Each has en suite facilities, a hospitality tray, soft bathrobes, direct dial phone and colour television. Closed Christmas Day and Boxing Day.

Places of interest nearby: Ross-on-Wye, Hay-on-Wye, the Welsh Marches, Hereford Cathedral and the Brecon Beacons.

Directions: From M50 junction 4 follow A40 signposted Monmouth. 1 mile past Wilton roundabout turn right to Glewstone; the Court is 1/2 mile on left.

Wilton Court Hotel

WILTON, ROSS-ON-WYE, HEREFORDSHIRE HR9 6AQ
TEL: 01989 562569 FAX: 01989 768460 E-MAIL: info@wiltoncourthotel.com

OWNERS: Helen and Roger Wynn
CHEF: Josèphine Marangon

SMALL HOTEL

S: £45–£65
D: £65–£95
Suite: £100–£120

Offering abundant peace and tranquillity on the banks of the River Wye, this property is a true gem, surrounded by walled gardens with mature shrubs, sloping lawns and an enchanting river.

Leaded windows and stone mullions are some of the many vestiges of the hotel's 15th century origins. Affording a view of either the gardens or the river, the recently refurbished en suite bedrooms are well-appointed, complete with trouser press, tea and coffee making facilities, direct dial telephones and colour televisions.

Guests may dine in the cosy bar, with its warm fire in winter, the light Conservatory with its view of the gardens or enjoy bar snacks alfresco. The very best of fresh local produce is used wherever possible.

Sports enthusiasts will be pleased with the local facilities which include canoeing, salmon fishing on the River Wye, horse-riding, ballooning, tennis,cycling, bowling and golf. The hotel has ample car parking and is within walking distance from the bustling streets of Ross on Wye with its 16th century market place

Places of interest nearby: Tintern Abbey, The Malvern Hills, the Forest of Dean and The Cotswolds are some of the many areas that are worth exploring.

Directions: From the M50, exit at junction 4 and turn to Ross at the junction of A40 and A49. The hotel is on the first right before the Wye River Bridge.

White Vine House

HIGH STREET, RYE, EAST SUSSEX TN31 7JF
TEL: 01797 224748 FAX: 01797 223599 E-MAIL: irene@whitevinehouse.freeserve.co.uk

GENERAL MANAGER: Irene Cheetham
CHEF:Anna Moore

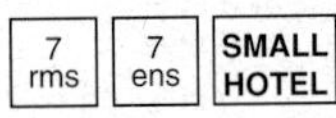

S: from £40
D: £70–£110

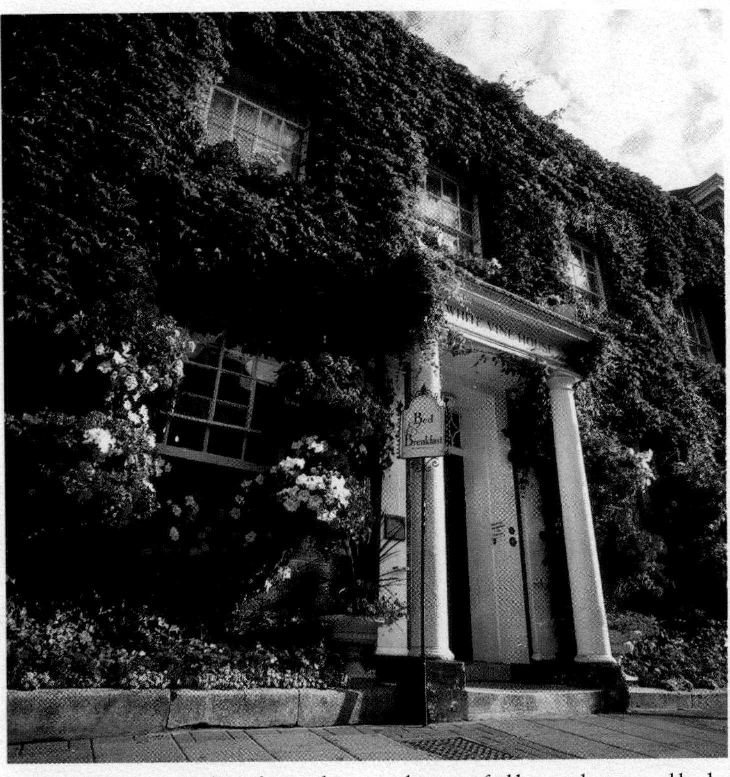

Despite its Georgian exterior this fine timber framed house is much older. Originally built around a courtyard that now forms the reception hallway, the hotel stands over Medieval cellars on the site of the ancient Whyte Vyne Inn. At the hub of the daytime bustle of this fascinating little market town, the house retains a unique character and restful atmosphere.

In the morning guests can savour the pleasant surroundings while enjoying breakfast from an impressive choice. Lunch is served daily with an interesting selection of dishes from light options to the more traditional, complemented by a range of good value wines. Small meetings and private dining are offered and the beautifully oak panelled Elizabethan Room is a comfortable residents lounge. Staff will happily recommend good restaurants from the many within strolling distance of the hotel door and make dinner reservations on behalf of guests to match individual preferences. Complimentary aperitifs are available every evening.

Places of interest nearby: Rye is a town of great historical interest and boasts many art galleries, potteries, antique dealers and book sellers. **Directions: Take the A21 to Flimwell, then the A268 to Rye. Telephone first for parking advice.**

THE COUNTRYMAN AT TRINK HOTEL

OLD COACH ROAD, ST IVES, CORNWALL TR26 3JQ
TEL: 01736 797571 FAX: 01736 797571

OWNERS: Howard and Cathy Massey

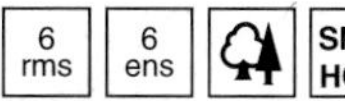

S: £38
D: £60–£70

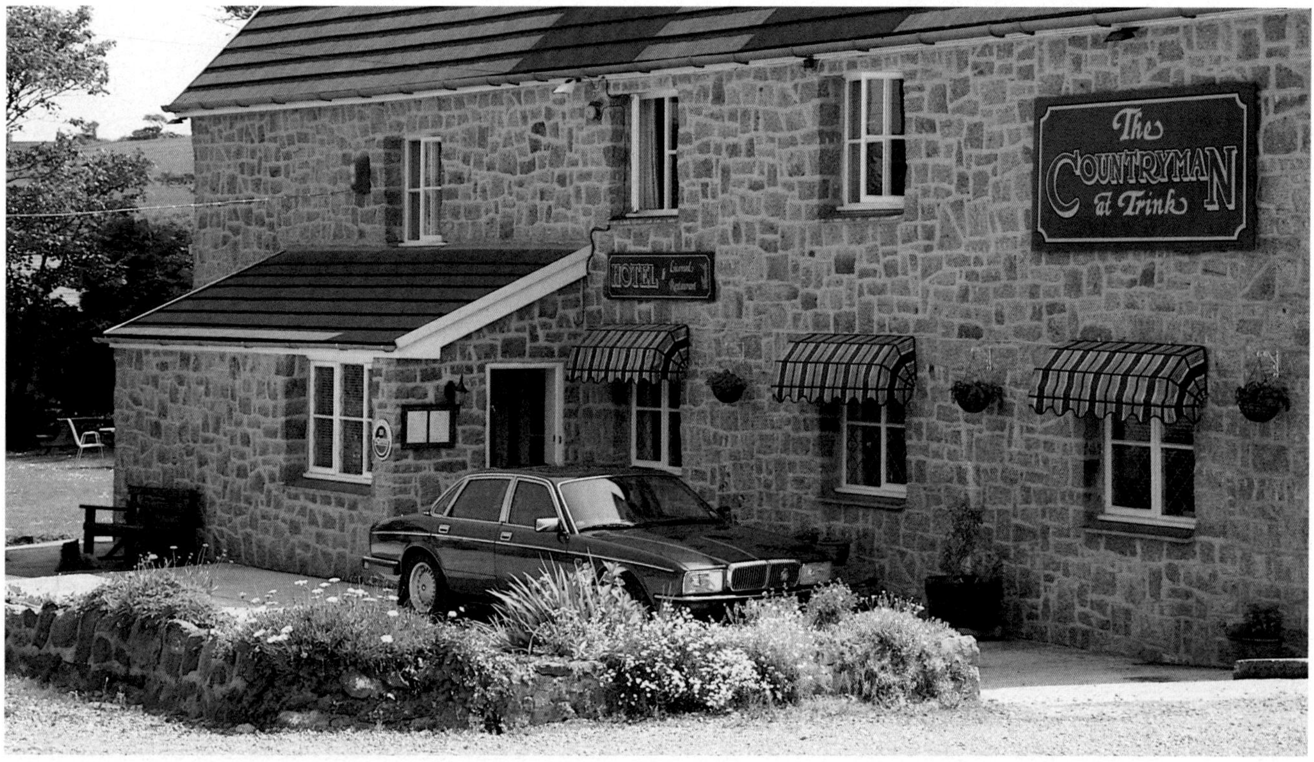

Five minutes drive from the quaint town of St Ives is the Countryman Hotel at Trink. St Ives has become a mecca for artists and one of the latest attractions is the new Tate Gallery with its collection of modern paintings and contemporary exhibits. Cornwall has a wealth of interesting things to see not least its dramatic coastline ideal for lovers of nature and walkers.

The Countryman dates from the 17th century. Today the small hotel has been renovated to meet the needs of the modern visitor, all rooms have en suite shower and toilet, colour television and tea making facilities.

The atmosphere of the hotel is friendly and inviting, the emphasis being on cheerful service and good value for money. This is a totally no smoking hotel. In the restaurant, Howard Massey, the chef-patron, likes cooking to order from his varied and interesting menu containing Cornish fish supported by a sensibly priced wine-list. St Ives has always had a tradition for generous hospitality. A former mayor, the legendary John Knill, bequeathed £10 for an annual banquet. Prices may have altered a little but the high quality of the local cooking has not changed. **Places of interest nearby:** Tate Gallery, Lands End. Barbara Hepworth's house, St Michael's Mount. Golf, riding and the sea. **Directions: A30, A3074 to St Ives, then B3311 for about two miles.**

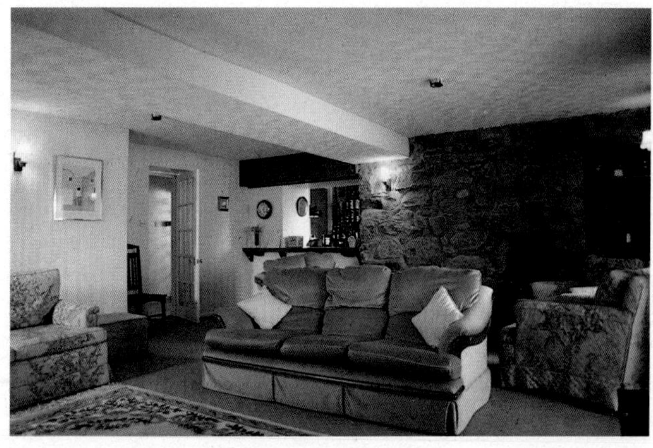

THE OLD RECTORY COUNTRY HOUSE HOTEL

ST KEYNE, LISKEARD, CORNWALL PL14 4RL
TEL: 01579 342617 FAX: 01579 342293 E-MAIL: savillelyons@freenet.co.uk

OWNERS: Bunny Saville and Michael Lyons
CHEF: Glenn Gatland

  SMALL HOTEL

 **S: £63–£85**
D: £85–£120

This beautiful old rectory lies in the tranquil Looe Valley, and is just five miles from the picturesque fishing village itself. Set in 4 acres of its own grounds, and having recently been the subject of a substantial restoration and refurbishment programme by its new owners, it is now an exquisite and intimate hotel, offering guests every comfort and total seclusion.

The bedrooms have been carefully presented with striking fabrics and clever co-ordination, and all the bathrooms have fluffy bathrobes and exotic Molton Brown cosmetics.

The drawing room overlooks the delightful grounds and is a luxurious place to relax with a pre-dinner drink or coffee; whilst the restaurant prides itself on its use of local ingredients incorporated into a varied and tempting menu, which has already been awarded 2 AA Rosettes.

Places of interest nearby: This is an area bursting with Heritage walks and National Trust properties to explore, and the coast with its stunning beaches is only 6 miles away. The Lost Gardens of Heligan, The Eden project and Pencarrow House & Gardens are all nearby, and The Cornwall Gardens Festival is held not far away in the Spring. **Directions: From M5 Exeter, stay on A38 past Plymouth and over Tamar Bridge. Turn off at Liskeard exit, and follow signs for Town Centre and pick up B3254 to St Keyne.**

The Hundred House Hotel

RUAN HIGHLANES, NR TRURO, CORNWALL TR2 5JR
TEL: 01872 501336 FAX: 01872 501151

OWNERS: Mike and Kitty Eccles

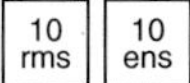

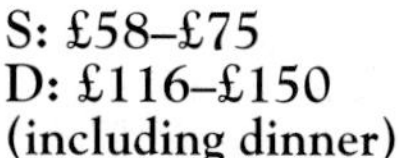

S: £58–£75
D: £116–£150
(including dinner)

Situated on Cornwall's beautiful Roseland Peninsula is The Hundred House Hotel, an 18th century Cornish country house set in three acres of gardens. It commands panoramic views over the countryside and is close to the sea and the lovely Fal estuary.

Once inside the wide hall with its handsome Edwardian staircase, there is the feeling of an elegant English home. Mike and Kitty Eccles have created a delightful hotel where guests can relax in the pretty sitting room, furnished with antiques and browse among the books of local interest. On cooler days they can enjoy a Cornish cream tea by a log fire and in the summer a game of croquet on the lawn. Each bedroom is individually decorated and has full en suite bath or shower room.

Guests regularly return to enjoy the delicious imaginative dinners and the hearty Cornish breakfast prepared by Kitty Eccles who has been awarded a Red Rosette by the AA. She uses fresh seasonal ingredients and specialities include baked avocado, fillet of lemon sole with a salmon mousse and a honey and lavender ice cream.

Places of interest nearby: Picturesque fishing villages, superb cliff walks and sandy beaches. Heligan Gardens, Eden project, sailing and boat trips on Fal Estuary. Lanhydrock House (NT). Cathedral city of Truro 12 miles away. **Directions: A390 from St Austell, left on B3278 to Tregony, then A3078 to St Mawes. Hotel is then 4 miles on.**

Preston House Hotel

SAUNTON, BRAUNTON, NORTH DEVON EX33 1LG
TEL: 01271 890472 FAX: 01271 890555 E-MAIL: prestonhouse-saunton@zoom.co.uk

OWNER: Jan Poole
CHEF: Kevin Little

12 rms | 12 ens | SMALL HOTEL

S: £65–£95
D: £90–£150

Miles of flat, golden sands and white-capped Atlantic rollers greet guests seeking peace and relaxation at Preston House, standing high on the glorious coastline of North Devon. Terraced, lawned gardens sweep down to the sea and an atmosphere of undisturbed continuity and tranquillity surrounds the hotel which has been extensively and sympathetically refurbished to its Victorian origins.

Most of the en suite bedrooms face seawards, all are individually decorated, tastefully furnished and contain all modern amenities from colour television and direct dial telephone to tea and coffee facilities. Some have a four-poster bed, balcony and the added luxury of a Jacuzzi.

A spacious and comfortable lounge provides perfect relaxation. Breakfast can be leisurely enjoyed in the hotel's conservatory which overlooks the garden, sands and ocean. Chef Kevin Little has won an AA rosette for his delicious and imaginative cuisine, which is served in the elegant restaurant or overlooking the magnificent view in the conservatory. The hotel, which is non-smoking throughout, provides out of seasons special breaks.

Places of interest nearby: Lynton, Lynmouth, Exmoor and many National Trust properties. **Directions: From the M5, exit at junction 27 and take the A361 towards Barnstaple. Continue on to Braunton and then turn left at traffic lights towards Croyde. The hotel is on the left after approximately two miles.**

The Grange Hotel and Restaurant

OBORNE, NR SHERBORNE, DORSET DT9 4LA
TEL: 01935 813463 FAX: 01935 817464 E-MAIL: karen@thegrangehotel–dorset.co.uk

OWNERS: Karen and Jonathan Arthur
MANAGERS: Manuela and Riccardo Petterlin
CHEF: Martin Barrett

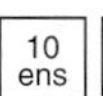

S: £60–£65
D: £85–£105

This 200 year old country house nestles peacefully in formal gardens, situated only 1½ miles from historic Sherborne. The welcome here is both personal and unobtrusive and the attentive hosts, Jonathan and Karen Arthur, have completed a most splendid refurbishment which includes a fine new conservatory.

The ten spacious bedrooms are well appointed with a number of modern facilities. Guests may enjoy dinner in a most pleasant ambience, overlooking the attractive floodlit gardens and log fires. The restaurant specialises in both international and traditional British cuisine and has recently been awarded 2 AA Rosettes. For diners with a sweet tooth, the dessert trolley is sure to tempt!

For those who are planning a very special occasion, the hotel can provide facilities for up to 40 guests which are also suited to conferences and business meetings alike. This quiet haven is a most ideal escape from city life and guests will be able to unwind whilst horse riding, fishing, enjoying a game of croquet or simply taking in the local scenery.

Places of interest nearby: Air enthusiasts will not be left out and they will be pleased to hear that the Fleet Aviation Museum can be found nearby. Keen golfers may use the golf course in close proximity of the hotel. Popular daytime excursions include visits to the abbey at Sherborne or the gardens at Stourhead. **Directions: Oborne can be found just off the A30 in between Sherborne and Milborne Port.**

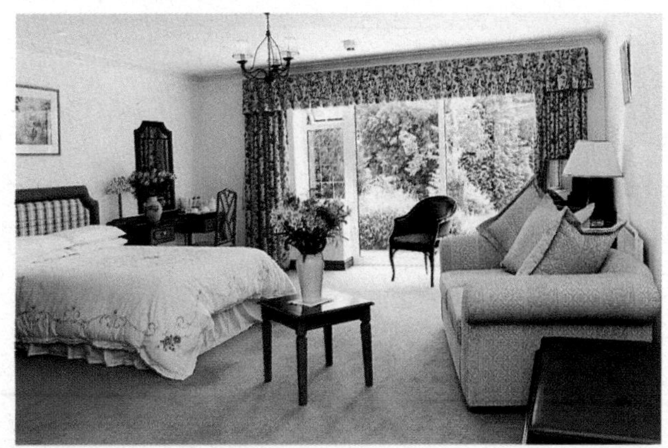

THE SHAVEN CROWN HOTEL

HIGH STREET, SHIPTON-UNDER-WYCHWOOD, OXFORDSHIRE OX7 6BA
TEL: 01993 830330 FAX: 01993 832136

OWNERS: Mr and Mrs Robert Burpitt

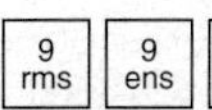

S: £55
D: £85–£120

Built of honey-coloured stone around an attractive central courtyard, The Shaven Crown Hotel dates back to the 14th century, when it served as a monks' hospice. The proprietors have preserved the inn's many historic features, such as the medieval hall with its ancient timbered roof. This is now the residents' lounge. Each of the bedrooms has en suite facilities and has been sympathetically furnished in a style befitting its own unique character. Rooms of various style and sizes are available, including a huge family room and ground-floor accommodation. Dining in the intimate, candlelit room is an enjoyable experience, with meals served at the tables beautifully laid with fine accessories. The best ingredients are combined to create original dishes with a cosmopolitan flair. The table d'hôte menu offers a wide and eclectic choice with a daily vegetarian dish among the specialities. An imaginative selection of dishes is offered every lunchtime and evening in the Monks Bar.

Places of interest nearby: The Shaven Crown is ideal for day trips to the Cotswolds, Oxford, Stratford-upon-Avon and Bath. There are three golf courses and tennis courts close by. Trout fishing and antique-hunting are popular activities in the area. **Directions: Take the A40 Oxford–Cheltenham road. At Burford follow the A361 towards Chipping Norton. The inn is situated directly opposite the village green in Shipton-under-Wychwood.**

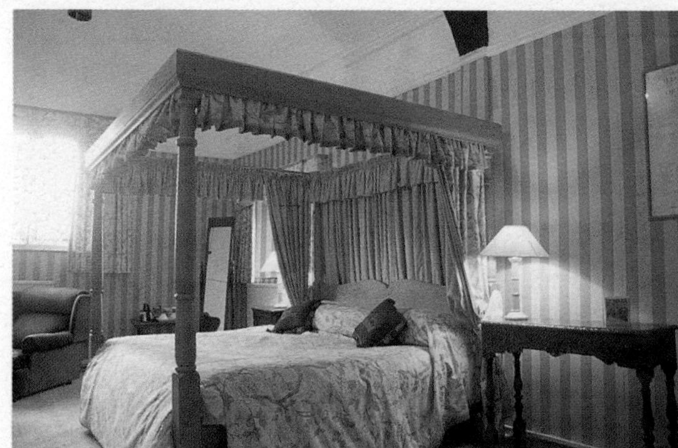

Rowton Castle Hotel

SHREWSBURY, SHROPSHIRE SY5 9EP
TEL: 01743 884044 FAX: 01743 884949 E-MAIL: post@rowtoncastle.c

OWNERS: Jack de Sousa and Nick Hollingshead
CHEF: Steve Parke

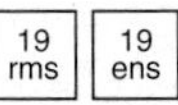
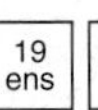

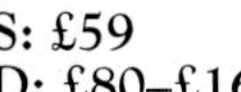

S: £59
D: £80–£160

Rowton Castle Hotel and Restaurant is just ten minutes from the medieval town of Shrewsbury. Set in 17 acres of grounds the entrance to the Grade II listed building is dominated by an impressive Cedar of Lebanon, reputed to be the largest of its kind in Europe.

A Victorian walled garden and two recently restored trout lakes are some of the many pleasures that await guests wishing to stroll through the tranquil grounds.

Situated within the walls of the historic castle, the 19 en suite bedrooms are well appointed. There are three four-poster beds and a four-poster Jacuzzi bath.

The tastefully refurbished Cedar Restaurant features a 17th century carved oak fireplace and offers a wide range of mouthwatering cuisine, whilst the oak-panelling provides a cosy and convivial ambience.

The Georgian Dining Room, with its hand painted murals, gilt panelling and crystal chandeliers, caters for private dinners for up to 10 guests. The Cardeston Suite can accommodate up to 110 banquet style and has private bar facilities. The hotel may be booked exclusively for large groups and special occasions.

Places of interest nearby: Shrewsbury Castle, Ironbridge and Llangollen. Golf, shooting, fishing and croquet are available.

Directions: Five miles from Shrewsbury on the A458 Welshpool road.

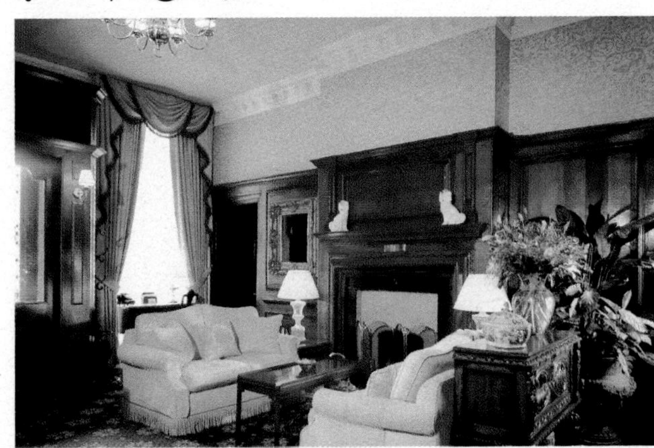

The Brompton

UPPER BROMPTON FARM, CROSS HOUSES, SHREWSBURY, SHROPSHIRE SY5 6LE
TEL: 01743 761629 FAX: 01743 761679 E-MAIL: chris@upperbromptonfarm.com

OWNERS: Christine and George Yates-Roberts
CHEF: Gareth Morgan

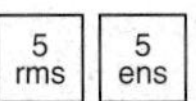

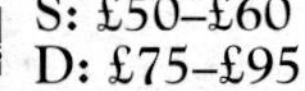

S: £50–£60
D: £75–£95

This elegant Georgian farmhouse is situated in the heart of rural Shropshire yet only 5 minutes from the town of Shrewsbury. Set in 315 acres of arable farmland it is an ideal spot from which to walk and enjoy the abundance of wildlife. Convenient for a host of local golf courses.

Winner of the Heart of England Tourist Board's 'Bed & Breakfast of the Year 1999' Award, The Brompton is a welcome retreat from urban life. The classically furnished drawing room with its open fire offers peace and relaxation at any time of day. The accommodation is splendidly decorated and English to the core: florals and chintz, soft carpets and deliciously comfortable four-posters.

Fine china, candles and contemporary glassware display Gareth Morgan's exciting and creative talents to their best advantage. Using best local produce, he artistically presents dishes such as warm salad of fresh tuna, monkfish and a sicilian caponata or roast Aberdeen Angus served with seared calves liver and a pickled walnut and olorosso sherry sauce, rounded off with fresh apricot and almond tart served with brandied mascarpone.

Places of interest nearby: National Trust properties, Ironbridge Gorge, Severn Valley Railway at Bridgnorth, walks on the Longmynd and Wenlock Edge. **Directions: From Shrewsbury on A458 Much Wenlock/Bridgnorth road (approx. 4 miles). On entering Cross Houses, go left at petrol station, after 1 mile right up lane to Brompton.**

Tree Tops Country House Hotel

SOUTHPORT OLD ROAD, FORMBY, NR SOUTHPORT, LANCASHIRE L37 0AB
TEL: 01704 572430 FAX: 01704 572430

OWNERS: Lesley Winsland
CHEF: David Oakes

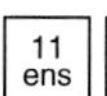

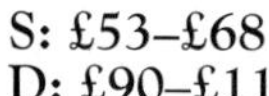

S: £53–£68
D: £90–£115

The Former Dower House of Formby Hall, Tree Tops, still retains all the elegance of a bygone age, set in five acres of lawns and woods. Over the last 18 years, Lesley Winsland has restored the house to its true glory and has installed all the modern conveniences sought after by today's visitor.

Spacious accommodation is available in well-appointed en suite lodges with all the facilities a discerning guest would expect. An outdoor-heated swimming pool has direct access to the sumptuously decorated Cocktail Lounge. Rich, dark leather seating, oynx-and-gilt tables and subtle lighting all contribute to the overall ambience, complemented by a truly welcoming and friendly staff.

Highly polished Regency furnishings, silver tableware and crystal chandeliers set the scene for culinary delights involving only the finest fresh ingredients. The new conservatory restaurant has a totally relaxed atmosphere with a superb new à la carte menu serving modern and interesting dishes together with a special snack selection.

Places of interest nearby: Tree Tops is only 7 mins drive from Southport with its sweeping sands and famous Lord street shopping centre. 20 mins from Liverpool. 10 golf courses can be found within a 5 mile radius, including 6 championship courses. **Directions: From M6 take M58 to Southport to the end of motorway. Follow signs to Southport on A565. Bypass Formby on dual carriageway and as it changes to single carriageway, turn right at traffic lights to Tree Tops.**

Horsley Hall

EASTGATE, NR STANHOPE, BISHOP AUCKLAND, CO. DURHAM DL13 2LJ
TEL: 01388 517239 FAX: 01388 517608 E-MAIL: hotel@horsleyhall.co.uk

OWNERS: Derek Glass and Liz Curry

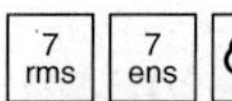

S: £47–£55
D: £62.50–£70
Family: £99

Horsley Hall is an elegant, three-story manor house nestling in the heart of Weardale, a designated area of outstanding natural beauty. Situated on the road south of the River Wear between Stanhope and Eastgate the hotel enjoys magnificent views across the Dale and easy access to local attractions.

The Hall dates back to the 17th century and was once the home of the Hildyard family, whose existence in the Dale can be traced back nearly 500 years. The owners offer a warm, friendly North East welcome, attentive personal service and are justly proud of their hotel's reputation for homely comfort and good food.

Liz is the chef and produces delicious cuisine and a varied choice of menus using the freshest of local produce. There are fine furnishings and fabrics, stylish décor and open fires throughout the Hall. The en suite bedrooms are extremely comfortable and have all the facilities to make a stay relaxing and enjoyable. They are all non smoking. The Hall is licensed for weddings and the Baronial Hall accommodates up to 80 guests for these, other private functions or business meetings. **Places of interest nearby:** Bowes Museum, High Force waterfall, Killhope Wheel and Lead Mining Centre, Derwent Reservoir, Beamish Open Air Museum, Durham Cathedral and Castle. **Directions: From the A68 take the A689 west to Stanhope. Then take the B6278 towards Brotherlee and Hasswicks. Horsley Hall (signposted) is on the right after approximately two miles.**

KINGSTON HOUSE

STAVERTON, TOTNES, DEVON TQ9 6AR
TEL: 01803 762 235 FAX: 01803 762 444 E-MAIL: info@kingston–estate.net

OWNERS: Michael and Elizabeth Corfield

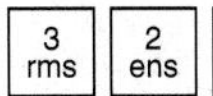

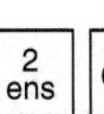

S: £80–£90
D: £120
Suite: £130–£140

The Kingston Estate nestles amongst the rolling hills and valleys of the South Hams region of Devon, bounded by Dartmoor and the sea, with the focal point, Kingston House, commanding sweeping views of the moor.

The Mansion, together with the superb self-catering cottages, have been sympathetically restored by the Corfield family to their former glory and now offer some of the highest standard accommodation to be found in the South West. The House boasts three period suites, (reached by way of the finest example of a marquetry staircase in England), which are hung with authentic wall papers and fabrics and include a 1735 Angel tester bed and an 1830 four-poster.

Dinner guests dine by candlelight in the elegant dining room at tables set with sparkling crystal, shining silver and starched linen. In winter, log fires crackle in the hearths, whilst in the summer pre-dinner drinks may be taken on the terrace overlooking the formal 18th century gardens. For every visitor to Kingston, hospitality and comfort are assured in this magnificent historic setting.

Places of interest nearby: Dartington Hall, Dartmouth, Totnes, Dartmoor & Devon's famous coastline.

Directions: Take A38 from Exeter or Plymouth, at Buckfastleigh take A384 Totnes road for two miles. Turn left to Staverton. At Sea Trout Inn, take left fork to Kingston and follow signs.

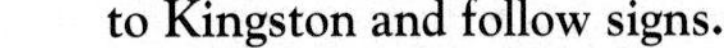

REDCOATS FARMHOUSE HOTEL AND RESTAURANT

REDCOATS GREEN, NEAR HITCHIN, HERTS SG4 7JR
TEL: 01438 729500 FAX: 01438 723322 E-MAIL: info@redcoats.co.uk

OWNERS: The Butterfield Family
CHEF: John Ruffell

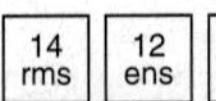       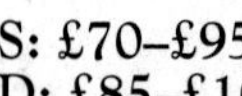

S: £70–£95
D: £85–£105

This 15th century farmhouse has been in the Butterfield family for generations, and in 1971, Peter and his sister converted it into a hotel. They preserved its traditional character of original beams, exposed brickwork and inglenook fireplaces and furnished it in a comfortable and inviting fashion.

Redcoats is set in tranquil gardens in the middle of rolling countryside yet not far from the A1(M). There are three dining rooms; the Oak Room (below left) with beams, oak panelling and log fires in winter, has 15th century charm. The elegant Victorian Room offers a more subtle ambience, eminently suitable for small wedding parties or conferences. Largest of all is the conservatory with its friendly bustle, also affording views of the beautiful gardens.

Redcoats has an excellent reputation for its cuisine, which uses predominantly local produce, and a wine list which is as wide-ranging geographically as it is in prices.

Places of interest nearby: Redcoats is close to several historic houses including Knebworth House, Hatfield House, Luton Hoo and Woburn Abbey and Wildlife Park. The Roman city of St Albans, the traditional market town of Hitchin and Cambridge University are all within a 30 minute drive. **Directions: Leave the A1(M) at junction 8 for Little Wymondley. At mini-roundabout turn left. At T-Junction go right, hotel is on left.**

The Tollgate Inn

CHURCH STREET, KINGHAM, OXFORDSHIRE OX7 6YA
TEL: 01608 658389 FAX: 01608 659467

OWNER: Penny Simpson
CHEF: Robert Ingleston

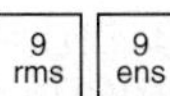
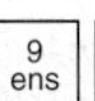

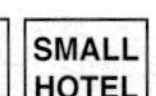

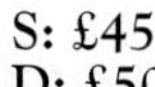

S: £45
D: £50

An 18th century former farmhouse, this beautiful Cotswold stone, Grade II listed building is situated in the centre of the unspoilt village of Kingham, ideally located for visiting the most popular tourist destinations.

Completely refurbished in contemporary style, The Tollgate retains a fresh country feel. The open-plan restaurant with coir matting and sanded wood furniture is the focal point of the hotel, and guests can enjoy drinks by the fire in the flagstoned, beamed Bar. In summer, there are tables in the walled lavender garden for lunch or dinner.

The bedrooms, some of which look out over the village, are individually decorated with simple yet striking furnishings and paint effects. The family room, a converted Hayloft with vaulted beamed ceiling, can accommodate up to five people. All the bedrooms are non-smoking, as is the Restaurant, but guests are welcome to smoke in the Bar.

Chef Robert Ingleston uses an eclectic mix of local and organic produce. His food spans the continents in style, but is firmly rooted in his classical training. There's always a good choice of fish and vegetarian dishes, as well as beef and pork from local farms, and mouth-watering snacks.

Places of interest nearby: Burford, Bourton-on-the-Water and many other Cotswold towns and villages, Blenheim Palace, Stratford-upon-Avon and Oxford. **Directions: The hotel is in the centre of Kingham, which lies between the B4450 and A436 to the east of Stow.**

Glebe Farm House

LOXLEY, WARWICKSHIRE CV35 9JW
TEL/FAX: 01789 842501 E-MAIL: scorpiolimited@msn.com

OWNER: Kate McGovern

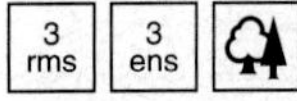

S: £69.50
D: £90–£100
Suite: £120

The pleasure of staying at this delightful country house is like that of visiting a private home. Just three miles from historic Stratford-upon-Avon and eight miles from Warwick, Glebe Farm is surrounded by a superb expanse of secluded lawned garden which opens on to 30 acres of beautiful farmland where one can ramble and enjoy the sounds and sights of local wildlife.

Owner Kate McGovern is an accomplished cook and her dinners, served in the attractive surroundings of a conservatory overlooking the gardens, will tempt every palate. Whenever possible fresh organic produce from the kitchen garden are used. Kate is a talented water colour artist and many of her paintings adorn the walls throughout the house which is furnished and decorated with immaculate taste.

There are three pretty en suite bedrooms with four-poster beds and television and tea and coffee facilities. From all bedrooms and the lounge there are splendid views of the countryside. Local sporting activities include golf, shooting and riding.

Places of interest nearby: The hotel is an ideal base for visiting Shakespeare's Stratford-upon-Avon, Warwick's imposing castle, Ragley Hall, Birmingham N.E.C., the Heritage Motor Museum and the Cotswolds. **Directions: From the M40, exit at junction 15. Join the A429 and follow the signs to Wellsbourne and then Loxley. Glebe Farm is on the right as you leave Loxley.**

Willington Hall Hotel

WILLINGTON, NR TARPORLEY, CHESHIRE CW6 0NB
TEL: 01829 752321 FAX: 01829 752596 E-MAIL enquiries@willingtonhall.co.uk

OWNERS: Stuart and Diana Begbie

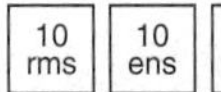
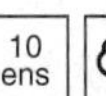

S: £68–£80
D: £100–£120

Built by Cheshire landowner Charles Tomkinson, Willington Hall was converted into a hotel by one of his descendants and in 1999 was bought by Stuart and Diana Begbie. Set in 17 acres of woods and parkland, the hotel affords wonderful views across the Cheshire countryside towards the Welsh mountains. There are both formally landscaped and 'wild' gardens, which create a beautiful backdrop for the handsome architectural proportions of the house. The hotel is a comfortable and friendly retreat for those seeking peace and seclusion. Under the personal supervision of Diana and Stuart, Willington Hall has acquired a good reputation with local people for its extensive bar meals and à la carte restaurant, along with friendly and attentive service. The menus offer traditional English cooking, with a French influence.

Places of interest nearby: It is an ideal location for visiting the Roman city of Chester, Tatton Park, Beeston Castle and Oulton Park racetrack. North Wales is easily accessible from Willington Hall. The hotel is closed on Christmas Day. **Directions: Take the A51 from Tarporley to Chester and turn right at the Bull's Head public house at Clotton. Willington Hall Hotel is one mile ahead on the left.**

Browns Hotel, Wine Bar & Brasserie

80 WEST STREET, TAVISTOCK, DEVON PL19 8AQ
TEL: 01822 618686 FAX: 01822 618646 E-MAIL: enquiries@brownsdevon.co.uk

14 rms | 14 ens | SMALL HOTEL

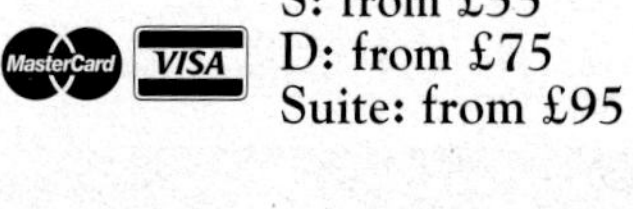

S: from £55
D: from £75
Suite: from £95

The ancient Stannary town of Tavistock is nestled in the valley of the River Tavy on the western slopes of Dartmoor and has been the western gateway to the moor for over a 1000 years. Against the background of the beautiful Dartmoor National Park, Browns Hotel, located in the town centre, extends a warm welcome to its visitors.

Formerly an old coaching inn, the hotel has a wealth of stone walls, slate floors, beams and log fires creating a wonderful atmosphere. The beautiful bedrooms offer total luxury and comfort with first-class en suite bathrooms.

During the summer guests enjoy eating alfresco in the beautifully presented courtyard with its colourful parasols and flowers. Browns has an extensive and lively a la carte menu prepared using local fresh produce.

Places of interest nearby: Guests can browse in the individual specialist shops or visit the remains of Benedictine Abbey, founded in AD 974. The beautiful Lydford Gorge, Buckland Abbey, once home of Sir Francis Drake and Morwellham Quay are all close by. Plymouth is 15 miles away, most famous for its' historic Barbican and Hoe. Other leisure activities include moor walking, fishing in the river Tavy or at superb local fishing venues, golf, horse-riding and cycling. Also nearby are The Wharf Theatre and cinema, leisure pool and tennis courts.

Directions: From A30, take A386 to Tavistock. From the square turn left into West Street.

Broom Hall Country Hotel

RICHMOND ROAD, SAHAM TONEY, THETFORD, NORFOLK IP25 7EX
TEL: 01953 882125 FAX: 01953 882125 E-MAIL: enquiries@broomhallhotel.co.uk

OWNERS: Nigel and Angela Rowling
MANAGER: Simon Rowling

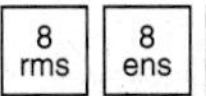
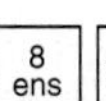

S: £52
D: £75–£98

Situated in 15 acres of mature gardens and parkland Broom Hall is a charming Victorian country house offering peace and tranquillity. Airy and spacious bedrooms each individually furnished and most offering lovely views provide guests with both comfort and a range of modern amenities.

A feature of the public rooms are the ornate ceilings and in the lounge a large open fire can be enjoyed in the winter months. An indoor heated swimming pool and full size snooker table are available for guests' use.

Fresh vegetables, from Broom Hall's own garden when in season, and many old fashioned desserts ensure that dinner in the dining room overlooking the garden is an enjoyable occasion. Small conferences can be arranged and the entire house can be 'taken over' for your family reunion or celebration. Seasonable breaks are available.

Places of interest nearby: Norwich, Cambridge, Ely and Bury St Edmunds are within easy reach. Sandringham and many National Trust properties, Thetford Forest, Norfolk Broads and coastline offering nature reserves and bird sanctuaries are also close by. **Directions: Half mile north of Watton on B1077 towards Swaffham.**

TREBREA LODGE

TRENALE, TINTAGEL, CORNWALL PL34 0HR
TEL: 01840 770410 FAX: 01840 770092

OWNERS: John Charlick and Sean Devlin

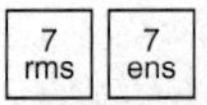 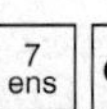  

  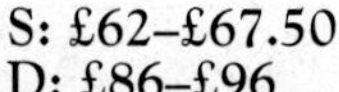

S: £62–£67.50
D: £86–£96

Winner of the Johansens 1994 Country House Award, Trebrea Lodge overlooks the beauty and grandeur of the North Cornish coast and is set in $4^1/_2$ acres of wooded hillside. This Grade II listed house was built on land granted to the Bray family by the Black Prince in the 14th century and has been lived in and improved by successive generations of the Brays for almost 600 years.

All the bedrooms are individually decorated with traditional and antique furniture and they offer uninterrupted views across open fields to the Atlantic Ocean. The elegant first-floor drawing room also boasts spectacular views, while there is a comfortable smoking room downstairs with an open log fire.

A full English breakfast and four course dinner are served in the oak-panelled dining room with the menu changing daily. Fresh local ingredients are used to create a selection of both traditional and modern British and European cuisine. The hotel has been awarded an AA rosette.

Places of interest nearby: Tintagel Island and Boscastle. Bodmin Moor, Lanhydrock House and gardens, Pencarrow House and extensive coastal walks. **Directions: From Launceston take Wadebridge–Camelford road. At A39 follow Tintagel sign – turn left for Trenale $^1/_2$ mile before reaching Tintagel.**

Hooke Hall

HIGH STREET, UCKFIELD, EAST SUSSEX TN22 1EN
TEL: 01825 761578 FAX: 01825 768025 E-MAIL: a.percy@virgin.net

OWNERS: Alister and Juliet Percy

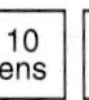
10 rms | 10 ens | SMALL HOTEL

S: from £55
D: from £75

Uckfield lies on the borders of Ashdown Forest, near the South Downs and resorts of Brighton and Eastbourne and 40 minutes from Gatwick Airport. Hooke Hall is an elegant Queen Anne town house, the home of its owners, Juliet and Alister Percy, who have carried out extensive renovations.

The comfortable bedrooms are individually decorated to a high standard with private facilities. In the panelled study guests can relax by the open fire and enjoy sampling the excellent range of malt whiskies on offer from the well-stocked 'Honesty Bar'. Breakfast is served in a delightful room with french windows opening onto the terrace and the garden beyond. There are several restaurants within easy walking distance of the hotel and further choices only minutes away by car.

Places of interest nearby: Within easy reach are Leeds, Hever and Bodiam Castles, Penshurst Place and Battle Abbey. The gardens of Sissinghurst, Nymans, Great Dixter, Sheffield Park, Wakehurst Place and Leonardslee are no distance nor is Batemans, Rudyard Kipling's home. Glyndebourne Opera is only 15 minutes by car. There are several English vineyards nearby to be visited. Closed for Christmas. **Directions: From M25 take the exit for East Grinstead and continue South on the A22 to Uckfield. Hooke Hall is at the northern end of the High Street.**

Tredethy House

HELLAND BRIDGE, BODMIN, CORNWALL PL30 4QS
TEL: 01208 841262 FAX: 01208 841707 E-MAIL: amandarose@tredethyhouse.co.uk

OWNERS: Amanda Rose
CHEF: Graham Holder

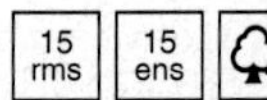

S: £51–£73
D: £115–£150
Suite: £135

In a central location, just west of Bodmin Moor, Tredethy House is the ideal base for exploring Cornwall. Set in 9 acres of grounds and with beautiful views over the countryside, this elegant manor house dates back to Tudor times, with later Victorian additions providing spacious accommodation in beautifully proportioned rooms.

The 15 bedrooms are all individual in their design and style – 11 in the main house and 4 courtyard suites – yet are united by their elegant décor and excellent facilities. Families will love the spacious courtyard suites with their additional sitting rooms, and dogs are welcome too with blankets and throws provided.

Local Cornish produce features prominently in the exciting dinner menu with unusual dishes such as "Fried Parmesan crumbed Cornish brie with a Lemon and Lime Gremolata" or "Pan fried medallions of prime Cornish Beef wrapped in bacon with seared Aubergine and Smoked Cheese on a rich pan Gravy". Children are also extremely well catered for with a two-course high tea prepared nightly.

Places of interest nearby: Pencarrow House and the local vineyard are well worth a visit, and there are plenty of walks along Bodmin Moor or the Camel Trail.

Directions: From A30 exit Bodmin, take the exit marked Helland from the roundabout and after 1½ miles turn left again signposted Helland.

Trehellas House & Memories of Malaya Restaurant

WASHAWAY, BODMIN, CORNWALL PL30 3AD
TEL: 01208 72700 FAX: 01208 73336 E-MAIL: trehellashouse@btinternet.com

OWNERS: Robin and Lee Boyle
CHEF: Lee Boyle

S: £37
D: £60
Suite: £100

This early 18th century former posting inn, steeped in history, is surrounded by two acres of grounds. The bedrooms are charming, varying in size, with five in the main house and others in the former coach house and barn. Following a recent refurbishment, the rooms are enhanced by the comfortable furnishings including patchwork quilts, iron bedsteads and en suite facilities.

The Memories of Malaya restaurant, with its beautifully preserved slate floor and elegant décor, serves a unique style of cuisine known as Nonya. Originating from the Pacific Rim, the dishes are authentically reproduced and flavoured with aromatic herbs and spices. Cornish breakfasts are served with locally produced organic bacon, sausages and free-range eggs.

Guests may wish to stroll in the pleasant gardens or enjoy the heated swimming pool. There are ample parking facilities.

Places of interest nearby: Pencarrow House and Lanhydrock House and Gardens are both within easy reach. The village of Rock is a popular base for sailing and fishing whilst cyclists and ramblers will enjoy the trails to Padstow and the Bodmin Moor. **Directions: Washaway is located on the A389 half-way between the towns of Bodmin and Wadebridge. Approaching from Bodmin, Trehellas House is situated to the right, set back from the main road and accessed by a slip road.**

THE ARDENCOTE MANOR HOTEL AND COUNTRY CLUB

LYE GREEN ROAD, CLAVERDON, WARWICKSHIRE CV35 8LS
TEL: 01926 843111 FAX 01926 842646 E-MAIL: hotel@ardencote.com

MANAGER: Paul Williams
CHEF: Simon Douglas

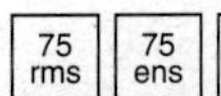 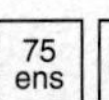   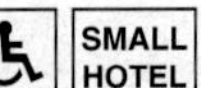

75 rms 75 ens SMALL HOTEL

   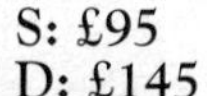

S: £95
D: £145

Two large stone lions guard the impressive arched entrance to this charming Edwardian-style hotel standing in 42 acres of grounds in the heart of Shakespeare Country. It is a peaceful, privately owned retreat within easy reach of historic Warwick and Stratford-upon-Avon. Ardencote Manor is a former gentleman's residence and has been sympathetically extended whilst retaining its unique ambience and appealing intimacy. All bedrooms are beautifully decorated, equipped to a high standard, and many have spectacular views.

Guests have a choice of three restaurants. The Oak Room offers imaginative and delightfully presented award-winning table d' hôte cuisine while there is an excellent range of pub food in the informal Lodge Bar and Restaurant which overlooks the lake. Alternatively, guests can enjoy an eclectic range of Mediterranean meals in the relaxed setting of the conservatory-style Leisure Bar.

Superb Leisure Club facilities include an indoor pool and spa, two gymnasia, sauna and steam rooms, squash and tennis courts and a health and beauty saloon. There is fishing for trout in the lake, and from summer 2001 a 9-hole golf course will be available.

Places of interest nearby: Birmingham City's attractions and the NEC, Warwick Castle, Stratford-upon-Avon. **Directions: From M40 follow signs to Henley-in-Arden. Lye Green Road is off the A4189 Henley-in-Arden/Warwick Road at Claverdon Village Green.**

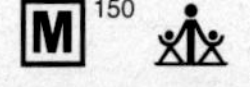  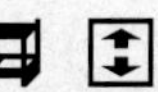   

www.johansens.com/ardencotemanor

BERYL

WELLS, SOMERSET BA5 3JP
TEL: 01749 678738 FAX: 01749 670508 E-MAIL: stay@beryl-wells.co.uk

OWNERS: Eddie and Holly Nowell

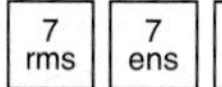 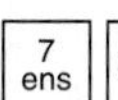  

S: £50–£70
D: £70–£95

This nineteenth century Gothic mansion is tastefully furnished with antiques. It also offers hospitality of the highest order.

The host is a famous antique dealer, with a long established shop in Wells, his gardening talents are reflected in the 13 acres of parkland which he has restored with great skill.

His wife is a charming and talented hostess, evident in the attention paid to detail and an excellent cook. Dinner is served by arrangement in the elegant dining room, with a set menu and house wines, pre-dinner and after-dinner drinks are available. It is possible to have small conferences or private celebrations. The en suite bedrooms have interesting views, with all the requisites for modern comfort.

Places of interest nearby: Wells Cathedral (1 mile), The Roman Baths at Bath, Glastonbury Abbey, Longleat House, Stourhead, Farleigh Castle, theatres in Bath and Bristol and many more fascinating places. For more active guests, there is marvellous golf, fishing, riding, excellent walking and a nearby leisure centre. **Directions: Leave Wells on Radstock Road B3139. Follow the signs to 'The Horringtons' and the 'H' sign for hospital. Opposite the Shell garage turn left into Hawkers Lane, Beryl is signed at the top with a leafy 500 yard drive to the main gate.**

GLENCOT HOUSE

GLENCOT LANE, WOOKEY HOLE, NR WELLS, SOMERSET BA5 1BH
TEL: 01749 677160 FAX: 01749 670210 E-MAIL: Glencot@ukonline.co.uk

OWNER: Jenny Attia
CHEF: Andrew Palmer

S: £64–£80
D: £88–£110

Idyllically situated in 18 acres of sheltered gardens and parkland with river frontage, Glencot House is an imposing Grade II listed Victorian mansion built in grand Jacobean style. It has been sensitively renovated to its former glory to provide comfortable country house accommodation and a homely atmosphere.

This elegantly furnished hotel has countless beautiful features: carved ceilings, walnut panelling, mullioned windows, massive fireplaces, antiques and sumptuous chandeliers. The bedrooms are decorated and furnished with period pieces. All have full en suite facilities and splendid views. Many have four-poster or half tester beds.

Guests can enjoy pleasant walks in the garden, trout fishing in the river, snooker, table tennis, a sauna or a dip in the jet-stream pool. The small, intimate bar has a balcony overlooking the grounds and diverse and delicious fare is served in the restaurant, enriched by beautiful glassware, silver and china.

Places of interest nearby: The caves at Wookey Hole, the cathedral town of Wells, the houses and gardens of Longleat, Stourhead and Montacute, Glastonbury, Bath, the Mendip Hills and the Cheddar Gorge. **Directions: From the M4, exit at junction 18. Take the A46 to Bath and then follow the signs to Wells and Wookey Hole. From the M5, exit at junction 22. Join the A38 and then the A371 towards Wells and Wookey Hole.**

SOULTON HALL

NR WEM, SHROPSHIRE SY4 5RS
TEL: 01939 232786 FAX: 01939 234097 E-MAIL: j.a.ashton@farmline.com

OWNERS: John and Ann Ashton
CHEF: Ann Ashton

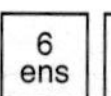  

S: £38–£49
D: £76–£99

Historic and imposing Soulton Hall stands in 550 acres of beautiful Shropshire parkland two miles east of the ancient market town of Wem. Dating from the 15th and 17 centuries, this Tudor brick built manor, with a magnificent pillared courtyard and beautiful walled garden, retains much of the grandeur and character of those bygone days, enhanced with all modern facilities.

Ann and John Ashton, descendants of the Protestant Lord Mayor of London who bought Soulton in 1556, have created a hotel of warmth whilst retaining many of the unique features in the four spacious bedrooms in the house. The two more modern bedrooms in the coach house are equally comfortably and provide total privacy.

Ann Ashton presides in the kitchen where her skills in traditional English cooking are enhanced by imagination and flair. Specialities might include hand-raised game pie or butter baked salmon served with saffron oil. The restaurant is open to non residents for dinner. There is a congenial bar and ample parking space.

Places of interest nearby: Hawkstone country park, Hodnet Hall and gardens, Grinshill, Nescliffe Hill, Ironbridge and Shrewsbury. Chester, Stoke and Worcester are within easy reach. **Directions: M54 to end, then A5 to junction with A49. North on A49, then join B5065 west to Wem.**

BEECHLEAS

17 POOLE ROAD, WIMBORNE MINSTER, DORSET BH21 1QA
TEL: 01202 841684 FAX: 01202 849344

OWNER: Josephine McQuillan

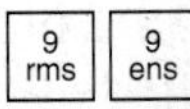 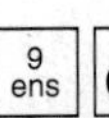  

S: £69–£89
D: £89–£99

Beechleas is a delightful Georgian Grade II listed town house hotel. It has been carefully restored and offers guests comfortable accommodation in beautifully furnished quality en suite bedrooms.

The hotel's own charming restaurant, which overlooks a pretty walled garden, is bright and airy in the summer and warmed by cosy log fires in the winter. The carefully prepared menu is changed daily and offers dishes using natural produce wherever possible along with the finest fresh ingredients available from the local market.

Sailing trips are available from Poole Harbour, where guests may choose to go fishing. They can play golf on one of the many local courses. It takes just five minutes to walk into the centre of Wimborne, a historic market town with an interesting twin tower church built on the site of its old Saxon Abbey during the 12th and 13th centuries.

The hotel, which is closed from 24 December to mid January, has been awarded two Red Stars by the AA and two Rosettes for its restaurant along with a Blue Ribbon from the RAC.

Places of interest nearby: There are many National Trust properties within easy reach, including Kingston Lacy House, Badbury Rings and Corfe Castle. Bournemouth and Poole are a 20 minute drive away. **Directions: From London take M3, M27, A31 and then B3073 to Wimborne.**

BROADOAKS COUNTRY HOUSE

BRIDGE LANE, TROUTBECK, WINDERMERE, CUMBRIA LA23 1LA
TEL: 01539 445566 FAX: 01539 488766 E-MAIL: trev@broadoaksf9.co.uk

OWNERS: Trevor and Joan Pavelyn
CHEF: Joan Pavelyn and Tarran Baxter

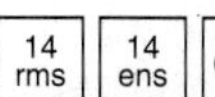

S: £65–£160
D: £110–£210

Tucked away in Troutbeck, one of the prettiest areas of the Lake District, Broadoaks is a wonderful retreat from which to explore this beautiful part of England.

Views from the first floor are truly breathtaking, reaching over Lake Windermere and the Troutbeck Valley into the ten acres of private grounds that belong to the hotel.

Designed to be relaxing and luxurious, yet mindful of the graceful building's Victorian past, all bedrooms are furnished with four poster or antique brass bedsteads, and are fully equipped with the latest Jacuzzi, spa whirlpool and sunken bath. Rich oak panelling runs from the entrance hall into the cosy music room with Bechstein piano and open fire, where guests can enjoy pre-dinner drinks or after dinner coffee. Rich red damask compliments the Victorian dining-room and is a splendid setting for the award-winning restaurant, that has a wide reputation and a choice of a la carte and house menus.

All guests have use of a local private leisure club, and complimentary mountain bike hire or can relax in the grounds trying their hand at pitch and put. Golf, fishing and clay-pigeon shooting can also be arranged.

Places of interest nearby: Exploring the beauty of the Lake District, guests many enjoy total relaxation. **Directions: M6 junction 36, A590/591 to Windermere. Go over small roundabout towards Ambleside, then right into Bridge Lane. Broadoaks is ½ mile on right.**

Fayrer Garden House Hotel

LYTH VALLEY ROAD, BOWNESS-ON-WINDERMERE, CUMBRIA LA23 3JP
TEL: 015394 88195 FAX: 015394 45986 E-MAIL: lakescene@fayrergarden.com

OWNERS: Iain and Jackie Garside

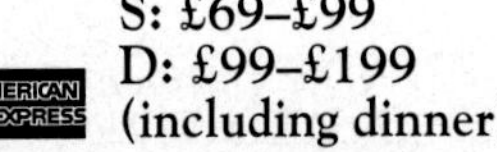

S: £69–£99
D: £99–£199
(including dinner)

Overlooking Lake Windermere in spacious gardens and grounds this lovely Victorian House is a very comfortable hotel where guests enjoy the spectacular views over the water, a real welcome and marvellous value for money.

The delightful lounges and bar and the superb air-conditioned restaurant all enjoy Lake views. There is an excellent table d'hôte menu in the award-winning restaurant changing daily using local produce where possible, fish, game and poultry and also a small à la carte choice. The wine list is excellent and very reasonably priced.

Many of the attractive bedrooms face the Lake, some having four- poster beds and whirlpool baths en suite. There are also ground floor rooms suitable for the elderly or infirm.

The nearby Parklands Leisure Complex has an indoor pool, sauna, steam room, badminton, snooker and squash complimentary to hotel residents. Special breaks available. **Places of interest nearby:** The Windermere Steamboat Museum, Boating from Bowness Pier and golf at Windermere Golf Club and The Beatrix Potter Attraction are all close by. **Directions: Junction 36 off the M6, A590 past Kendal. Take B5284 at the next roundabout, turn left at the end and the hotel is 350 yards on the right.**

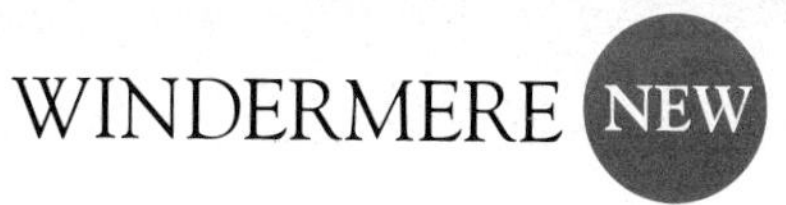

Lakeshore House

ECCLERIGG, WINDERMERE, CUMBRIA LA23 1LJ
TEL: 015394 33202 FAX: 015394 33213 E-MAIL: lakeshore@lakedistrict.uk.com

OWNERS: Keith and Penelope Robinson

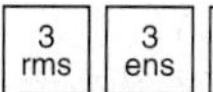

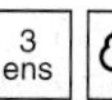

S: £85
D: £130–£170

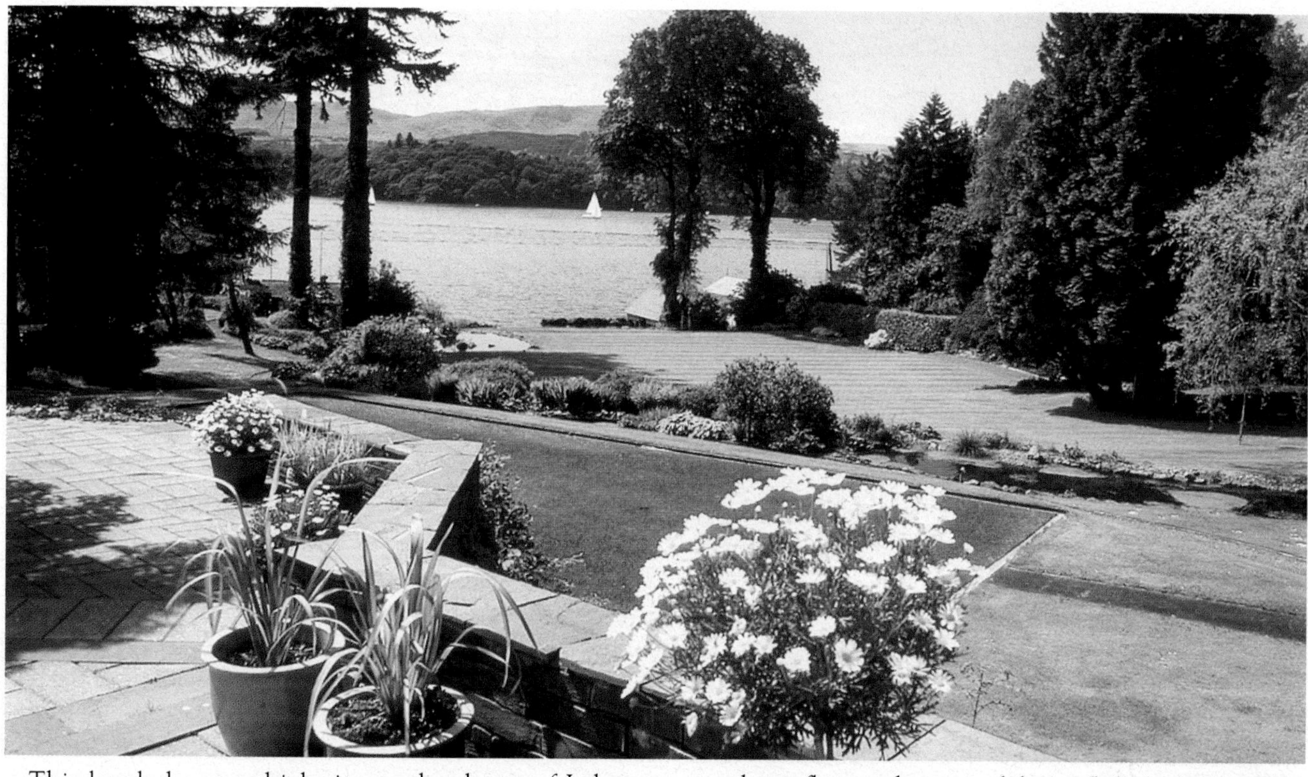

This lovely house, which sits on the shores of Lake Windermere, is a peaceful retreat from hectic modern life with some of the finest views imaginable. From its attractive modern exterior, manicured gardens, shaded by mature willows, firs and larches, lead down to the lake. The majestic background incorporates some of Lakelands finest fells, Coniston Old man, Wetherlam, Cringle Crags and the Langdales. Owners Keith and Penelope Robinson have spared no expense in making their home a place to enjoy.

The ground floor Beatrix Potter Suite offers total privacy and its sitting room with patio overlooks the lake towards Epely Head. Upstairs are two equally exquisitely furnished and decorated en suite bedrooms with balconies. Leather armchairs, flowers, decanter of sherry, fluffy bathrobes, TV, video and direct dial telephones perpetuate the feeling of care and luxury. All suites have seperate access.

Great emphasis is placed on the traditional Cumbrian or Continental breakfast which is enjoyed around a heated swimming pool in an "air-conditioned" conservatory. There is a sauna and facilities to practice tennis, badminton, croquet and putting. Although dinner is not available at Lakeshore House, some of the best restaurants in the area are close by. **Places of interest nearby:** Bowness, Ambleside, Beatrix Potter's "Hill Top" Farm. **Directions: Take A591 towards Windermere. Lakeshore House is approximately 1 mile north of Windermere.**

M 10 12 VCR

The Old Vicarage Country House Hotel

CHURCH ROAD, WITHERSLACK, NR GRANGE-OVER- SANDS, CUMBRIA LA11 6RS
TEL: 015395 52381 FAX: 015395 52373 E-MAIL: hotel@oldvicarage.com

OWNERS: Roger and Jill Brown, Stan and Irene Reeve
CHEF: James Brown MCGB

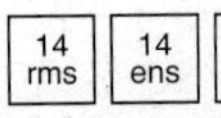  

S: £65–£95
D: £98–£175

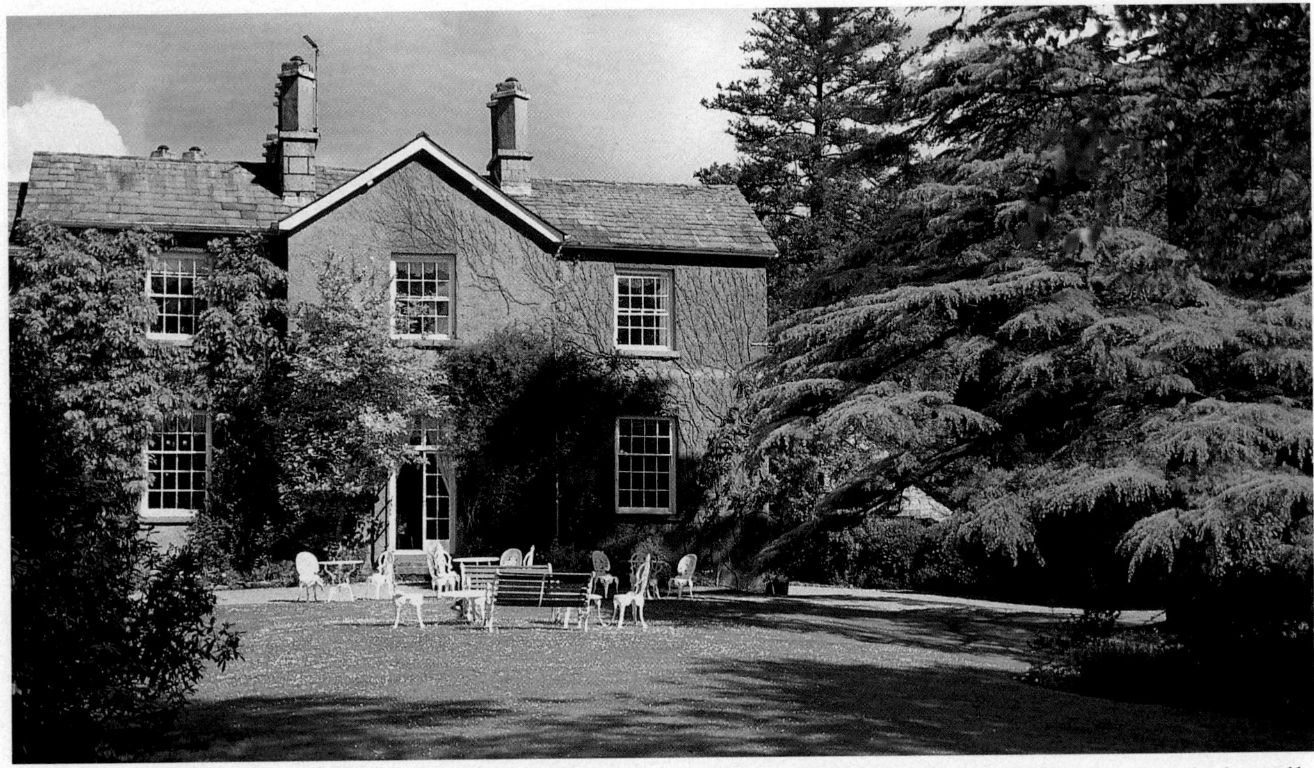

Near to the lakes...far from the crowds, this lovely old, family-run historic house offers the tranquil timeless atmosphere that reflects the calm and beauty of the surrounding Lake District National Park.

The delightful, mature garden is stocked with many interesting plants and part of it is left natural for wild flowers, unusual orchids, butterflies, dragonflies and birds. An all-weather tennis court in a delightful setting is for guests' use. Guests also have free use of the nearby Cascades Leisure Club.

In the old house, each of the comfortable bedrooms has its own particular character yet with all the modern facilities. The Orchard House, close by, is set beside an ancient damson orchard and has particularly well-equipped, spacious rooms each with its own woodland terrace. With top culinary awards, the well-planned menus include interesting, good quality locally-produced specialities. Diets can, of course, easily be catered for. **Places of interest nearby:** Windermere, Wordsworth Heritage and Sizergh Castle (a member of The National Trust) are all within easy reach. Nature enthusiasts will be delighted to visit the famous topiary gardens at Levens Hall. **Directions: From M6 junction 36, follow A590 to Barrow. After 6 miles turn right into Witherslack, then first left after the telephone box.**

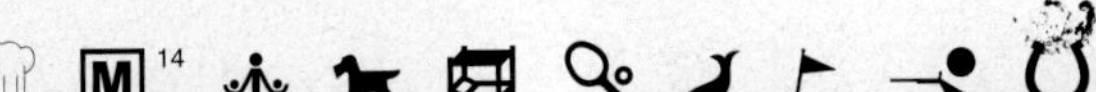

THE PARSONAGE COUNTRY HOUSE HOTEL

ESCRICK, YORK, NORTH YORKSHIRE YO19 6LF
TEL: 01904 728111 FAX: 01904 728151 E-MAIL: reservations@parsonagehotel.co.uk

OWNERS: Paul and Karan Ridley
MANAGER: Frank McCarten

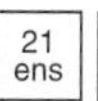

S: £75–£95
D: £110–£140

Surrounded by wide expanses of lawn, formal gardens and wild woodland, The Parsonage Country House Hotel provides an oasis of comfort and tranquillity.

In the nearby valleys are hidden ancient hamlets and villages still immersed in the old way of life. The Parsonage has been passed down through various noble families and baronies from Count Alan of Brittany in the early 11th century, to the de Lascelles, the Knyvetts, Thompsons, Lawleys and finally the Forbes Adams retaining all of its charm and many original features.

Each bedroom has been furnished with comfort and luxury in mind and features a full range of modern facilities. Two of the larger rooms contain magnificent four poster beds, ground floor rooms available. 4 individual air conditioned banqueting and conference rooms available to accommodate 150. Large car park. Large conservatory overlooking garden which serves light lunch or afternoon tea.

A highly appetising selection of dishes is created by the chef, who uses only the freshest, high quality local ingredients. A varied and carefully selected wine list is available to complement any meal.

Places of interest nearby: The Parsonage is a perfect base from which to visit York and Harrogate, the estates of Castle Howard, the three Cistercian Abbeys, the Yorkshire coastline or the Yorkshire Dales. **Directions: Escrick is on the A19 a few miles south of York.**

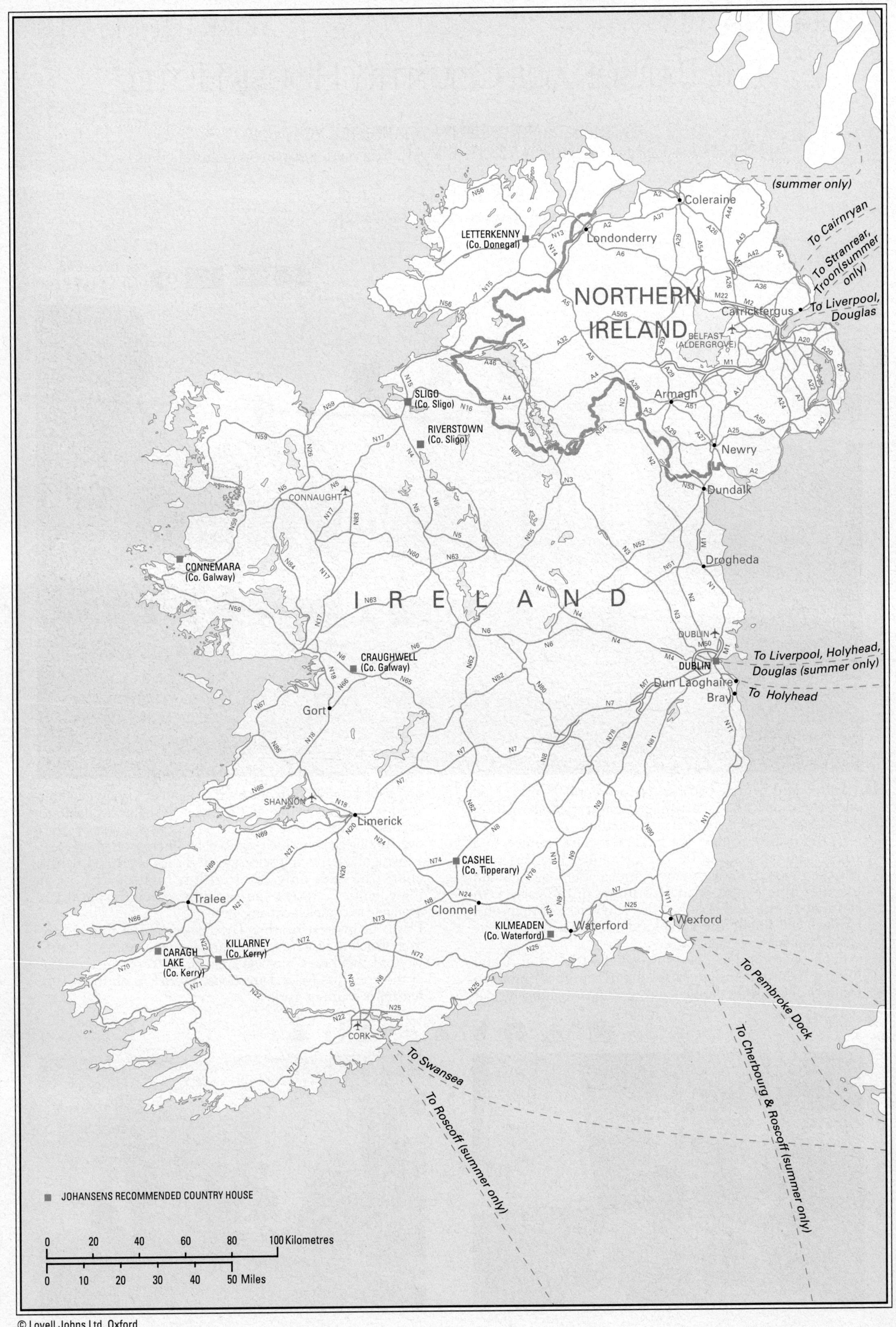
NORTHERN IRELAND
IRELAND
Coleraine
Londonderry
LETTERKENNY
(Co. Donegal)
Carrickfergus
BELFAST
(ALDERGROVE)
Armagh
Newry
Dundalk
SLIGO
(Co. Sligo)
RIVERSTOWN
(Co. Sligo)
CONNAUGHT
CONNEMARA
(Co. Galway)
Drogheda
DUBLIN
DUBLIN
Dun Laoghaire
Bray
CRAUGHWELL
(Co. Galway)
Gort
SHANNON
Limerick
CASHEL
(Co. Tipperary)
Tralee
Clonmel
KILMEADEN
(Co. Waterford)
Waterford
Wexford
CARAGH
LAKE
(Co. Kerry)
KILLARNEY
(Co. Kerry)
CORK
(summer only)
To Cairnryan
To Stranrear, Troon(summer only)
To Liverpool, Douglas
To Liverpool, Holyhead, Douglas (summer only)
To Holyhead
To Pembroke Dock
To Cherbourg & Roscoff (summer only)
To Swansea
To Roscoff (summer only)
JOHANSENS RECOMMENDED COUNTRY HOUSE
0 20 40 60 80 100 Kilometres
0 10 20 30 40 50 Miles

Ireland

A blend of verdant countryside, vast coastlines, rich cultural traditions, celtic legends and fine foods are all on offer in Ireland.

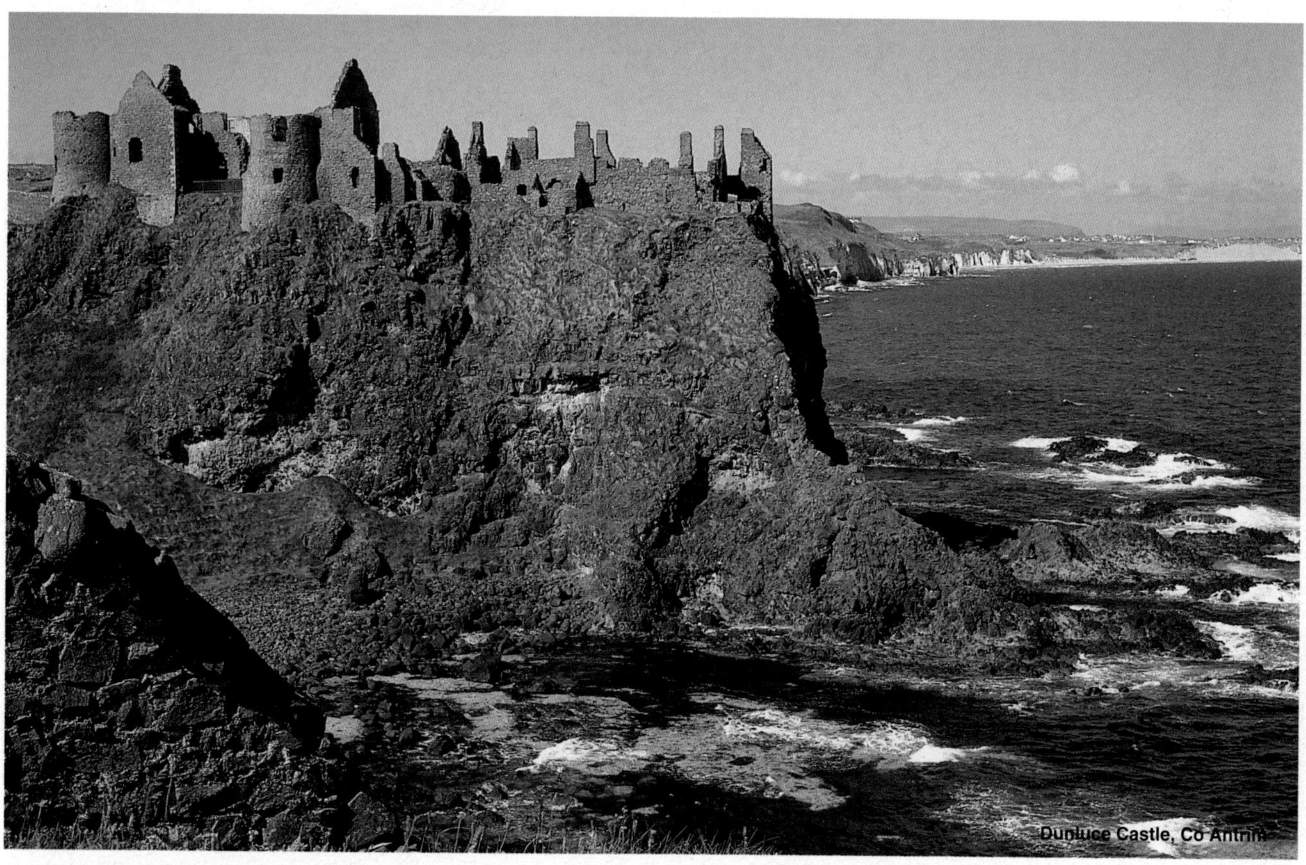
Dunluce Castle, Co Antrim

What's happening in Ireland?

• **International Jazz & Blues Festival** – this festival celebrates the important role that music plays in Irish culture. Visitors are able to get involved in workshops, performances and city wall parades. Held in Londonderry throughout May.

• **Castlewood Opera** – set in the beautiful Castlewood National Trust attraction, this event comprises 18 performances all held throughout June. For more information call 028 9066 1090.

• **Aspects Irish Literature Festival** – held towards the end of September at the Bangor Heritage Centre, this annual festival is an opportunity to soak up Ireland's literary culture. For more information call 028 9127 8032.

For more information about Ireland and Northern Ireland please contact:

The Irish Tourist Board
St Andrews Church
Suffolk Street
Dublin 2
Tel: 00 353 1 602 4000

Northern Ireland Tourist Board
St Anne's Court
59 North Street
Belfast BT1 1NB
Tel: 028 9024 6609

CARAGH LODGE

CARAGH LAKE, CO KERRY
TEL: 00 353 66 9769115 FAX: 00 353 66 9769316 E-MAIL: caraghl@iol.ie

OWNER: Mary Gaunt

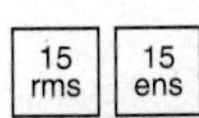

S: IR£85
D: IR£125–IR£160
Suite: IR£220

The breathtaking slopes of Ireland's highest mountain range, McGillycuddy Reeks, rise majestically above this elegant Victorian hotel whose award-winning gardens run gently down to the shore of Caragh Lake. Less than a mile from the spectacular Ring of Kerry, Caragh Lodge offers an unsurpassed blend of luxury, heritage, tranquillity, hospitality and service. It is excellent in every way and an ideal base for the sightseeing, golfing and fishing enthusiast.

All the en suite bedrooms are decorated with period furnishings and antiques, with the converted garden rooms looking over magnificent displays of magnolias, camellias, rhododendrons, azaleas and rare subtropical shrubs. The exquisite dining room overlooks the lake and Mary Gaunt personally prepares menus of the finest Irish food, including freshly caught salmon, succulent Kerry lamb, garden grown vegetables and home-baked breads. Open 13 Apr–14 Oct.

Caragh Lodge's gardens conceal an all-weather tennis court and sauna chalet. Salmon and trout swim in the lake and two boats are available for angling guests. Ghillies or permits for fishing in the two local rivers can be arranged. There are also local golf courses, where tee off times can be organised.

Places of interest nearby: The Ring of Kerry, Dingle Peninsula, Gap of Dunloe, Killarney and Tralee. **Directions: From Killorglin travel on N70 towards Glenbeigh and take second road signposted for Caragh Lake. At lake turn left, Caragh Lodge is on your right.**

CASHEL PALACE HOTEL

MAIN STREET, CASHEL, CO TIPPERARY
TEL: 00 353 62 62707 FAX: 00 353 62 61521 E-MAIL: reception@cashel–palace.ie

OWNERS: Silkestan Ltd
PROPRIETORS: Patrick and Susan Murphy

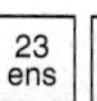  

S: IR£90–IR£155
D: IR£110–IR£155
Suite: IR£175–IR£225

This magnificent and luxurious 18th century hotel stands in the shadow of the famous Rock of Cashel. It is at the heart of a heritage town surrounded by a wealth of historical sites. Built in 1730 as a palace for Archbishop Theophilus Bolton it is a jewel of late Queen Anne and early Georgian style. Described as "A place of notable hospitality" in Loveday's Tour of 1732, the Cashel Palace Hotel's beauty is enhanced by 28 acres of walled gardens which includes a private walk to the Rock of Cashel and two Mulberry Trees planted in 1702 to commemorate the coronation of Queen Anne.

The hotel has been lovingly restored with great attention given to preserving its character and integrity. The spacious bedrooms of the main house echo the style and elegance of the 18th century and are individually furnished to the highest standards. The recent restoration of the Mews House, across the courtyard from the main house, has afforded the hotel ten beautifully appointed en suite bedrooms.

The tradition of fine food continues in the relaxed ambience of the Bishops Buttery which specialises in lighter modern Irish cuisine with classical influences.

Local leisure activities include pony trekking, horse riding, golf, tennis, trout and salmon fishing.

Places of interest nearby: Cashel is an ideal base from which to tour Munster and the South East and is within easy reach of Cahir Castle, the Devil's Bit Mountain and Holy Cross.

Directions: Cashel is on the junction of the N8 and N74.

Ross Lake House Hotel

ROSSCAHILL, OUGHTERARD, CO GALWAY, IRELAND
TEL: 00 353 91 550109 FAX: 00 353 91 550184 E-MAIL:rosslake@iol.ie

OWNERS: Henry and Elaine Reid

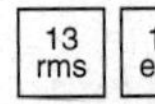

S: £65–£100
D: £100–£170
Suite: £180

Homeliness and relaxation are the hallmarks of this elegant 19th century hotel situated in the beautiful County Galway countryside unspoilt by the advance of time. It is an attractive old house whose former glory has been carefully and tastefully revived by owners Henry and Elaine Reid.

Surrounded by rambling woods and magnificent lawned gardens studded with colourful flowers and evergreen shrubs, Ross Lake was formerly an estate house of landed gentry who prized it for its serenity. The owners pride themselves that the hotel is a haven of peace where recreation comes naturally and service and hospitality are of the highest order.

Public rooms are spacious and combine the elegance of an earlier age with modern comforts. The drawing room, is particularly attractive. Comfort and good taste are also reflected in the hotel's 12 bedrooms which are all en suite and offer lovely views over the gardens.

Quality Irish food is excellently prepared and presented in the intimate restaurant with dishes enhanced by fresh produce from the Connemara hills, streams and lakes.

For the active there is tennis in the grounds, golfing at the Oughterard 18-hole parkland course, game and course fishing. **Places of interest nearby:** Aughnanure Castle, Kylemore Abbey, Connemara National Park, the Aran Islands, Cliffs of Moher and the Burren. **Directions: Ross Lake House is off N59, 14 miles north west of Galway.**

St Clerans

CRAUGHWELL, CO GALWAY, IRELAND
TEL: 00 353 91 846555 FAX: 00 353 91 846600 E-MAIL: stclerans@iol.ie

OWNERS: Merv Griffin Hotels
CHEF: Hisashi Kumagai

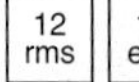 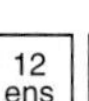 

  Rooms: IR£230–IR£380

Situated in the heart of beautiful County Galway, the magnificent Georgian manor house, St Clerans, is one of the most attractive houses in Ireland. At least that is what the former owner, Hollywood legend John Huston thought. St Clerans was built by the Burke family in 1784 and remained in their possession for nearly two centuries. Under its current owner, Merv Griffin, the house has been restored to its former glory and offers visitors the chance to enjoy the magic that so beguiled royalty and Hollywood celebrities in days gone by.

With its elegant period furniture, works of art collected from all over the world, blazing fires and peaceful gardens, St Clerans offers country house living at its very best. Twelve spacious guest rooms, beautifully and luxuriously appointed, look out over the glorious Galway countryside. One, a circular bedroom, was the former playroom of Angelica Huston.

The magnificent dining room serves food prepared from the fines and freshest local ingredients. Outdoor pursuits abound and guests may enjoy horse-riding, clay pigeon shooting, croquet, putting green and driving range all on site, fishing, horse-racing and hunting with the Galway Blazers.

Places of interest nearby: Connemara and the Cliffs of Moher can be explored. Golf enthusiasts may enjoy the courses at Galway Bay, Lahinch and Ballybunion. **Directions: On Galway-Dublin road N6, take 2nd left after passing through Craughwell. Follow road for 2 miles until you come to black gates of house on your right (30 mins from Galway City).**

Earls Court House

WOODLAWN JUNCTION, MUCKROSS ROAD, KILLARNEY, CO KERRY
TEL: 00 353 64 34009 FAX: 00 353 64 34366 E-MAIL: earls@eircon.net

OWNERS: Ray and Emer Moynihan

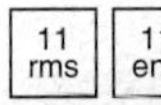

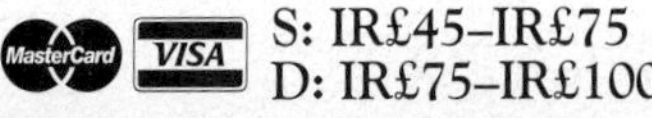

S: IR£45–IR£75
D: IR£75–IR£100

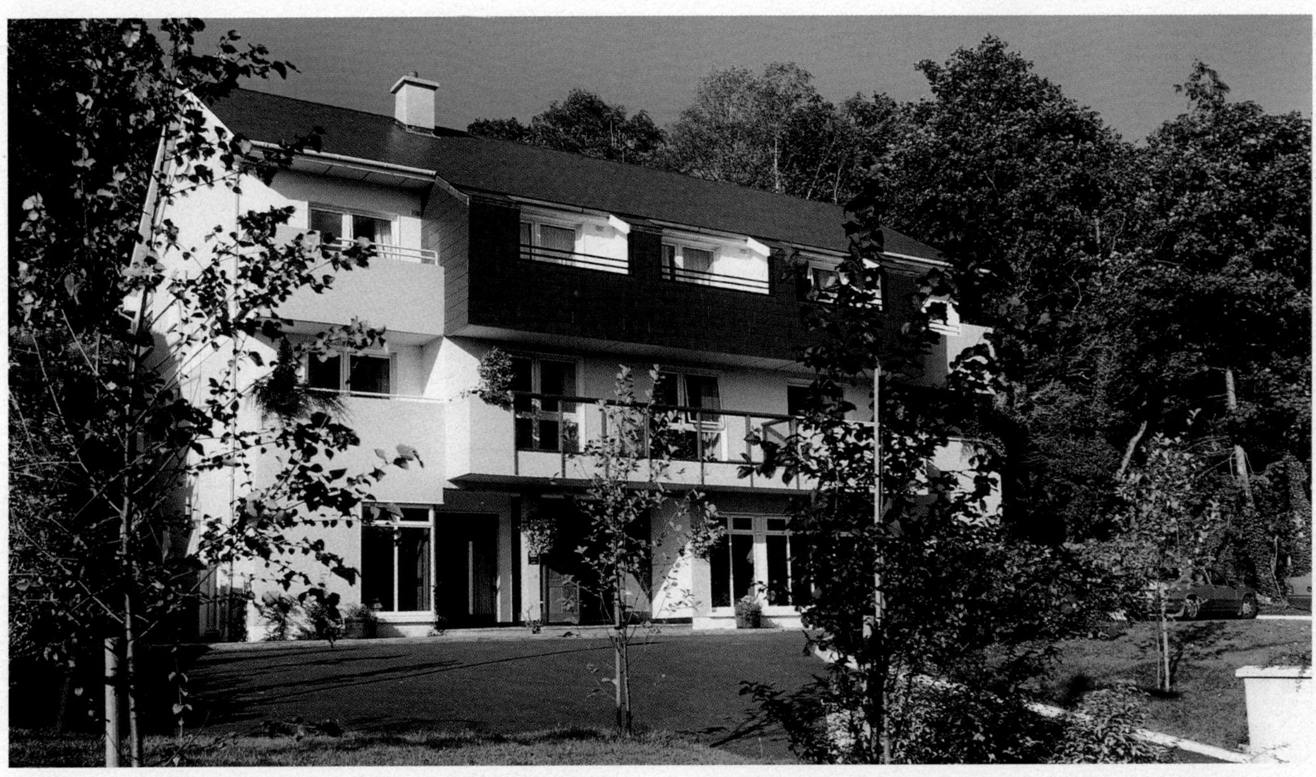

Earls Court House stands elevated and shadowed by tall, whispering trees just a five minutes walk from the bustling town centre of Killarney. It is in the heart of beautiful Co Kerry, surrounded by the 25,000 acres of Killarney National Park with its lakes, mountains and magnificent gardens where giant rhododendrons and tropical plants grow in abundance. Owners Ray and Emer Moynihan pride themselves that the hotel is a haven of tranquillity where relaxation comes naturally and service and hospitality is of the highest standards.

Earls Court is a purpose built, spacious hotel in the country house tradition. Fine antiques, prints and fabrics adorn the rooms throughout. Magnificent carved beds complement the charming, en suite bedrooms which are furnished with all modern amenities. Most of the bedrooms have private balconies with views over the open spaces of Muckross Park.

The hotel is an ideal base from which to tour Kerry, to explore Killarney National Park, or play south west Ireland's premier golf courses. Pony trekking, salmon and trout fishing can be arranged. Dinner is not available, but there are many good restaurants close by. The hotel is closed from November 5 to February 28.

Places of interest nearby: Killarney National Park. **Directions: Earls Court House is close to the centre of Killarney, just off the N71 Muckross Road.**

KILLARNEY ROYAL HOTEL

COLLEGE STREET, KILLARNEY, CO KERRY, IRELAND
TEL: 00 353 64 31853 FAX: 00 353 64 34001 E-MAIL: royalhot@iol.ie

OWNERS: Joe and Margaret Scally

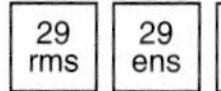

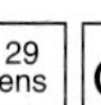

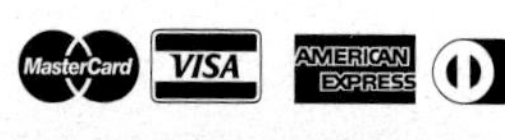

S: IR£90–IR£120
D: IR£140–IR£170
Suite: IR£190–IR£220

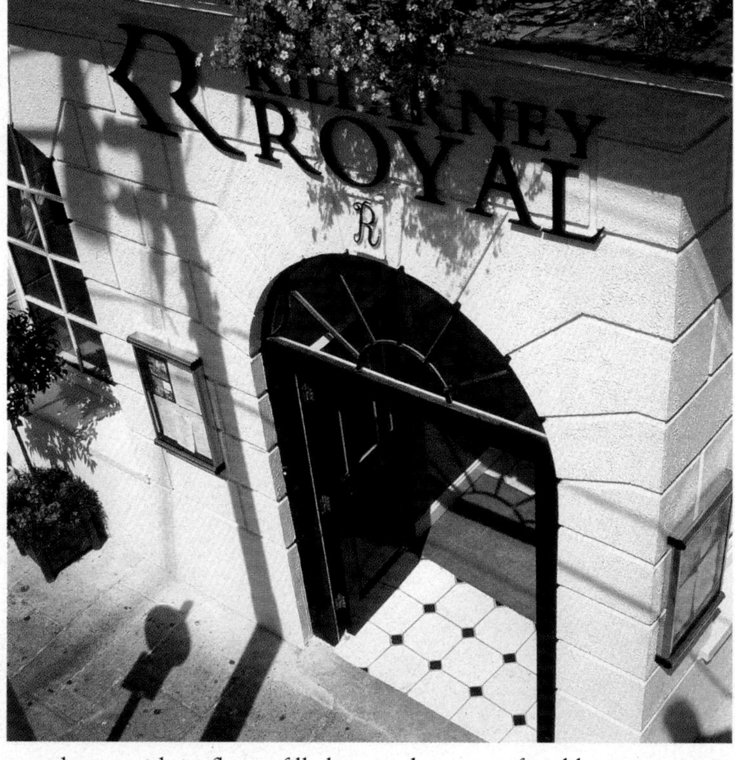

This attractive Victorian town house with its flower-filled window boxes stands in the centre of bustling Killarney and is ideal for touring South West Ireland. At the heart of beautiful County Kerry, it is surrounded by Killarney National Park with its lakes, mountains and gardens where giant rhododendrons and tropical plants grow in abundance.

Owners Joe and Margaret Scally pride themselves in their hospitality and meticulous high standards of service that ensure guests enjoy the hotel's charm and grace. Nothing is taken for granted once the visitor steps through the shining black entrance door into the black and white tailed lobby. Each individually designed bedroom has unique features, is delightfully decorated, furnished with elegant antiques and has a comfortable sitting area and lovely marble bathroom. All rooms are air-conditioned.

The attractive restaurant offers innovative cuisine, complemented by a selection of wines from a well-stocked cellar. There are numerous challenging golf courses in the vicinity as well as an almost endless variety of outdoor pursuits. The hotel can arrange fishing, shooting, riding and day trips to such attractions as the Ring of Kerry, Dingle peninsula and the Lakes of Killarney.

Places of interest nearby: Killarney National Park, Muckross House and gardens, Ross Castle, St Mary's Cathedral and Demesne. **Directions: In the centre of Killarney off the N22.**

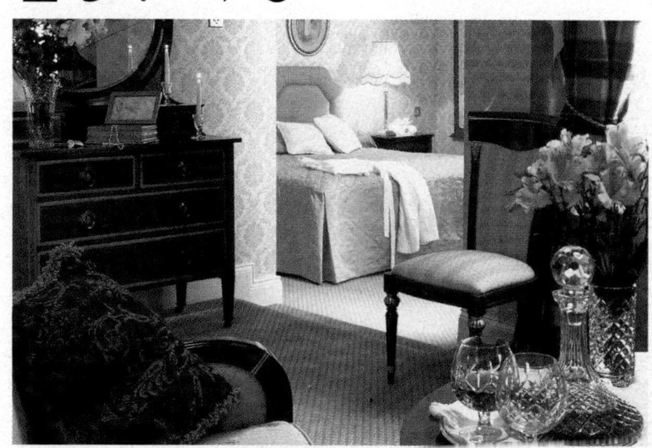

THE OLD RECTORY – KILMEADEN HOUSE

KILMEADEN, CO WATERFORD, IRELAND
TEL: 00 353 51 384254 FAX: 00 353 51 384884 E-MAIL: kilmeadenhouse@eircom.net

OWNERS: Jerry and Patricia Cronin

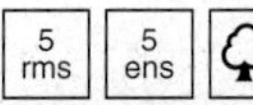

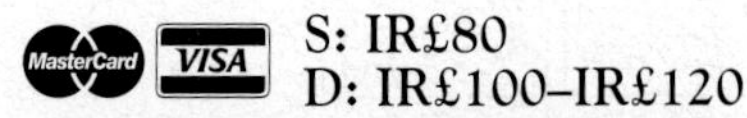

A truly warm and friendly Irish welcome awaits visitors as they arrive at the lovely Old Rectory situated in seclusion in County Waterford's beautiful landscape, capped from the west by the majestic Comeragh and Monavullagh ranges.

Constructed in the mid 19th century, this solidly built house stands serenely and imposingly in 12 acres of paddock, woodland and gardens just a short drive from Waterford City. The vision of the owners, Jerry Cronin, a local surgeon, and his wife Patricia, is to create simple elegance.

The charm of this country house is in its warm and comfortable atmosphere. Each of the tastefully decorated, non-smoking bedrooms is en suite and designed in complete harmony with the house. They are individually furnished with antiques, high ceilings, wooden sash windows and many personal touches to help guests feel at home. Views from their windows over the delightful garden which contains rare and well known plants are particularly delightful.

Light meals are available in the evening; guests must give 24 hours notice. Closed from 1st October to 30th April. **Places of interest nearby:** Dunmore East - a picturesque fishing village, the Comeragh and Monavullagh mountains and Waterford with its busy harbour. There are five major golf courses within easy reach whilst riding and fishing can be enjoyed locally. **Directions: Approximately 10 miles west of Waterford just off N25 road to Cork.**

Castle Grove Country House Hotel

RAMELTON ROAD, LETTERKENNY, CO DONEGAL
TEL: 00 353 74 51118 FAX: 00 353 74 51384

OWNER: Mary T and Raymond Sweeny

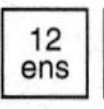

S: IR£45–£50
D: IR£60–IR£100
Suite: IR£130–IR£200

This elegant Georgian House, reached by a mile long avenue through parkland, is in a sheltered position with a spectacular view of Lough Swilly.

True Irish hospitality is offered at this family-owned country residence with its gracious reception rooms and the charming drawing room looking out on the extensive grounds. There is a separate television room.

The dining room is very popular with the people who live in the neighbourhood, so reservations are necessary. The succulent dishes offered on the extensive menu reflecting the marvellous local produce – especially the fish – are served in great style accompanied by wines from a list of the highest calibre. Small corporate lunches are a speciality.

The bedrooms are spacious, all recently refurbished and equipped with modern necessities.

Donegal is famous for its white sand beaches and clean seas. The scenery is superb along the coast roads and in the mountains. Glenveagh National Park is fascinating, with its castle and famous gardens. One can meet Derek Hill at his fine Art Gallery at Churchill. Activities nearby include golf and fishing (lake, river and deep sea). Riding can be arranged on request. **Directions: Castle Grove is three miles from Letterkenny, off the R245.**

Coopershill House

RIVERSTOWN, CO SLIGO
TEL: 00 353 71 65108 FAX: 00 353 71 65466 E-MAIL: ohara@coopershill.com

OWNERS: Brian and Lindy O'Hara

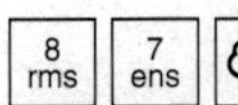   

S: IR£66–IR£73
D: IR£112–IR£126

Winner of Johansens 1995 Country House Award, Coopershill is a fine example of a Georgian family mansion. Home to seven generations of the O'Hara family since 1774, it combines the spaciousness and elegance of an earlier age with modern comforts. Public rooms are furnished in period style with gilt-framed portraits, hunting trophies and antiques. Six of the bedrooms have four-poster or canopy beds and all have private bathrooms.

Dinner is served by candlelight in the elegant dining room, where good cooking is complemented by a wide choice of wines. Open log fires and personal attention from owners Brian and Lindy O'Hara help to create the warm atmosphere and hospitality that typify Coopershill. Out of season the house is open to parties of 12 to 16 people at a special rate. Tariffs are reduced if guests stay for three consecutive nights or more.

The River Arrow winds through the 500-acre estate and boating, trout and coarse fishing are available. Shooting is not permitted, leaving the abundant wildlife undisturbed. There is an excellent hard tennis court and also a croquet lawn. There are marvellous mountain and lakeside walks to enjoy in the area. Closed 1st November to 1st April. **Places of interest nearby:** Sligo and Yeats country. **Directions: Leave N4 Sligo–Dublin road at Drumfin follow signs for Coopershill. One mile on, turn left.**

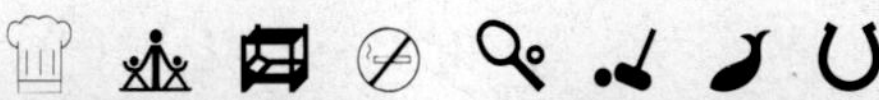

ORDER FORM

order 3 titles get £5 off • order 4 titles get £10 off • order 5 titles get £20 off

or you can order the Chairman's collection and save £35

Simply indicate the quantity of each title you wish to order, total up the cost and then make your appropriate discount. Complete your order below and choose your preferred method of payment. Then send it to Johansens, FREEPOST (CB 264), 43 Millharbour, London E14 9BR (no stamp required). FREE gifts will automatically be dispatched with your order. Fax orders welcome on 0207 537 3594.

ALTERNATIVELY YOU CAN ORDER IMMEDIATELY ON FREEPHONE 0800 269 397 and quote ref B13

Recommended Hotels - Great Britain & Ireland 2001
Publication date: October 2000
I wish to order QUANTITY copy/ies priced at £19.95 each. Total cost £

Recommended Country Houses - Great Britain & Ireland 2001
Publication date: October 2000
I wish to order QUANTITY copy/ies priced at £11.95 each. Total cost £

Recommended Traditional Inns, Hotels & Restaurants - Great Britain 2001
Publication date: October 2000
I wish to order QUANTITY copy/ies priced at £11.95 each. Total cost £

Historic Houses, Castles & Gardens 2001 (incorporating Museums & Galleries)
Publication date: December 2000
I wish to order QUANTITY copy/ies priced at £7.95 each. Total cost £

Recommended Hotels - Europe & The Mediterranean 2001
Publication date: October 2000
I wish to order QUANTITY copy/ies priced at £16.95 each. Total cost £

Recommended Hotels - North America, Bermuda & The Caribbean 2001
Publication date: October 2000
I wish to order QUANTITY copy/ies priced at £12.95 each. Total cost £

Recommended Hotels, Country Houses & Game Lodges – Southern Africa, Mauritius, The Seychelles 2001 Publ. date: October 2000
I wish to order QUANTITY copy/ies priced at £9.95 each. Total cost £

Recommended Hotels & Lodges Australia, New Zealand, The Pacific 2001
Publication date: October 2000
NEW
I wish to order QUANTITY copy/ies priced at £9.95 each. Total cost £

Recommended Business Meeting Venues 2001
Publication date: February 2001
I wish to order QUANTITY copy/ies priced at £25.00 each. Total cost £

Johansens Pocket Guide 2001
Publication date: January 2001
NEW
I wish to order QUANTITY copy/ies priced at £7.95 each. Total cost £

The Chairman's Collection

order the complete collection of Johansens Recommended Guides for only £99.55 a saving of £35

***PLUS FREE P&P** worth £4.50*

***PLUS FREE Luxury Luggage Tag** worth £15*

***PLUS FREE Privilege Card** worth £20*

The Chairman's Collection contains the following titles:

•Business Meetings Venues •Traditional Inns, Hotels & Restaurants - GB •Hotels - GB & Ireland •Country Houses - GB & Ireland •Historic Houses, Castles & Gardens •Hotels, Country Houses & Game Lodges - Southern Africa •Hotels - North America, Bermuda, The Caribbean •Hotels - Europe & The Mediterranean •Hotels & Lodges - Australia, New Zealand, The Pacific • Johansens Pocket Guide 2001

Now please complete your order and payment details

I have ordered 3 titles - £5 off		–£5.00
I have ordered 4 titles - £10 off		–£10.00
I have ordered 5 titles - £20 off		–£20.00
Total cost of books ordered minus discount (not including the Chairman's Collection)	£	
Privilege Card - FREE WITH ANY ORDER Additional cards can be ordered for £20		£
Luxury Luggage Tag - Johansens branded polished steel tag at £15. Quantity and total cost:		£
POSTAGE & PACKING (UK) for a single item add £2.50 / More than one item add £4.50 / (Outside) UK for a single item add £4.00 / More than one item add £6.00		£
I wish to order the Chairman's collection at £99.55 (no P&P required) **Enter quantity and total cost:**		£
Johansens Gold Blocked SLIP CASE at £5 for the Chairman's Collection. Quantity and total cost:		£
GRAND TOTAL	£	

I have chosen my Johansens Guides and (please tick)

I enclose a cheque payable to Johansens ☐

I enclose my order on company letterheading, please invoice (UK only) ☐

Please note that books will be sent upon payment being received

Please debit my credit/charge card account (please tick) ☐

☐ **MasterCard** ☐ **Amex** ☐ **Visa** ☐ **Switch** (Issue Number)

Card Holders Name (Mr/Mrs/Miss)

Address

Postcode

Telephone

Card No. Exp Date

Signature

NOW simply detach the order form and send it to Johansens, FREEPOST (CB264), 43 Millharbour, London E14 9BR (no stamp required)

FREE gifts will be dispatched with your order. Fax orders welcome on 0207 537 3594

NO STAMP REQUIRED

Johansens
FREEPOST (CB 264)
43 Millharbour
London
E14 9BR

MARKREE CASTLE

COLLOONEY, COUNTY SLIGO, IRELAND
TEL: 00 353 71 67800 FAX: 00 353 71 67840 E-MAIL: markree@iol.ie

OWNER: Charles Cooper

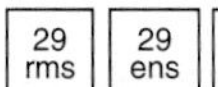 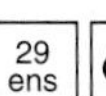   

 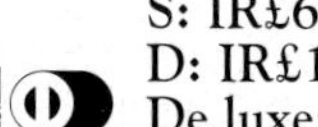

S: IR£67.50
D: IR£116
De luxe: IR£156

Regarded as one of Ireland's major architectural masterpieces, Markree Castle is Sligo's oldest inhabited castle. It has been the home of the Cooper family since 1640, but over the years the house has undergone a number of transformations. Today, the castle retains its family atmosphere and the character of the old building, while providing every modern comfort.

The interior boasts a spectacular oak staircase. This is overlooked by a stained glass window, purportedly tracing the Cooper family tree back to the time of King John of England. There are a variety of notable reception rooms, in addition to the interconnecting dining rooms which feature Louis-Philippe style plasterwork created by Italian craftsmen in 1845. An imaginative menu is provided

The bedrooms vary in character and style, but all offer views over the gardens or surrounding countryside.

Markree is in the heart of "Yeats Country", with magnificent scenery all around. The Rosses Point golf course and the Strandhill course are within a few miles. Trout and salmon fishing can be arranged nearby. **Places of interest nearby:** Carrowmore, which has Europe's largest and oldest collection of megalithic remains; Lissadell House; Yeats's grave at Drumcliffe; and the town of Donegal. **Directions: Nine miles from Sligo airport, 125 from Dublin via N4. Collooney is just south of Sligo town.**

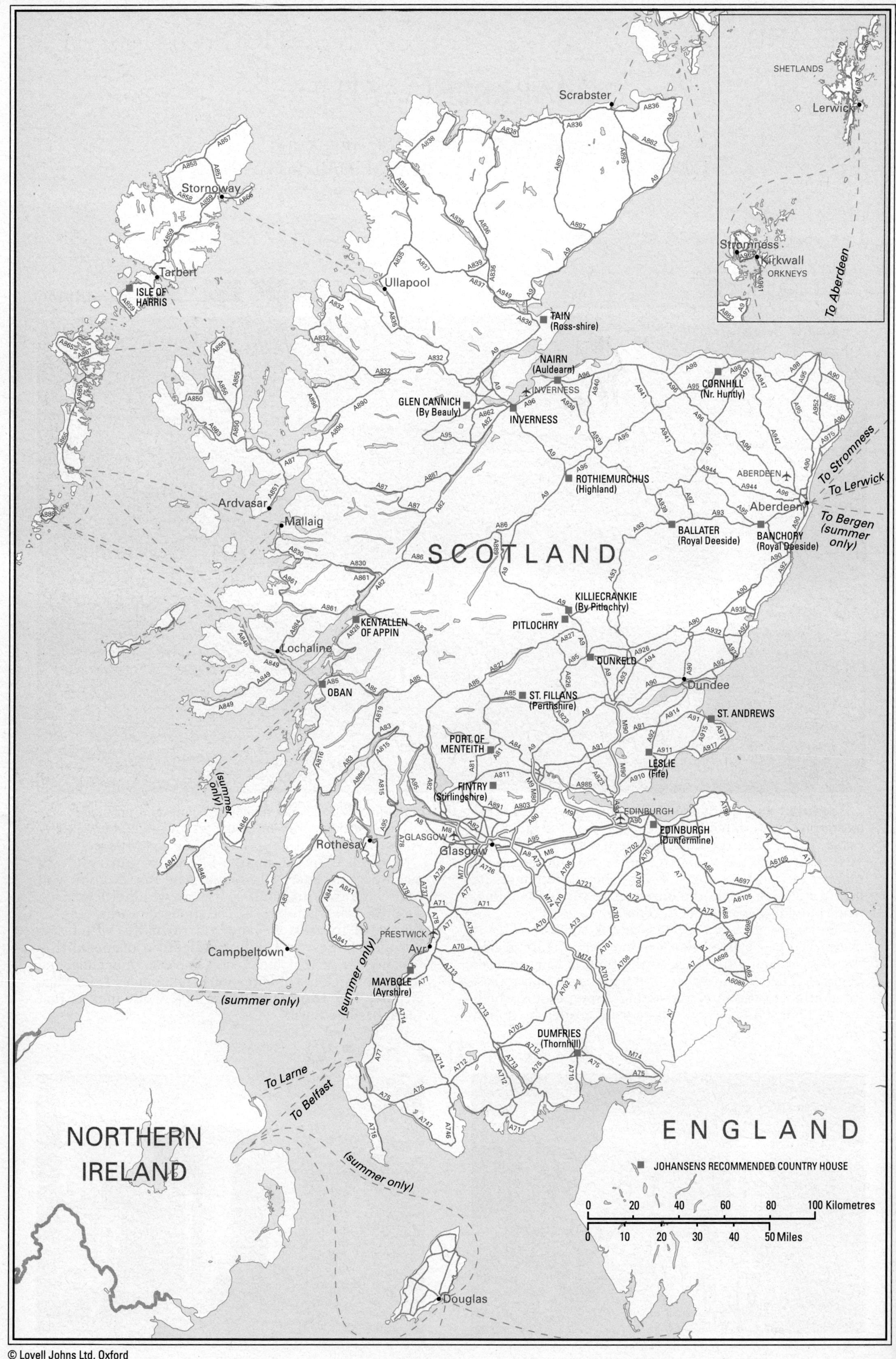
SHETLANDS
Lerwick
Stromness
Kirkwall
ORKNEYS
To Aberdeen
Scrabster
Stornoway
Tarbert
ISLE OF HARRIS
Ullapool
TAIN (Ross-shire)
NAIRN (Auldearn)
INVERNESS
CORNHILL (Nr. Huntly)
GLEN CANNICH (By Beauly)
INVERNESS
ABERDEEN
To Stromness
To Lerwick
ROTHIEMURCHUS (Highland)
Aberdeen
Ardvasar
Mallaig
BALLATER (Royal Deeside)
BANCHORY (Royal Deeside)
To Bergen (summer only)
SCOTLAND
KILLIECRANKIE (By Pitlochry)
PITLOCHRY
KENTALLEN OF APPIN
Lochaline
DUNKELD
OBAN
Dundee
ST. FILLANS (Perthshire)
ST. ANDREWS
PORT OF MENTEITH
LESLIE (Fife)
FINTRY (Stirlingshire)
(summer only)
EDINBURGH
EDINBURGH (Dunfermline)
GLASGOW
Glasgow
Rothesay
PRESTWICK
Ayr
Campbeltown
MAYBOLE (Ayrshire)
(summer only)
(summer only)
DUMFRIES (Thornhill)
To Larne
To Belfast
NORTHERN IRELAND
ENGLAND
(summer only)
JOHANSENS RECOMMENDED COUNTRY HOUSE
0 20 40 60 80 100 Kilometres
0 10 20 30 40 50 Miles
Douglas

Johansens Recommended Country Houses & Small Hotels

Scotland

With a fusion of Highland festivals, Celtic ancestry and breathtaking landscape, Scotland is the traveller's perfect host.

Eilean Donan Castle, Highland, Dornie

What's happening in Scotland?

• **Western Isles Challenge** – early in May, this spectacular three day multi sport team event includes hill running, mountain biking and sea canoeing.

•**Edinburgh Festival Fringe** – the most renowned and largest arts festival in the world offers visitors daily theatre, dance, music and comedy shows in over 200 venues. Held from 3rd to 25th August. For more information call 0131 226 5257.

•**Pitlochry Festival of Walking** – this event gives visitors the chance to experience the walks through the hills, forests, lochs and rivers of the Highland Perthshire. Held from 14th to 21st October. For more information call 01796 472 215.

For further information, please contact:

The Scottish Tourist Board
23 Ravelston Terrace
Edinburgh
EH4 3TP

Tel: 0131 332 2433

Balgonie Country House

BRAEMAR PLACE, BALLATER, ROYAL DEESIDE, ABERDEENSHIRE AB35 5NQ
TEL: 013397 55482 FAX: 013397 55482 E-MAIL: balgonie@lineone.net

OWNERS: John and Priscilla Finnie

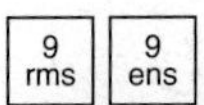   

 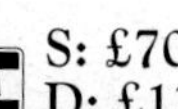

S: £70
D: £120

In the heart of one of Scotland's most unspoilt areas, on the outskirts of the village of Ballater, lies Balgonie House. Winner of the 1997 Johansens Country House Award for Excellence. This Edwardian-style building is set within four acres of mature gardens and commands wonderful views over the local golf course towards the hills of Glen Muick beyond. Balgonie's nine bedrooms are each named after a fishing pool on the River Dee. They are individually decorated and furnished and most offer lovely outlooks from their windows. Amenities include private bathrooms, colour television and direct-dial telephones. At the heart of the hotel is the dining room, offering superb Scottish menus: including fresh salmon from the Dee, succulent local game, high quality Aberdeen Angus beef and seafood from the coastal fishing ports and vintage wine chosen from an excellent list. Balgonie has won the coveted Taste of Scotland Prestige Award for its cuisine, also 2 AA Red Star and 2 Rosettes. **Places of interest nearby:** The village of Ballater, a five minute walk away, is a thriving community. As suppliers to the Queen, many of its shops sport Royal Warrant shields. This is an ideal centre for golf, hillwalking, sightseeing and touring. Balmoral Castle is within easy reach, as are both the Malt Whisky Trail and Castle Trail. **Directions: Upon entering Ballater from Braemar on the A93, Balgonie House is signposted on the right.**

Every Drop Helps

After much time spent planning and organising, The Hildon Foundation is ready to start changing young lives.

Devised as means of helping talented youngsters to further their ambitions, The Hildon Foundation is now starting to raise the money. For every bottle of Hildon *Sport* mineral water sold a 1p donation will be made to the Foundation. The target for the first year is £100,000 and all of the money raised will go directly to the Foundation as Hildon Ltd will meet all the administrative costs and make-up any shortfall in the funds.

Some of the anticipated recipients of grants from The Hildon Foundation will be budding sportsmen and women, others may be musicians, dancers or actors; wherever their talents lie.

continued overleaf...

Every Drop Helps

"Helping young people is the best possible foundation for the future."

David Gower OBE, patron.

I enclose a donation of ______________________
(Please enclose with postcard in an envelope)

Please send details with regard to making a committed gift ☐

Please send general information about The Hildon Foundation ☐

Name ______________________

Address ______________________

____

______________________ Postcode ______

Daytime Telephone Number ______________________

Every Drop Helps

"Helping young people is the best possible foundation for the future."

David Gower OBE, patron.

I enclose a donation of ______________________
(Please enclose with postcard in an envelope)

Please send details with regard to making a committed gift ☐

Please send general information about The Hildon Foundation ☐

Name ______________________

Address ______________________

____

______________________ Postcode ______

Daytime Telephone Number ______________________

Every Drop Helps

"Helping young people is the best possible foundation for the future."

David Gower OBE, patron.

I enclose a donation of ______________________
(Please enclose with postcard in an envelope)

Please send details with regard to making a committed gift ☐

Please send general information about The Hildon Foundation ☐

Name ______________________

Address ______________________

____

______________________ Postcode ______

Daytime Telephone Number ______________________

Please
Affix
Stamp
Here

THE HILDON FOUNDATION

PO BOX 1
BROUGHTON SO20 8WP

Please
Affix
Stamp
Here

THE HILDON FOUNDATION

PO BOX 1
BROUGHTON SO20 8WP

Please
Affix
Stamp
Here

THE HILDON FOUNDATION

PO BOX 1
BROUGHTON SO20 8WP

...continuation

It is also important that the Foundation has an appropriate and enthusiastic patron, so, The Hildon Foundation is particularly pleased that its first patron will be the much respected former England Cricket captain, David Gower OBE.

Since he retired from professional cricket, David Gower has developed his talents as an accomplished broadcaster on television and radio, and as a witty and interesting motivational after dinner speaker. Still a keen sportsman in his spare time – he is a talented tennis player, skier and bobsleigh enthusiast – David is the ideal figure to encourage youngsters in their chosen paths.

As well as actively supporting and promoting the Foundation, David will play a key role in deciding who the recipients should be, with the first awards being presented in summer 2001.

Tyddyn Iolyn Farm Guest House

PENTREFELIN, NR CRICCIETH, GWYNEDD, NORTH WALES LL52 0RB
TEL/FAX: 01766 522509 : TEL: 01766 522537 E-MAIL: tiol@nildram.co.uk

OWNER: Mrs Charlotte Lowe
CHEF: Ellen Dennis

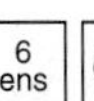

FARM HOUSE

S: £30–£50
D: £60–£100

This unique conversion of a working farm, complete with cats, ponies, ducks and hens, affords spectacular views over Harlech, the Rhinog Mountains and the breathtaking landscape of Snowdonia. Inglenook fireplaces, wooden beams and a countryman-style stove add character to this charming, peaceful atmosphere. Guests are accommodated in delightful bedrooms which are located in the 16th century barn and former outhouses. Each is Victorian in style featuring old-fashioned décor, beautiful fabrics and attractive baths.

After a hearty breakfast of fresh farm eggs and home-made muesli and jams, guests may explore the surrounding countryside and indulge in pursuits nearby such as clay pigeon shooting, fishing, riding or playing golf. The impressive backdrop is ideal for long rambles or hikes. An indoor swimming pool is planned for 2001. Hungry appetites may be quelled by a 3-course evening meal, which is prepared upon request. Owner Charlotte Lowe and her creative chef are justifiably proud of the cuisine which is based on local produce, organic ingredients and herbs from the garden. Special diets are catered for by arrangement. The property is totally non-smoking. WTB 3 star, AA 3 diamonds, Farm Tourism Award, member of the Taste of Wales and Calon Eryri Farm Group. **Places of interest nearby:** Portmeirion village, the Rhinog Mountains and Snowdonia are worth exploring. **Directions: The farmhouse is signed from A497 in Pentrefelin, midway between Porthmadog and Criccieth.**

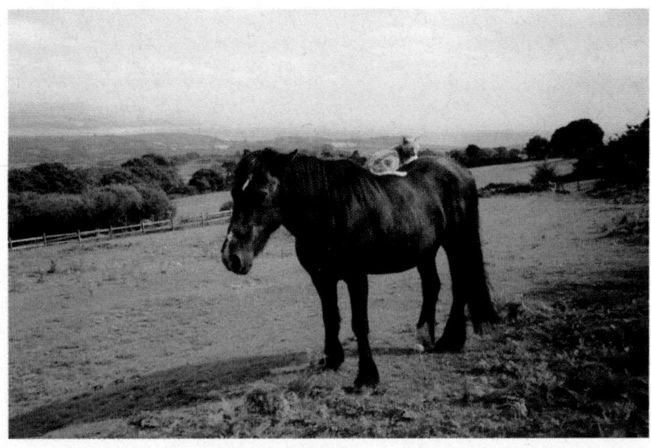

Abergwynant Hall

DOLGELLAU, SNOWDONIA, WALES LL40 1YF
TEL: 01341 422160 FAX: 01341 422046 E-MAIL: relax@abergwynant.co.uk

OWNERS: Sandra and Bob Armstrong

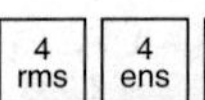

S: £75–£90
D: £100–£150

Located between the mountains and the sea, in the heart of the Snowdonia National Park, this haven of peace is ideal for those wishing to escape from the pressures of modern life and relax amidst glorious countryside. The 23 acres of landscaped grounds were designed in Victorian times and boast colourful rhododendrons, azaleas, ancient oak woodland and a monkey puzzle tree.

Four beautifully appointed, sumptuous bedrooms feature antique brass beds or four-poster beds. Those wishing to be pampered will be impressed by the truly decadent en suite bathrooms, some of which offer original roll top baths. The service afforded by owners Sandra and Bob Armstrong are excellent and the extra touches, such as afternoon tea with home-made treats on the terrace, add to the appeal.

Guests work up an appetite cycling or walking in the surrounding countryside before returning to the hotel and feasting on hearty British dishes, which might include traditional roast Welsh black beef with Yorkshire pudding rounded off by white chocolate cheesecake with a red berry fruit coulis. The intimate ambience of the hall makes it an ideal venue for house parties, reunions and special occasions.

Places of interest nearby: The summit of Cadair Idris, the Mawddach trail and the stunning walks above the Cambrian coast must be explored. **Directions: Abergwynant Hall is situated in the Snowdonia National Park, one mile past Penmaenpool on A493.**

Plas Dolmelynllyn

GANLLWYD, DOLGELLAU, GWYNEDD LL40 2HP
TEL: 01341 440273 FAX: 01341 440640 E-MAIL: info@dolly–hotel.co.uk

OWNERS: Jon Barkwith and Joanna Reddicliffe
CHEF: Joanna Reddicliffe

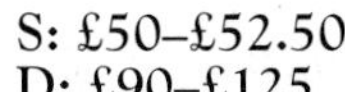

S: £50–£52.50
D: £90–£125

The approach to Plas Dolmelynllyn, which is entirely non-smoking, set in the amazing scenery of south Snowdonia, leads through a winding, beech-lined drive that brings guests to the doorway. A house has stood on the site since the 1500s, extended in the 18th and 19th centuries. Bedrooms are individually decorated and comfortably furnished. Joanna Reddicliffe, the daughter of the house, prepares an interesting and varied daily changing menu with several choices in each course including vegetarian dishes.

There is a conservatory bar and a large sitting room with full-length windows overlooking the valley. Dogs are allowed in two of the bedrooms only.

The hotel is surrounded by three acres of formal gardens, bounded by a swiftly running stream which flows into a small lake. Guests can take advantage of the hotel's fishing on 10 miles of river and three local lakes.

Places of interest nearby: Adjoining the grounds are 1,200 acres of mountains, meadow and forest, where it is possible to walk all day without seeing a car or crossing a road. Castles, slate caverns, waterfalls and a gold mine can all be visited nearby, but the theme here is relaxation amid wonderful surroundings, comfort, and only the gentlest of activities.

Directions: Plas Dolmelynllyn is off the main A470 Dolgellau– Llandudno road, just north of Dolgellau. Dinner, bed and breakfast, combined rates and short breaks are available.

THE CAWDOR ARMS HOTEL

RHOSMAEN STREET, LLANDEILO, CARMARTHENSHIRE SA19 6EN
TEL: 01558 823500 FAX: 01558 822399 E-MAIL: cawdor.arms@btinternet.com

OWNERS: John and Sylvia Silver
CHEF: Rod Peterson and Jane Silver

S: £45–£60
D: £60–£75

With tall pillars flanking an impressive entrance below a wrought-iron balcony and a road running just a few steps from the door this is not a typical country house hotel, but it has very much of a country house atmosphere, elegance and charm.

This historic coaching hotel of Georgian design is situated in the centre of a picturesque market town on the north bank of the River Tywi. The poet Edmund Spenser, in his Faerie Queene, cites Merlin's cave among the wooded hills around Llandeilo. The town is also famous for Dynevor Castle, seat of Lord Dynevor, whose family has held it since the 9th century.

The hotel's 16 en suite bedrooms have been tastefully and individually refurbished to a standard which will satisfy the most discerning visitor. Extensive lounge areas have Persian carpets, leather sofas, fine oil paintings and a wealth of antique furniture.

The award-winning, 18th century dining room is superb. Head Chef Rod Petersen, assisted by the daughter of the owners, prepares imaginative 2 Rosette cuisine using the freshest of local produce. Specialities include St David's Duck, Towy Salmon, Carmarthenshire Lamb and Welsh Black Beef. **Places of interest nearby:** The National Botanic Garden of Wales, Aberglasney Gardens, Carreg Cennen, Dryslwyn Castle, Goldengrove Country Park, Carmathen's Norman castle. **Directions: Exit the M4 at junction 49. Take the A48 to Cross Hands and then join the A476 to Llandeilo.**

The Crown At Whitebrook

WHITEBROOK, MONMOUTHSHIRE NP25 4TX
TEL: 01600 860254 FAX: 01600 860607 E-MAIL: crown@whitebrook.demon.co.uk

OWNERS: Angela and Elizabeth Barbara
CHEF: Mark Turton

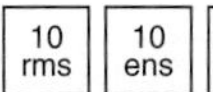
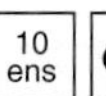

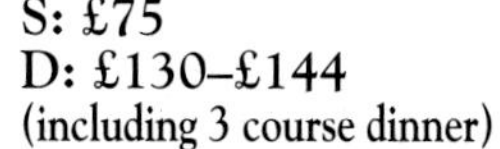

S: £75
D: £130–£144
(including 3 course dinner)

A romantic small hotel nestling deep in the Wye Valley, a designated area of outstanding natural beauty, The Crown is ideally situated for those seeking peace and tranquillity, with its two and three night breaks providing particularly good value for money.

Located up the wooded Whitebrook Valley on the fringe of Tintern Forest and only one mile from the River Wye, this is a place where guests can enjoy spectacular scenery. Angela and Elizabeth Barbara offer their guests a genuinely friendly welcome amid the tranquil comforts of the cosy lounge and bar.

Mark Turton cooking has earned the Restaurant 3 AA Rosettes and numerous prestigious awards for excellence. Dishes include local Welsh lamb and Wye salmon cooked in a modern Anglo-European style, followed by a choice of delicious home-made puddings and a selection of British farm cheeses. Most dietary requirements can be catered for as all food is freshly cooked to order. The wine list is carefully chosen and extensive.

Places of interest nearby: Tintern Abbey, racing at Chepstow, Chepstow Castle and the Brecon Beacons National Park are all within easy reach. **Directions: Whitebrook is situated between the A466 and the B4293 approximately five miles south of Monmouth.**

M[20]

NORTON HOUSE HOTEL AND RESTAURANT

NORTON ROAD, MUMBLES, SWANSEA SA3 5TQ
TEL: 01792 404891 FAX: 01792 403210 E-MAIL: nortonhouse@btconnect.com

OWNERS: Jan and John Power
CHEF: Mark Comisini

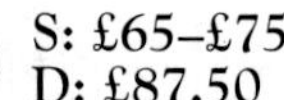

S: £65–£75
D: £87.50

A really warm Welsh welcome and home-from-home hospitality are generously offered by this elegant hotel's resident proprietors Jan and John Power. Nothing is too much trouble and they are justly proud of the attentive and friendly atmosphere that pervades the whole hotel.

Norton House is attractively Georgian in style. It stands in lovely gardens set back from the Mumbles seafront and although not exactly rural it is run as a country house. Décor, furnishings and fabrics throughout are a tasteful delight.

The bedrooms all have up-to-date private amenities with four of the more spacious rooms offering four-poster beds. The majority of rooms are in a newer wing and are slightly smaller. Ground floor rooms have easy access from a private terrace.

The charming restaurant overlooks the terrace and gardens and chef Mark Comisini has earned a high reputation for tasty and imaginative cuisine with the emphasis on local produce and traditional flavours. Dinner menus are written in Welsh with English translations and include tempting dishes such as Penclawdd cockles and local laverbread and rack of Welsh lamb with black peppercorns and minted sauce.

Places of interest nearby: Sandy beaches of the Gower Peninsula, Swansea's maritime quarter and market.

Directions: Exit M4 at Jct42. Take A483 to Swansea, then A4067 alongside Swansea Bay. 1 mile beyond the Mumbles sign, the hotel is signposted on the right.

Waterwynch House Hotel

WATERWYNCH BAY, TENBY, PEMBROKESHIRE SA70 8JT
TEL: 01834 842464 FAX: 01834 845076 E-MAIL: enquiries@waterwynchhousehotel.co.uk

OWNERS: Bette and Geoff Hampton

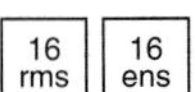
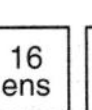

S: £40–£55
D: £52–£88
Suite: £76–£116

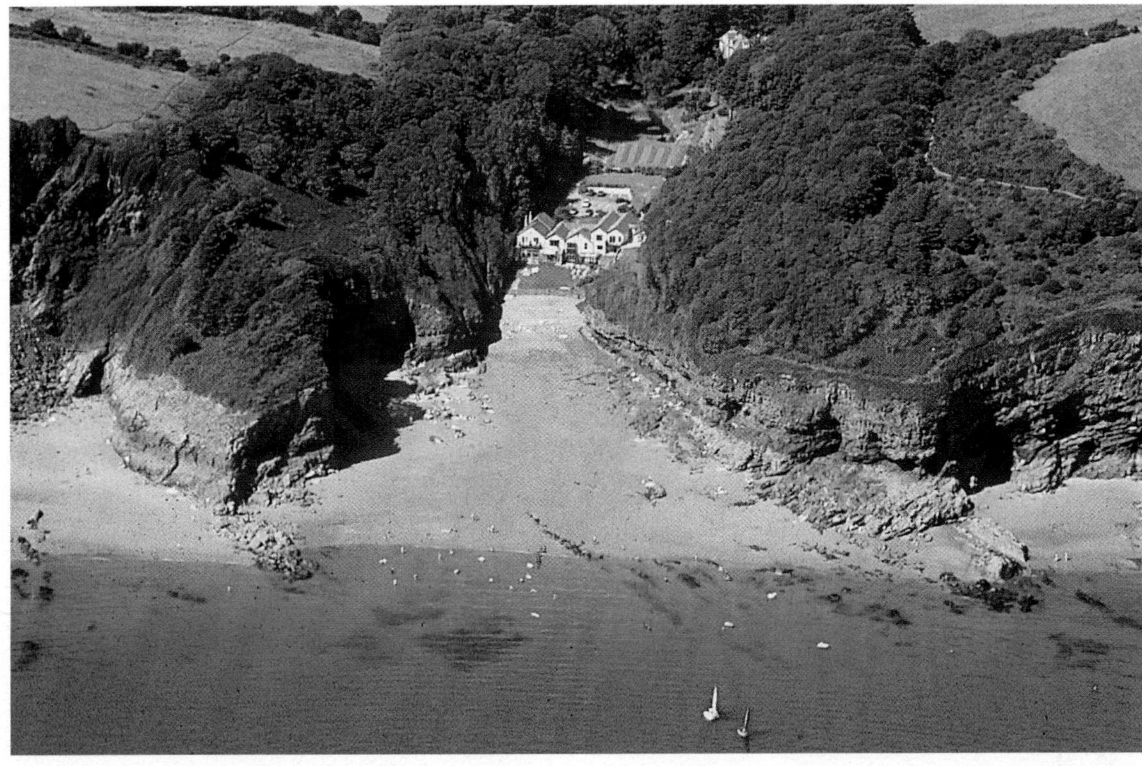

Waterwynch House is a uniquely secluded retreat nestling in a pretty little cove on the beautiful shores of Carmathen Bay. Surrounded by the Pembrokeshire Coastal National Park and 27 acres of its own woodland and gardens, it is a quiet, intimate hotel with an enviable reputation for friendly hospitality and personal service.

Dating from 1820 when it was built as a family home for Tenby based artist Charles Norris, the hotel retains its peaceful charm of the past. It is an ideal base from which to enjoy coastal walks, the wildlife and superb scenery, or just to relax on the private beach.

The 16 tastefully furnished and decorated bedrooms, all of which are non smoking, offer every modern comfort. Some have balconies and sea views, others overlook the gardens. The superior lounge suites feature Jacuzzi baths in their newly refurbished bathrooms.

A nightly table d'hôte menu caters for the most discerning connoisseur in the dining room with its panoramic view over the bay. As well as some unusual speciality dishes there are a good selection of fish courses. The hotel is closed from November to February.

Places of interest nearby: Superb walking along the adjacent Pembrokeshire coastal path, bird-watching, painting, fishing, golf and croquet, bowls and putting. **Directions: Off the A478 Kilgetty to Tenby road. Signposted on the left half a mile after the New Hedges roundabout.**

Parva Farmhouse and Restaurant

TINTERN, CHEPSTOW, MONMOUTHSHIRE NP16 6SQ
TEL: 01291 689411 FAX: 01291 689557

OWNERS: Dereck and Vickie Stubbs
CHEF: Dereck Stubbs

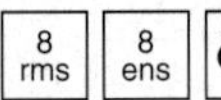   

S: £50
D: £68–£78

Surrounded by the glorious, wooded hillsides of the beautiful lower Wye Valley and just a mile from 12th century Tintern Abbey, one of the finest relics of Britain's monastic age, Parva Farmhouse is a homely haven where visitors can relax and forget the pressures of their daily world. This is an ideal spot for country lovers. The salmon and trout teeming River Wye flows just 50 yards from the hotel's small, flower-filled garden, there is an abundance of wildlife and hundreds of tempting walks.

Built during the 17th century, Parva today provides every comfort. The bedrooms are well-furnished and most have pretty views across the River Wye. The beamed lounge with its log-burning fireplace, "Honesty Bar" and deep Chesterfield sofas and chairs is the perfect place to relax and chat over the day's happenings.

The crowning glory of Parva is the excellent food, home-cooked by chef-patron Dereck Stubbs and served in the AA Rosette Inglenook Restaurant before a 14-foot beamed fireplace. Golf, shooting and riding are close by and there is horse-racing at Chepstow. Two night breaks inclusive of dinner are especially popular and good value for money.

Places of interest nearby: Tintern Abbey, castles at Abergavenny and Chepstow, Offa's Dyke, the Royal Forest of Dean, many old ruins and ancient monuments. **Directions: Leave M48 at Jct2 and join A466 towards Monmouth. The hotel is on the north edge of Tintern Village.**

MOËT
BRUT IMPÉRIAL
MOËT & CHANDON
CHAMPAGNE
the preferred
champagne
of johansens

Johansens Recommended Traditional Inns, Hotels & Restaurants in Great Britain

ENGLAND

Ashbourne – Red Lion Inn, Main Street, Hognaston, Ashbourne, Derbyshire DE6 1PR. Tel: 01335 370396

Ashbourne/Uttoxeter – Beeches Restaurant, Waldley, Doveridge, Nr Ashbourne, Derbyshire DE6 5LR. Tel: 01889 590288

Bakewell – The Peacock Hotel at Rowsley, Rowsley, Near Matlock, Derbyshire DE4 2EB. Tel: 01629 733518

Belford – The Blue Bell Hotel, Market Place, Belford, Northumberland NE70 7NE. Tel: 01668 213543

Brancaster Staithe – The White Horse, Brancaster Staithe, Norfolk PE31 8BW. Tel: 01485 210262

Bridport – The Manor Hotel, West Bexington, Dorchester, Dorset DT2 9DF. Tel: 01308 897616

Brighton – The Old Tollgate Restaurant And Hotel, The Street, Bramber, Steyning, West Sussex BN44 3WE. Tel: 01903 879494

Burford – The Lamb Inn, Sheep Street, Burford, Oxfordshire OX18 4LR. Tel: 01993 823155

Burnsall – The Red Lion, By the bridge at Burnsall, Near Skipton, North Yorkshire BD23 6BU. Tel: 01756 720204

Burton Upon Trent – Boar's Head Hotel, Lichfield Road, Sudbury, Derbyshire DE6 5GX. Tel: 01283 820344

Burton-on-Trent – Ye Olde Dog & Partridge, High Street, Tutbury, Burton upon Trent, Staffordshire DE13 9LS. Tel: 01283 813030

Calver – The Chequers Inn, Froggatt Edge, Nr Calver, Derbyshire S30 1ZB. Tel: 01433 630231

Camborne – Tyacks Hotel, 27 Commercial Street, Camborne, Cornwall TR14 8LD. Tel: 01209 612424

Cambridge – The White Horse Inn, Hollow Hill, Withersfield, Haverhill, Suffolk CB9 7SH. Tel: 01440 706081

Carlisle – The Tarn End House Hotel, Talkin Tarn, Brampton, Cumbria CA8 1LS. Tel: 016977 2340

Chesterfield / Sheffield – Manor House Hotel & Restaurant, High Street, Old Dronfield, Derbyshire S18 1PY. Tel: 01246 413971

Christchurch – The Lord Bute, 181 / 185 Lymington Road, Highcliffe on Sea, Christchurch , Dorset BH23 4JS. Tel: 01425 278884

Cirencester – The New Inn at Coln, Coln St-Aldwyns, Nr Cirencester, Gloucestershire GL7 5AN. Tel: 01285 750651

Clare – The Plough Inn, Brockley Green, Sudbury, Nr Hundon, Suffolk CO10 8DT. Tel: 01440 786789

Clavering – The Cricketers, Clavering, Nr Saffron Walden, Essex CB11 4QT. Tel: 01799 550442

Coleford – The New Inn, Coleford, Crediton, Devon EX17 5BZ. Tel: 01363 84242

Compton Bassett – White Horse Inn, Compton Bassett, Calne, Wiltshire SN11 8RG. Tel: 01249 813118

Coningsby – The Lea Gate Inn, Leagate Road, Coningsby, Lincolnshire LN4 4RS. Tel: 01526 342370

Cranbrook – The George Hotel , Stone Street, Cranbrook, Kent TN17 3HE. Tel: 01580 713348

Ditcheat – The Manor House Inn, Ditcheat, Somerset BA4 6RB. Tel: 01749 860276

Dorchester-On-Thames – The George Hotel, High Street, Dorchester-On-Thames, Oxford OX10 7HH. Tel: 01865 340404

East Witton – The Blue Lion, East Witton, Nr Leyburn, North Yorkshire DL8 4SN. Tel: 01969 624273

Egton – The Wheatsheaf Inn, , Egton, Nr Whitby, North Yorkshire YO21 1TZ. Tel: 01947 895271

Eton – The Christopher Hotel, High Street, Eton, Windsor, Berkshire SL4 6AN. Tel: 01753 811677 / 852359

Evershot – Acorn Inn, Fore Street, Evershot, Nr Dorchester, Dorset DT2 0JW. Tel: 01935 83228

Evesham – Riverside Restaurant And Hotel, The Parks, Offenham Road, Nr Evesham, Worcestershire WR11 5JP. Tel: 01386 446200

Exmoor – The Royal Oak Inn, Winsford, Exmoor National Park, Somerset EX24 7JE. Tel: 01643 851455

Falmouth – Trengilly Wartha Country Inn & Restaurant, Nancenoy, Constantine, Falmouth, Cornwall TR11 5RP. Tel: 01326 340332

Fordingbridge – The Three Lions Restaurant, Stuckton, Fordingbridge, Hampshire SP6 2HF. Tel: 01425 652489

Goring-On-Thames – The Leatherne Bottel Riverside Inn & Restaurant, The Bridleway, Goring-On-Thames, Berkshire RG8 0HS. Tel: 01491 872667

Grimsthorpe – The Black Horse Inn, Grimsthorpe, Bourne, Lincolnshire PE10 0LY. Tel: 01778 591247

Grindleford – The Maynard Arms, Main Road, Grindleford, Derbyshire S32 2HE. Tel: 01433 630321

Halifax/Huddersfield – The Rock Inn Hotel, Holywell Green, Halifax, West Yorkshire HX4 9BS. Tel: 01422 379721

Handcross – The Chequers At Slaugham, , Slaugham, Nr Handcross, West Sussex RH17 6AQ. Tel: 01444 400239/400996

Harrogate – The George, Wormald Green, Nr Harrogate, North Yorkshire HG3 3PR. Tel: 01765 677214

Harrogate – The Boar's Head Hotel, Ripley, Harrogate, North Yorkshire HG3 3AY. Tel: 01423 771888

Hathersage – The Plough Inn, Leadmill Bridge, Hathersage, Derbyshire S30 1BA. Tel: 01433 650319

Hayfield – The Waltzing Weasel, New Mills Road, Birch Vale, High Peak, Derbyshire SK22 1BT. Tel: 01663 743402

Helmsley – The Feathers Hotel, Market Place, Helmsley, North Yorkshire YO6 5BH. Tel: 01439 770275

Helmsley – The Feversham Arms Hotel, , Helmsley , North Yorkshire YO6 5AG. Tel: 01439 770766

Hindon – The Grosvenor Arms, Hindon, Salisbury, Wiltshire SP3 6DJ. Tel: 01747 820696

Holt – The Roman Camp Inn, Holt Road, Aylmerton, Norwich, Norfolk NR11 8QD. Tel: 01263 838291

Honiton – Home Farm Hotel, , Wilmington, Nr Honiton, Devon EX14 9JR. Tel: 01404 831278

Huddersfield – The Weavers Shed Restaurant with Rooms, Knowl Road, Golcar, Huddersfield, West Yorkshire HD7 4AN. Tel: 01484 654284

Kenilworth – Clarendon House Bar Brasserie Hotel, Old High Street, Kenilworth, Warwickshire CV8 1LZ. Tel: 01926 857668

Knutsford – Longview Hotel And Restaurant, 51/55 Manchester Road, Knutsford, Cheshire WA16 0LX. Tel: 01565 632119

Leek – The Three Horseshoes Inn & Kirk's Restaurant, Buxton Road, Blackshaw Moor, Nr Leek, Staffordshire ST13 8TW. Tel: 01538 300296

Longleat – The Bath Arms, Horningsham, Warminster, Wiltshire BA12 7LY. Tel: 01985 844308

Lymington – Gordleton Mill Inn, Silver Street, Hordle, Nr Lymington, Hampshire SO41 6DJ. Tel: 01590 682219

Lynmouth – The Rising Sun, Harbourside, Lynmouth, Devon EX35 6EQ. Tel: 01598 753223

Maidstone – Ringlestone Inn and Farmhouse Hotel, 'Twixt Harrietsham and Wormshill, Nr Maidstone, Kent ME17 1NX. Tel: 01622 859900

Malmesbury – The Horse And Groom Inn, Charlton, Near Malmesbury, Wiltshire SN16 9DL. Tel: 01666 823904

Mells – The Talbot Inn at Mells, , Mells, Nr Bath, Somerset BA11 3PN. Tel: 01373 812254

Mildenhall – The Bell Hotel, High Street, Mildenhall, Suffolk IP28 7EA. Tel: 01638 717272

Newby Bridge – The Swan Hotel, Newby Bridge, Nr Ulverston, Cumbria LA12 8NB. Tel: 015395 31681

Nottingham – Hotel Des Clos, Old Lenton Lane, Nottingham, Nottinghamshire NG7 2SA. Tel: 01159 866566

Oxford – Holcombe Hotel, High Street, Deddington, Nr Woodstock, Oxfordshire OX15 0SL. Tel: 01869 338274

Oxford – The Jersey Arms, , Middleton Stoney, Oxfordshire OX6 8SE. Tel: 01869 343234

Padstow – The Old Custom House Hotel, South Quay, Padstow, Cornwall PL28 8BL. Tel: 01841 532359

Pangbourne – The George Hotel, The Square, Pangbourne, Nr Reading, Berkshire RG8 7AJ. Tel: 01189 842237

Pelynt – Jubilee Inn, Pelynt, Nr Looe, Cornwall PL13 2JZ. Tel: 01503 220312

Penzance – The Summer House, Cornwall Terrace, Penzance, Cornwall TR18 4HL. Tel: 01736 363744

Pickering – The White Swan, The Market Place, Pickering, North Yorkshire YO18 7AA. Tel: 01751 472288

Port Gaverne – The Port Gaverne Inn, , Nr. Port Isaac, North Cornwall PL29 3SQ. Tel: 01208 880244

Preston – Ye Horn's Inn, Horn's Lane, Goosnargh, Nr Preston, Lancashire PR3 2FJ. Tel: 01772 865230

Rugby – The Golden Lion Inn of Easenhall, Easenhall, Nr Rugby, Warwickshire CV23 0JA. Tel: 01788 832265

Saddleworth – The Old Bell Inn Hotel, Huddersfield Road, Delph, Saddleworth, Nr Oldham, Greater Manchester OL3 5EG. Tel: 01457 870130

Shipton Under Wychwood – The Shaven Crown Hotel, High Street, Shipton Under Wychwood, Oxfordshire OX7 6BA. Tel: 01993 830330

Snettisham – The Rose & Crown, Old Church Road, Snettisham, Norfolk PE31 7LX. Tel: 01485 541382

Stamford – The Crown Hotel, All Saints Place, Stamford, Lincolnshire PE9 2AG. Tel: 01780 763136

Stamford – Black Bull Inn, Lobthorpe, Nr Grantham, Lincolnshire NG33 5LL. Tel: 01476 860086

Stanton Wick – The Carpenters Arms, Stanton Wick, Nr Pensford, Somerset BS39 4BX. Tel: 01761 490202

Stow-On-The-Wold – The Kings Head Inn & Restaurant, The Green, Bledington, Oxfordshire OX7 6XQ. Tel: 01608 658365

Telford – The Hundred House Hotel, Bridgnorth Road,Norton, Nr Shifnal, Telford, Shropshire TF11 9EE. Tel: 01952 730353

Thaxted – Recorders House Restaurant (With Rooms), 17 Town Street, Thaxted, Essex CM6 2LD. Tel: 01371 830438

Thirsk – Crab & Lobster, Asenby, North Yorkshire YO7 3QL. Tel: 01845 577286

Thornham – The Lifeboat Inn, Ship Lane, Thornham, Norfolk PE36 6LT. Tel: 01485 512236

Thorpe Market – Green Farm Restaurant And Hotel, North Walsham Road, Thorpe Market, Norfolk NR11 8TH. Tel: 01263 833602

Tintagel – The Port William, Trebarwith Strand, Nr Tintagel, Cornwall PL34 0HB. Tel: 01840 770230

Totnes – The Sea Trout Inn, , Staverton, Nr Totnes, Devon TQ9 6PA. Tel: 01803 762274

Upton-Upon-Severn,Nr Malvern – The White Lion Hotel, High Street, Upton-Upon-Severn, Nr Malvern, Worcestershire WR8 0HJ. Tel: 01684 592551

West Auckland – The Manor House Hotel & Country Club, The Green, West Auckland, County Durham DL14 9HW. Tel: 01388 834834

Whitewell – The Inn At Whitewell, Forest Of Bowland, Clitheroe, Lancashire BB7 3AT. Tel: 01200 448222

Wisbech – Crown Lodge Hotel, Downham Road, Outwell, Wisbech , Cambridgeshire PE14 8SE. Tel: 01945 773391

Wooler – The Tankerville Arms Hotel, Wooler, Northumberland NE71 6AD. Tel: 01668 281581

SCOTLAND

Annan – The Powfoot Hotel, Powfoot, Near Annan, Dumfriesshire DG12 5PN. Tel: 01461 700254

Edinburgh – Bank Hotel, 1 South Bridge, Edinburgh EH1 1LL. Tel: 0131 622 6800

Isle Of Skye – Hotel Eilean Iarmain, , Sleat, Isle Of Skye IV43 8QR. Tel: 01471 833332

Kylesku – Kylesku Hotel, Kylesku, Via Lairg, Sutherland IV27 4HW. Tel: 01971 502231/502200

Loch Earn – Achray House on Loch Earn, Loch Earn, St Fillan, Perthshire PH6 2NF. Tel: 01764 685231

Moffat – Annandale Arms Hotel, High Street, Moffat, Dumfriesshire DG10 9HF. Tel: 01683 220013

Oldmeldrum – The Redgarth, Kirkbrace, Oldmeldrum, Aberdeenshire AB51 0DJ. Tel: 01651 872 353

Plockton – The Plockton Hotel & Garden Restaurant, Harbour Street, Plockton, Wester Ross IV52 8TN. Tel: 01599 544274

Poolewe – Pool House Hotel, Poolewe, Achnasheen, Wester Ross IV22 2LD. Tel: 01445 781272

Stirling – Sheriffmuir Inn, Sheriffmuir, Nr Dunblane, Perthshire FK15 0LN. Tel: 01786 823285

Tighnabruaich – Royal Hotel, Tighnabruaich, Argyll, Argyllshire PA21 2BE. Tel: 01700 811239

WALES

Bridgend – The Great House, High Street, Bridgend, Laleston, Mid-Glamorgan CF32 0HP. Tel: 01656 657644

Llanarmon Dyffryn Ceiriog – The West Arms Hotel, Llanarmon D C, Nr Llangollen, Denbighshire LL20 7LD. Tel: 01691 600665

Presteigne – The Radnorshire Arms, High Street, Presteigne, Powys LD8 2BE. Tel: 01544 267406

CHANNEL ISLANDS

Guernsey – Les Rocquettes Hotel, Les Gravees, St Peter Port GY1 1RN. Tel: 01481 722176

L2
power is the same all over the UK
it's the people you deal
with which make the
difference
Value is what we strive for, which includes a competitive price, as well as a methodology to save you further money and management time.
Our annual customer retention rate is 97% and our surveys show 85% of our customers mark our service as "excellent".
Contact us for further details on a cheaper electricity price.
Lloyd Lewis Power
27 Shamrock Way, Hythe Marina Village, Hythe, Hampshire, SO45 6DY.
T 02380 841555 F 02380 841777
Email: power@lloydlewis.co.uk Website: www.lloydlewis.co.uk
preferred energy supplier

Johansens Recommended Country Houses & Small Hotels listed by name

To enable you to use your 2001 Johansens Recommended Country Houses & Small Hotels Guide more effectively, the following indexes are listed alphabetically, by property name within each country, by county and by location.

ENGLAND

Name	Location	Page
Abbots Oak	Coalville	65
Andrew's On The Weir	Porlock Weir	142
Appleton Hall	Appleton-Le-Moors	31
Apsley House	Bath	37
The Ardencote Manor Hotel	Warwick	172
Arrow Mill Hotel	Alcester	27
Ashelford	Combe Martin	66
Ashwick Country House Hotel	Dulverton	74
Aynsome Manor Hotel	Cartmel	57
Bath Lodge Hotel	Bath	38
The Beaufort Hotel	Portsmouth	145
The Beeches Hotel	Norwich	123
Beechleas	Wimborne Minster	176
Beechwood Hotel	North Walsham	121
Bel Alp House	Dartmoor	68
Beryl	Wells	173
Bibury Court	Bibury	46
Biggin Hall	Biggin-By-Hartington	47
Blackaller	North Bovey	119
Broadoaks Country House	Windermere	177
The Brompton	Shrewsbury	158
Broom Hall Country Hotel	Thetford	167
Browns Hotel Wine Bar	Tavistock	166
Burleigh Court	Minchinhampton	115
Burpham Country House Hotel	Arundel	32
Catton Old Hall	Norwich	124
Chalk Lane Hotel	Epsom	75
Chapel House	Atherstone	34
Charlton Kings Hotel	Cheltenham	59
Chase Lodge	Hampton Court	85
Chequers Hotel	Pulborough	146
Chippenhall Hall	Diss	70
Cockliffe Country House Hotel	Nottingham	128
Coombe House Country Hotel	Crediton	67
The Cormorant Hotel	Golant by Fowey	81
The Cottage Hotel	Nottingham	129
The Countryman At Trink Hotel	St Ives	151
The County Hotel	Bath	39
Crosby Lodge Hotel	Carlisle	56
Cross House Hotel	Padstow	139
Crouchers Bottom Country Hotel	Chichester	61
Dale Head Hall Lakeside Hotel	Keswick	98
Daneswood House Hotel	Cheddar	58
Dial House Hotel	Bourton-On-The-Water	50
Downrew House Hotel	Barnstaple	36
'Edge Hall' Hotel	Hadleigh	84
Elderton Lodge	North Walsham	122
Eleven Didsbury Park	Manchester	111
The Elms	Beccles	45
Fallowfields	Oxford	137
Fayrer Garden House Hotel	Windermere	178
Felbrigg Lodge	Holt	94
The George Hotel	Dorchester-On-Thames	72
Glebe Farm House	Stratford-upon-Avon	164
Glencot House	Wells	174
Glewstone Court	Ross-On-Wye	148
Grafton Manor Hotel	Bromsgrove	54
The Grange Hotel	Albrighton	26
The Grange Hotel & Restaurant	Sherborne	155
The Granville	Brighton	51
The Great Escape Holiday Company	North Norfolk Coast	120
Green Bough Hotel	Chester	60
Grove House	Hamsterley Forest	86
The Hautboy	Ockham	132
Hipping Hall	Kirkby Lonsdale	101
The Homestead	Derby	69
Hooke Hall	Uckfield	169
Horsley Hall	Stanhope	160
The Hundred House Hotel	St Mawes	153
Ilsington Country Hotel	Ilsington	96
Kingston House	Staverton	161
Lakeshore House	Windermere	179
Langar Hall	Nottingham	130
Langrish House	Petersfield	141
Little Offley	Luton	108
Lower Bache House	Leominster	103
Lower Brook House	Blockley	49
The Malt House	Chipping Campden	63
Melbourn Bury	Cambridge	55
The Mill House Hotel	Ashington	33
Moor View House	Lydford	109
Moortown Lodge	Ringwood	147
Nanny Brow Hotel & Restaurant	Ambleside	29
Nansloe Manor	Helston	91
Norfolk Mead Hotel	Norwich	125
The Nurse's Cottage	Lymington	110
Oak Lodge Hotel	Enfield	75
The Old Manor Hotel	Loughborough	106
The Old Priory Hotel	Bath	40
The Old Rectory	Great Snoring	83
The Old Rectory	Norwich	126
The Old Rectory	Ilminster	95
The Old Rectory Hotel	St Keyne	152
The Old Vicarage Hotel	Witherslack	180
The Old Windmill	Alcester	28
The Otterburn Tower	Otterburn	134
Overton Grange Hotel	Ludlow	107
Owlpen Manor	Owlpen	136
Oxenways	Membury	112
Paradise House	Bath	41
The Parsonage Hotel	York	181
Pen-y-Dyffryn Country Hotel	Oswestry	133
Penhallow Manor Hotel	Launceston	102
Periton Park Hotel	Middlecombe	113
The Pheasant	Helmsley	90
Porlock Vale House	Porlock Weir	143
Preston House Hotel	Saunton	154
The Pump House Apartment	Billericay	48
Redcoats Farmhouse Hotel	Stevenage	162
Romney Bay House	New Romney	117
Rookhurst Country House Hotel	Hawes	88
Rowton Castle Hotel	Shrewsbury	157
Rylstone Manor	Isle of Wight	97
Sandgate Hotel at Restaurant La Terrasse	Folkestone	78
Santo's Higham Farm	Higham	93
Sawrey House Country Hotel	Hawkshead	89
Sea Marge Hotel	Overstrand	135
Shallowdale House	Ampleforth	30
The Shaven Crown Hotel	Shipton Under Wychwood	156
Soulton Hall	Wem	175
Stanhill Court Hotel	Gatwick	79
Stanton Manor	Chippenham	62
The Steppes	Hereford	92
The Stower Grange	Norwich	127
Sutton Bonnington Hall	Nottingham	131
Swinside Lodge Hotel	Keswick	99
Temple Sowerby House Hotel	Penrith	140
Thatched Cottage Hotel	Brockenhurst	52
Three Choirs	Newent	118
The Tollgate Inn	Stow-On-The-Wold	163
Trebrea Lodge	Tintagel	168
Tredethy House	Wadebridge	170
Tree Tops Country House Hotel	Southport	159
Trehellas House	Wadebridge	171
Trelawne Hotel	Falmouth	77
Tudor Farmhouse Hotel	Clearwell	64
Tye Rock Country House	Porthleven	144
Villa Magdala	Bath	42
Wallett's Court	Dover	73
Waren House Hotel	Bamburgh	35
Washingborough Hall	Lincoln	104
Waterford House	Middleham	114
Westwood Country House	Oxford	138
The White House	Harrogate	87
The White House	Kingsbridge	100
White Moss House	Grasmere	82
White Vine House	Rye	150
Whitley Ridge Hotel	Brockenhurst	53
Widbrook Grange	Bath	43
Wigham	Morchard Bishop	116
Willington Hall Hotel	Tarporley	165
Wilton Court Hotel	Ross-on-Wye	149
The Wind In The Willows	Glossop	80
Winder Hall	Lorton	105
Woolverton House	Bath	44
Yalbury Cottage Hotel	Dorchester	71

WALES

Name	Location	Page
Abergwynant Hall	Dolgellau	226
The Cawdor Arms Hotel	Llandeilo	228
The Crown At Whitebrook	Monmouth	229
Llechwen Hall	Cardiff	223
Norton House Hotel	Swansea	230
The Old Rectory Country House	Conwy	224
Parva Farmhouse and Restaurant	Tintern	232
Plas Dolmelynllyn	Dolgellau	227
Plas Penhelig Hotel	Aberdovey	220
Tan-y-Foel	Betws-y-Coed	221
Ty'n Rhos Country Hotel	Caernarfon	222
Tyddyn Iolyn	Criccieth	225
Waterwynch House Hotel	Tenby	231

SCOTLAND

Name	Location	Page
Ardsheal House	Kentallen Of Appin	206
Ardvourlie Castle	Isle Of Harris	205
Balgeddie House Hotel	Leslie	208
Balgonie Country House	Ballater	196
Banchory Lodge Hotel	Banchory	197
Boath House	Nairn	210
Castle of Park	Cornhill	198
Corrour House	Rothiemurchus	214
Culcreuch Castle Hotel	Fintry	202
Culduthel Lodge	Inverness	204
Culzean Castle	Maybole	209
Dungallan House Hotel	Oban	211
The Four Seasons Hotel	St Fillans	216
Garvock House Hotel	Edinburgh	201
Glenmorangie House at Cadbol	Tain	217
The Inn on North Steet	St. Andrews	215
The Killiecrankie Hotel	Killiecrankie	207
Knockendarroch House	Pitlochry	212
The Lake Hotel	Port Of Menteith	213
Mullardoch House Hotel	Glen Cannich	203
The Pend	Dunkeld	200
Trigony House Hotel	Dunfries	199

IRELAND

Name	Location	Page
Caragh Lodge	Caragh Lake	184
Cashel Palace Hotel	Cashel	185
Castle Grove Hotel	Letterkenny	191
Coopershill House	Riverstown	192
Earls Court House	Killarney	188
Killarney Royal Hotel	Killarney	189
Markree Castle	"Sligo	193
The Old Rectory - Kilmeaden House	Kilmeaden	190
Ross Lake House Hotel	Connemara	186
St. Clerans	Craughwell	187

CHANNEL ISLES

Name	Location	Page
Bella Luce Hotel & Restaurant	Guernsey	17
La Favorita Hotel	Guernsey	16
La Sablonnerie	Sark Island	19
The White House	Herm Island	18

Johansens Recommended Country Houses & Small Hotels listed by county

ENGLAND

Cambridgeshire

Melbourn Bury ... Cambridge ... 55

Cheshire

Green Bough Hotel ... Chester ... 60
Willington Hall Hotel ... Tarporley ... 165

Co. Durham

Grove House ... Hamsterley Forest ... 86
Horsley Hall ... Stanhope ... 160

Cornwall

The Cormorant Hotel ... Golant by Fowey ... 81
The Countryman At Trink Hotel ... St Ives ... 151
Cross House Hotel ... Padstow ... 139
The Hundred House Hotel ... St Mawes ... 153
Nansloe Manor ... Helston ... 91
The Old Rectory Hotel ... St Keyne ... 152
Penhallow Manor Hotel ... Launceston ... 102
Trebrea Lodge ... Tintagel ... 168
Tredethy House ... Wadebridge ... 170
Trehellas House ... Wadebridge ... 171
Trelawne Hotel ... Falmouth ... 77
Tye Rock Country House ... Porthleven ... 144

Cumbria

Aynsome Manor Hotel ... Cartmel ... 57
Broadoaks Country House ... Windermere ... 177
Crosby Lodge Hotel ... Carlisle ... 56
Dale Head Hall Lakeside Hotel ... Keswick ... 98
Fayrer Garden House Hotel ... Windermere ... 178
Hipping Hall ... Kirkby Lonsdale ... 101
Lakeshore House ... Windermere ... 179
Nanny Brow Hotel & Restaurant ... Ambleside ... 29
The Old Vicarage Hotel ... Witherslack ... 180
Sawrey House Country Hotel ... Hawkshead ... 89
Swinside Lodge Hotel ... Keswick ... 99
Temple Sowerby House Hotel ... Penrith ... 140
White Moss House ... Grasmere ... 82
Winder Hall ... Lorton ... 105

Derbyshire

Biggin Hall ... Biggin-By-Hartington ... 47
The Homestead ... Derby ... 69
Santo's Higham Farm ... Higham ... 93
The Wind In The Willows ... Glossop ... 80

Devon

Ashelford ... Combe Martin ... 66
Bel Alp House ... Dartmoor ... 68
Blackaller ... North Bovey ... 119
Browns Hotel Wine Bar ... Tavistock ... 166
Coombe House Country Hotel ... Crediton ... 67
Downrew House Hotel ... Barnstaple ... 36
Ilsington Country Hotel ... Ilsington ... 96
Kingston House ... Staverton ... 161
Moor View House ... Lydford ... 109
Oxenways ... Membury ... 112
Preston House Hotel ... Saunton ... 154
The White House ... Kingsbridge ... 100
Wigham ... Morchard Bishop ... 116

Dorset

Beechleas ... Wimborne Minster ... 176
The Grange Hotel & Restaurant ... Sherborne ... 155
Yalbury Cottage Hotel ... Dorchester ... 71

East Sussex

The Granville ... Brighton ... 51
Hooke Hall ... Uckfield ... 169
White Vine House ... Rye ... 150

Essex

The Pump House Apartment ... Billericay ... 48

Gloucestershire

Bibury Court ... Bibury ... 46
Burleigh Court ... Minchinhampton ... 115
Charlton Kings Hotel ... Cheltenham ... 59
Dial House Hotel ... Bourton-On-The-Water ... 50
Lower Brook House ... Blockley ... 49
The Malt House ... Chipping Campden ... 63
Owlpen Manor ... Owlpen ... 136
Three Choirs ... Newent ... 118
Tudor Farmhouse Hotel ... Clearwell ... 64

Greater Manchester

Eleven Didsbury Park ... Manchester ... 111

Hampshire

The Beaufort Hotel ... Portsmouth ... 145
Langrish House ... Petersfield ... 141
Moortown Lodge ... Ringwood ... 147
The Nurse's Cottage ... Lymington ... 110
Thatched Cottage Hotel ... Brockenhurst ... 52
Whitley Ridge Hotel ... Brockenhurst ... 53

Herefordshire

Glewstone Court ... Ross-On-Wye ... 148
Lower Bache House ... Leominster ... 103
The Steppes ... Hereford ... 92
Wilton Court Hotel ... Ross-on-Wye ... 149

Hertfordshire

Little Offley ... Luton ... 108
Redcoats Farmhouse Hotel ... Stevenage ... 162

Isle of Wight

Rylstone Manor ... Isle of Wight ... 97

Kent

Romney Bay House ... New Romney ... 117
Sandgate Hotel ... Folkestone ... 78
Wallett's Court ... Dover ... 73

Lancashire

Tree Tops Restaurant & Hotel ... Southport ... 159

Leicestershire

Abbots Oak ... Coalville ... 65
The Old Manor Hotel ... Loughborough ... 106
Sutton Bonnington Hall ... Nottingham ... 131

Lincolnshire

Washingborough Hall ... Lincoln ... 104

Middlesex

Oak Lodge Hotel ... Enfield ... 75

Norfolk

The Beeches Hotel ... Norwich ... 123
Beechwood Hotel ... North Walsham ... 121
Broom Hall Country Hotel ... Thetford ... 167
Catton Old Hall ... Norwich ... 124
Elderton Lodge ... North Walsham ... 122
Felbrigg Lodge ... Holt ... 94
The Great Escape Holiday Company ... North Norfolk Coast ... 120
Norfolk Mead Hotel ... Norwich ... 125
The Old Rectory ... Great Snoring ... 83
The Old Rectory ... Norwich ... 126
Sea Marge Hotel ... Overstrand ... 135
The Stower Grange ... Norwich ... 127

North Yorkshire

Appleton Hall ... Appleton-Le-Moors ... 31
The Parsonage Hotel ... York ... 181
The Pheasant ... Helmsley ... 90
Rookhurst Country House Hotel ... Hawes ... 88
Shallowdale House ... Ampleforth ... 30
Waterford House ... Middleham ... 114
The White House ... Harrogate ... 87

Northumberland

The Otterburn Tower ... Otterburn ... 134
Waren House Hotel ... Bamburgh ... 35

Nottinghamshire

Cockliffe Country House Hotel ... Nottingham ... 128
The Cottage Hotel ... Nottingham ... 129
Langar Hall ... Nottingham ... 130

Oxfordshire

The George Hotel ... Dorchester-On-Thames ... 72
Fallowfields ... Oxford ... 137
The Shaven Crown Hotel ... Shipton Under Wychwood ... 156
The Tollgate Inn ... Stow-On-The-Wold ... 163
Westwood Country House ... Oxford ... 138

Shropshire

The Brompton ... Shrewsbury ... 158
Overton Grange Hotel ... Ludlow ... 107
Pen-y-Dyffryn Country Hotel ... Oswestry ... 133
Rowton Castle Hotel ... Shrewsbury ... 157
Soulton Hall ... Wem ... 175

Somerset

Andrew's On The Weir ... Porlock Weir ... 142
Apsley House ... Bath ... 37
Ashwick Country House Hotel ... Dulverton ... 74
Bath Lodge Hotel ... Bath ... 38
Beryl ... Wells ... 173
The County Hotel ... Bath ... 39
Daneswood House Hotel ... Cheddar ... 58
Glencot House ... Wells ... 174
The Old Priory Hotel ... Bath ... 40
The Old Rectory ... Ilminster ... 95
Paradise House ... Bath ... 41
Periton Park Hotel ... Middlecombe ... 113
Porlock Vale House ... Porlock Weir ... 143
Villa Magdala ... Bath ... 42
Woolverton House ... Bath ... 44

Staffordshire

The Grange Hotel ... Albrighton ... 26

Suffolk

Chippenhall Hall ... Diss ... 70
'Edge Hall' Hotel ... Hadleigh ... 84
The Elms ... Beccles ... 45

Surrey

Chalk Lane Hotel ... Epsom ... 75
Chase Lodge ... Hampton Court ... 85
The Hautboy ... Ockham ... 132
Stanhill Court Hotel ... Gatwick ... 79

Warwickshire

The Ardencote Manor Hotel ... Warwick ... 172
Arrow Mill Hotel ... Alcester ... 27
Chapel House ... Atherstone ... 34
Glebe Farm House ... Stratford-upon-Avon ... 164

West Sussex

Burpham Country House Hotel ... Arundel ... 32
Chequers Hotel ... Pulborough ... 146
Crouchers Bottom Country Hotel ... Chichester ... 61
The Mill House Hotel ... Ashington ... 33

Wiltshire

Stanton Manor ... Chippenham ... 62
Widbrook Grange ... Bath ... 43

Worcestershire

Grafton Manor Hotel ... Bromsgrove ... 54
The Old Windmill ... Alcester ... 28

WALES

Carmarthenshire

The Cawdor Arms Hotel ....Llandeilo 228

Conwy

The Old Rectory Country House .Conwy 224
Tan-y-Foel ....Betws-y-Coed 221

Glamorgan

Llechwen Hall ....Cardiff 223

Gwynedd

Abergwynant Hall ....Dolgellau 226
Plas Dolmelynllyn.........................Dolgellau 227
Plas Penhelig Hotel ....Aberdovey 220
Ty'n Rhos Country Hotel.............Caernarfon 222
Tyddyn Iolyn ....Criccieth 225

Monmouthshire

The Crown At Whitebrook ....Monmouth 229
Parva Farmhouse and Restaurant .Tintern 232

Pembrokeshire

Waterwynch House Hotel...........Tenby 231

West Glamorgan

Norton House Hotel.....................Swansea...................230

SCOTLAND

Aberdeenshire

Balgonie Country House ....Ballater 196
Banchory Lodge Hotel..................Banchory 197
Castle of Park................................Cornhill...................198

Argyllshire

Ardsheal House ....Kentallen Of Appin 206
Dungallan House Hotel................Oban........................211

Ayrshire

Culzean Castle ....Maybole...................209

Dunfriesshire

Trigony House Hotel....................Dunfries...................199

Fife

Balgeddie House Hotel................Leslie 208
Garvock House Hotel...................Edinburgh................201
The Inn on North Steet ....St. Andrews.............215

Inverness-shire

Boath House ....Nairn 210
Corrour House ....Rothiemurchus 214
Culduthel Lodge ....Inverness 204
Mullardoch House Hotel.............Glen Cannich 203

Perthshire

The Four Seasons Hotel ....St Fillans..................216
The Killiecrankie Hotel ....Killiecrankie 207
Knockendarroch House ....Pitlochry..................212
The Lake Hotel.............................Port Of Menteith 213
The Pend ....Dunkeld...................200

Ross-shire

Glenmorangie House at Cadbol...Tain 217

Stirling & Trossachs

Culcreuch Castle Hotel................Fintry 202

Western Isles

Ardvourlie Castle ....Isle Of Harris...........205

IRELAND

Co Donegal

Castle Grove Hotel........................Letterkenny 191

Co Galway

Ross Lake House Hotel.................Connemara.............186
St. Clerans ....Craughwell 187

Co Kerry

Caragh Lodge...............................Caragh Lake 184
Earls Court House........................Killarney 188
Killarney Royal Hotel...................Killarney 189

Co Sligo

Coopershill House ....Riverstown 192
Markree Castle.............................Sligo........................193

Co Tipperary

Cashel Palace Hotel ....Cashel......................185

Co Waterford

The Old Rectory...........................Kilmeaden 190

CHANNEL ISLES

Bella Luce Hotel & Restaurant ....Guernsey 17
The White House ....Herm Island..............18
La Sablonnerie ....Sark Island................19
La Favorita Hotel..........................Guernsey 16

Johansens Recommended Country Houses & Small Hotels listed by region

ENGLAND

Albrighton ....The Grange Hotel..........................26
Alcester ....Arrow Mill Hotel And Restaurant .27
Alcester ....The Old Windmill 28
Altarnun ....see Launceston
Ambleside ....Nanny Brow Hotel & Restaurant...29
Ampleforth ....Shallowdale House..........................30
Appleton-Le-Moors..Appleton Hall 31
Apuldram ....see Chichester
Arrow ....see Alcester
Arundel ....Burpham Country House Hotel......32
Ashington ....The Mill House Hotel 33
Atherstone ....Chapel House.................................34
Axminster ....see Membury
Bamburgh ....Waren House Hotel 35
Barnstaple ....Downrew House Hotel 36
Bath.........................Apsley House 37
Bath.........................Bath Lodge Hotel............................38
Bath.........................The County Hotel 39
Bath.........................The Old Priory Hotel......................40
Bath.........................Paradise House 41
Bath.........................Villa Magdala..................................42
Bath.........................Widbrook Grange 43
Bath.........................Woolverton House..........................44
Beccles.....................The Elms 45
Bibury ....Bibury Court 46
Biggin-By-Hartington .Biggin Hall 47
Billericay ....The Pump House Apartment 48
Bishops Tawton ......see Barnstaple
Blockley..................Lower Brook House.........................49
Bourton-On-The-Water .Dial House Hotel 50
Bowness..................see Windermere
Bradford-On-Avon .see Bath
Brighton ....The Granville 51
Broad Campden ......see Chipping Campden
Brockenhurst...........Thatched Cottage Hotel.................52
Brockenhurst...........Whitley Ridge Hotel.......................53
Bromsgrove ....Grafton Manor Hotel 54
Burpham.................see Arundel
Cambridge..............Melbourn Bury 55
Carlisle ....Crosby Lodge Hotel 56
Cartmel ....Aynsome Manor Hotel 57
Charlton Kings........see Cheltenham
Charlwood..............see Gatwick
Cheddar..................Daneswood House Hotel 58
Cheltenham ....Charlton Kings Hotel 59
Cheshire ....see Tarporley
Chester ....Green Bough Hotel.........................60
Chichester..............Crouchers Bottom Country Hotel..61
Chillington ....see Kingsbridge
Chippenham ....Stanton Manor...............................62
Chipping Campden The Malt House 63
Chipping Campden see Blockley
Clappersgate...........see Ambleside
Claverdon ....see Warwick
Clearwell ....Tudor Farmhouse Hotel.................64
Coalville.................Abbots Oak 65
Coleford ....see Crediton
Coltishall................see Norwich
Combe Martin ....Ashelford..66
Copt Oak ....see Coalville
Cotswolds...............see Minchinhampton
Crediton ....Coombe House Country Hotel.......67
Cricket Malherbie...see Ilminster
Cromer ....see Overstrand
Crosby-On-Eden .....see Carlisle
Dartmoor................Bel Alp House 68
Dartmoor................see Ilsington
Derby.......................The Homestead..............................69
Didsbury ....see Manchester
Diss..........................Chippenhall Hall 70
Dorchester..............Yalbury Cottage Hotel 71
Dorchester-On-Thames..The George Hotel 72
Dover.......................Wallett's Court 73
Drayton ....see Norwich
Dulverton................Ashwick Country House Hotel 74
East Down ....see Combe Martin
Enfield ....Oak Lodge Hotel............................75
Epsom ....Chalk Lane Hotel 75
Escrick ....see York
Falmouth ....Trelawne Hotel 77
Felbrigg...................see Holt
Folkestone ....Sandgate Hotel 78
Formby ....see Southport
Fressingfield............see Diss
Gatwick..................Stanhill Court Hotel.......................79
Glewstone ....see Ross-On-Wye
Glossop...................The Wind In The Willows 80
Golant by Fowey.....The Cormorant Hotel.....................81
Grasmere ....White Moss House..........................82
Great Burstead ....see Billericay
Great Snoring ....The Old Rectory 83
Hadleigh.................'Edge Hall' Hotel............................84
Hampton Court ......Chase Lodge 85
Hampton Wick ....see Hampton Court
Hamsterley Forest ...Grove House 86
Harome ....see Helmsley
Harrogate ....The White House 87
Hawes......................Rookhurst Country House Hotel...88
Hawkshead.............Sawrey House Country Hotel.........89
Haytor Vale............see Dartmoor
Helland Bridge ....see Wadebridge
Helmsley ....The Pheasant 90
Helston....................Nansloe Manor 91
Helston....................see Porthleven
Hereford ....The Steppes 92
Higham ....Santo's Higham Farm 93
Hinksey Hill............see Oxford
Hitchin....................see Stevenage
Holt ....Felbrigg Lodge 94
Ilminster.................The Old Rectory 95
Ilsington ....Ilsington Country Hotel 96
Inkberrow................see Alcester
Isle of Wight ....Rylstone Manor 97
Keswick ....Dale Head Hall Lakeside Hotel......98
Keswick ....Swinside Lodge Hotel.....................99
Kingham.................see Stow-On-The-Wold
Kingsbridge ....The White House 100
Kingston Bagpuize...see Oxford
Kirkby Lonsdale ......Hipping Hall 101
LakeThirlmere ....see Keswick
Langar ....see Nottingham
Langrish..................see Petersfield

Launceston.............Penhallow Manor Hotel 102
Leominster ....Lower Bache House 103
Lincoln...................Washingborough Hall...................104
Little Offley............see Luton
Littlestone..............see New Romney
London...................see Enfield
Lorton ....Winder Hall 105
Loughborough ....The Old Manor Hotel 106
Lower Bockhampton .see Dorchester
Loxley.....................see Stratford-upon-Avon
Ludlow ....Overton Grange Hotel 107
Luton......................Little Offley...................................108
Lydford ....Moor View House 109
Lymington..............The Nurse's Cottage 110
Manchester ....Eleven Didsbury Park....................111
Mawnan Smith ....see Falmouth
Melbourn................see Cambridge
Membury ....Oxenways......................................112
Middlecombe ....Periton Park Hotel........................113
Middleham.............Waterford House...........................114
Midsomer Norton ...see Bath
Minchinhampton....Burleigh Court 115
Minehead ....see Middlecombe
Moretonhamstead ......see North Bovey
Morchard Bishop ....Wigham...116
Near Durham ....see Hamsterley Forest
Near Sawrey ....see Hawkshead
New Romney ....Romney Bay House........................117
Newent...................Three Choirs.................................118
Newlands................see Keswick
North Bovey...........Blackaller 119
North Norfolk Coast ..The Great Escape Holiday Company..120
North Walsham ......Beechwood Hotel...........................121
North Walsham ......Elderton Lodge..............................122
Norton St Philip .....see Bath
Norwich ....The Beeches Hotel 123
Norwich ....Catton Old Hall.............................124
Norwich ....Norfolk Mead Hotel 125
Norwich ....The Old Rectory............................126
Norwich ....The Stower Grange.........................127
Nottingham............Cockliffe Country House Hotel....128
Nottingham............The Cottage Hotel.........................129
Nottingham............Langar Hall 130
Nottingham............Sutton Bonnington Hall...............131
Oborne ....see Sherborne
Ockham...................The Hautboy..................................132
Old Catton.............see Norwich
Oswestry.................Pen-y-Dyffryn Country Hotel.......133
Otterburn ....The Otterburn Tower 134
Overstrand ....Sea Marge Hotel 135
Overton..................see Ludlow
Owlpen...................Owlpen Manor...............................136
Oxford ....Fallowfields 137
Oxford ....Westwood Country House............138
Padstow ....Cross House Hotel 139
Penrith ....Temple Sowerby House Hotel......140
Petersfield...............Langrish House 141
Pickering ....see Appleton-Le-Moors
Porlock Weir..........Andrew's On The Weir 142
Porlock Weir..........Porlock Vale House 143
Porthleven..............Tye Rock Country House 144
Portsmouth.............The Beaufort Hotel.......................145
Pulborough.............Chequers Hotel.............................146
Ringwood ....Moortown Lodge...........................147
Ross-On-Wye.........Glewstone Court...........................148
Ross-on-Wye..........Wilton Court Hotel.......................149
Ruan Highlanes ......see St Mawes
Ruddington ....see Nottingham
Rydal Water...........see Grasmere
Rye ....White Vine House.........................150
Saham Toney ....see Thetford
Sandgate.................see Folkestone
Saunton..................Preston House Hotel.....................154
Shanklin.................see Isle of Wight
Sherborne...............The Grange Hotel & Restaurant..155
Shipham.................see Cheddar
Shipton Under Wychwood..The Shaven Crown Hotel 156
Shrewsbury............The Brompton 158
Shrewsbury............Rowton Castle Hotel 157
Southport...............Tree Tops Restaurant & Hotel.....159
Spondon.................see Derby
St Ives.....................The Countryman At Trink Hotel..151
St Keyne.................The Old Rectory Hotel.................152
St Mawes................The Hundred House Hotel...........153
Stanhope................Horsley Hall.................................160
Staverton................Kingston House.............................161
Stevenage...............Redcoats Farmhouse Hotel...........162
Stow-On-The-Wold.The Tollgate Inn...........................163
Stratford-upon-Avon.Glebe Farm House 164
Sutton Bonnington.see Nottingham
Sway ....see Lymington
Tarporley................Willington Hall Hotel 165
Tavistock................Browns Hotel Wine Bar................166
Telford....................see Albrighton
Temple Sowerby .....see Penrith
Thetford ....Broom Hall Country Hotel...........167
Thorpe St Andrew..see Norwich
Tintagel..................Trebrea Lodge 168
Toft Monks ....see Beccles
Totnes ....see Staverton
Trenale ....see Tintagel
Trink ....see St Ives
Uckfield..................Hooke Hall....................................169
Ullingswick ....see Hereford
Vale Down ....see Lydford
Wadebridge ....Tredethy House 170
Wadebridge ....Trehellas House 171
Warwick.................The Ardencote Manor Hotel 172
Washaway ....see Wadebridge
Washingborough.....see Lincoln
Weardale................see Stanhope
Wells ....Beryl 173
Wells ....Glencot House 174
Wem.......................Soulton Hall.................................175
Wensleydale...........see Hawes
Wensleydale...........see Middleham
West Cliffe.............see Dover
Wimborne Minster .Beechleas......................................176
Windermere ....Broadoaks Country House 177
Windermere ....Fayrer Garden House Hotel..........178
Windermere ....Lakeshore House 179
Witherslack............The Old Vicarage Hotel 180
Woolverton............see Bath
York........................The Parsonage Hotel 181

WALES

Abercynon ....see Cardiff
Aberdovey..............Plas Penhelig Hotel......................220
Betws-y-Coed.........Tan-y-Foel....................................221
Caernarfon ....Ty'n Rhos Country Hotel.............222
Cardiff ....Llechwen Hall..............................223
Conwy ....The Old Rectory Country House .224
Criccieth ....Tyddyn Iolyn.................................225
Dolgellau................Abergwynant Hall 226
Dolgellau................Plas Dolmelynllyn.........................227
Ganllwyd................see Dolgellau
Llandeilo ....The Cawdor Arms Hotel..............228
Monmouth ....The Crown At Whitebrook..........229
Mumbles.................see Swansea
Swansea..................Norton House Hotel.....................230
Tenby ....Waterwynch House Hotel 231
Tintern...................Parva Farmhouse and Restaurant .232
Waterwynch Bay.....see Tenby
Whitebrook............see Monmouth

SCOTLAND

Auldearn ....see Nairn
Ayrshire..................see Maybole
Ballater...................Balgonie Country House..............196
Banchory ....Banchory Lodge Hotel..................197
Beauly.....................see Glen Cannich
Cornhill..................Castle of Park 198
Dunfermline...........see Edinburgh
Dunfries..................Trigony House Hotel 199
Dunkeld..................The Pend.......................................200
Edinburgh...............Garvock House Hotel...................201
Fife..........................see Leslie
Fintry.....................Culcreuch Castle Hotel 202
Glen Cannich ....Mullardoch House Hotel 203
Highland ....see Rothiemurchus
Huntly ....see Cornhill
Inverness ....Culduthel Lodge 204
Isle Of Harris..........Ardvourlie Castle..........................205
Kentallen Of Appin .Ardsheal House.............................206
Killiecrankie...........The Killiecrankie Hotel................207
Leslie ....Balgeddie House Hotel 208
Maybole..................Culzean Castle 209
Nairn ....Boath House.................................210
Oban ....Dungallan House Hotel 211
Perthshire ....see St Fillans
Pitlochry.................Knockendarroch House 212
Port Of Menteith ....The Lake Hotel.............................213
Ross-shire ....see Tain
Rothiemurchus........Corrour House 214
Royal Deeside.........see Banchory
St. Andrews............The Inn on North Steet 215
St Fillans ....The Four Seasons Hotel................216
Stirlingshire............see Fintry
Tain........................Glenmorangie House at Cadbol ...217
Thornhill ....see Dunfries

IRELAND

Caragh Lake ....Caragh Lodge 184
Cashel ....Cashel Palace Hotel......................185
Co Donegal ....see Letterkenny
Co Galway ....see Connemara
Co.Galway ....see Craughwell
Co.Kerry.................see Killarney
Co. Waterford ....see Kilmeaden
Connemara ....Ross Lake House Hotel.................186
Craughwell.............St. Clerans....................................187
Killarney.................Killarney Royal Hotel 189
Killarney.................Earls Court House 188
Kilmeaden..............The Old Rectory 190
Letterkenny............Castle Grove Hotel.......................191
Riverstown ....Coopershill House 192
Sligo,Co Sligo ....Markree Castle..............................193
Fermain Bay ....see Guernsey

CHANNEL ISLANDS

Guernsey ....Bella Luce Hotel & Restaurant 17
Guernsey ....La Favorita Hotel...........................16
Guernsey ....see Herm Island
Guernsey ....see Sark Island
Herm Island ....The White House 18
Sark Island ....La Sablonnerie 19
St Martin................see Guernsey

Johansens Preferred Partners

AT&T...6
Barrels & Bottles.......................................11
Dorlux..13
Gordon & MacPhail 241
Hildon Ltd..................................9, 244 & IBC
Hotel Telephone Systems 242
Knight Frank...IFC
Lloyd Lewis Power 236
Marsh UK Ltd..20
Moët Hennessy......................................233
Pacific Direct..234

PREFERRED PARTNERS

Preferred partners are those organisations specifically chosen and exclusively recommended by Johansens for the quality and excellence of their products and services for the mutual benefit of Johansens recommendations, readers and independent travellers. For further details, please contact Fiona Patrick at Johansens on 0207 566 9700.

ORDER FORM

order 3 titles get £5 off • order 4 titles get £10 off • order 5 titles get £20 off

or you can order the Chairman's collection and save £35

Simply indicate the quantity of each title you wish to order, total up the cost and then make your appropriate discount. Complete your order below and choose your preferred method of payment. Then send it to Johansens, FREEPOST (CB 264), 43 Millharbour, London E14 9BR (no stamp required). FREE gifts will automatically be dispatched with your order. Fax orders welcome on 0207 537 3594.

ALTERNATIVELY YOU CAN ORDER IMMEDIATELY ON FREEPHONE 0800 269 397 and quote ref B13

Recommended Hotels - Great Britain & Ireland 2001
Publication date: October 2000
I wish to order QUANTITY copy/ies priced at £19.95 each. Total cost £

Recommended Country Houses - Great Britain & Ireland 2001
Publication date: October 2000
I wish to order QUANTITY copy/ies priced at £11.95 each. Total cost £

Recommended Traditional Inns, Hotels & Restaurants - Great Britain 2001
Publication date: October 2000
I wish to order QUANTITY copy/ies priced at £11.95 each. Total cost £

Historic Houses, Castles & Gardens 2001 (incorporating Museums & Galleries)
Publication date: December 2000
I wish to order QUANTITY copy/ies priced at £7.95 each. Total cost £

Recommended Hotels - Europe & The Mediterranean 2001
Publication date: October 2000
I wish to order QUANTITY copy/ies priced at £16.95 each. Total cost £

Recommended Hotels - North America, Bermuda & The Caribbean 2001
Publication date: October 2000
I wish to order QUANTITY copy/ies priced at £12.95 each. Total cost £

Recommended Hotels, Country Houses & Game Lodges – Southern Africa, Mauritius, The Seychelles 2001 Publ. date: October 2000
I wish to order QUANTITY copy/ies priced at £9.95 each. Total cost £

NEW
Recommended Hotels & Lodges Australia, New Zealand, The Pacific 2001
Publication date: October 2000
I wish to order QUANTITY copy/ies priced at £9.95 each. Total cost £

Recommended Business Meeting Venues 2001
Publication date: February 2001
I wish to order QUANTITY copy/ies priced at £25.00 each. Total cost £

NEW
Johansens Pocket Guide 2001
Publication date: January 2001
I wish to order QUANTITY copy/ies priced at £7.95 each. Total cost £

The Chairman's Collection

order the complete collection of Johansens Recommended Guides for only £99.55 a saving of £35

PLUS FREE P&P worth £4.50

PLUS FREE Luxury Luggage Tag worth £15

PLUS FREE Privilege Card worth £20

The Chairman's Collection contains the following titles:

•Business Meetings Venues •Traditional Inns, Hotels & Restaurants - GB •Hotels - GB & Ireland •Country Houses - GB & Ireland •Historic Houses, Castles & Gardens •Hotels, Country Houses & Game Lodges - Southern Africa •Hotels - North America, Bermuda, The Caribbean •Hotels - Europe & The Mediterranean •Hotels & Lodges - Australia, New Zealand, The Pacific • Johansens Pocket Guide 2001

Now please complete your order and payment details

I have ordered 3 titles - £5 off		−£5.00
I have ordered 4 titles - £10 off		−£10.00
I have ordered 5 titles - £20 off		−£20.00
Total cost of books ordered minus discount (not including the Chairman's Collection)		£
Privilege Card - FREE WITH ANY ORDER Additional cards can be ordered for £20		£
Luxury Luggage Tag - Johansens branded polished steel tag at £15. Quantity and total cost:		£
POSTAGE & PACKING (UK) for a single item add £2.50; More than one item add £4.50; (Outside) UK for a single item add £4.00; More than one item add £6.00		£
I wish to order the Chairman's collection at £99.55 (no P&P required) **Enter quantity and total cost:**		£
Johansens Gold Blocked SLIP CASE at £5 for the Chairman's Collection. Quantity and total cost:		£
GRAND TOTAL		£

I have chosen my Johansens Guides and (please tick)

I enclose a cheque payable to Johansens ☐

I enclose my order on company letterheading, please invoice (UK only) ☐
Please note that books will be sent upon payment being received

Please debit my credit/charge card account (please tick) ☐

☐ **MasterCard** ☐ **Amex** ☐ **Visa** ☐ **Switch** (Issue Number)

Card Holders Name (Mr/Mrs/Miss)

Address

Postcode

Telephone

Card No.

Exp Date

Signature

NOW simply detach the order form and send it to Johansens, FREEPOST (CB264), 43 Millharbour, London E14 9BR (no stamp required)

FREE gifts will be dispatched with your order. Fax orders welcome on 0207 537 3594

GUEST SURVEY REPORT

Your own Johansens 'inspection' gives reliability to our guides
and assists in the selection of Award Nominations

Name of Hotel: ______________________________

Location of Hotel: ______________________________

Page No: ______________________________

Date of visit: ______________________________

Name of GUEST: ______________________________

Address of GUEST: ______________________________

______________________________ **Postcode** __________

Please tick one box in each category below:	*Excellent*	*Good*	*Disappointing*	*Poor*
Bedrooms				
Public Rooms				
Restaurant/Cuisine				
Service				
Welcome/Friendliness				
Value For Money				

Occasionally we may allow other reputable organisations to write with offers which may be of interest.
If you prefer not to hear from them, tick this box ☐

To: Johansens, c/o Norwood Mailing CO Ltd, FREEPOST CB264, London SE27 0BR

ORDER FORM

order 3 titles get £5 off • order 4 titles get £10 off • order 5 titles get £20 off

or you can order the Chairman's collection and save £35

Simply indicate the quantity of each title you wish to order, total up the cost and then make your appropriate discount. Complete your order below and choose your preferred method of payment. Then send it to Johansens, FREEPOST (CB 264), 43 Millharbour, London E14 9BR (no stamp required). FREE gifts will automatically be dispatched with your order. Fax orders welcome on 0207 537 3594.

ALTERNATIVELY YOU CAN ORDER IMMEDIATELY ON FREEPHONE 0800 269 397 and quote ref B13

Recommended Hotels - Great Britain & Ireland 2001
Publication date: October 2000
I wish to order QUANTITY copy/ies priced at £19.95 each. Total cost £

Recommended Country Houses - Great Britain & Ireland 2001
Publication date: October 2000
I wish to order QUANTITY copy/ies priced at £11.95 each. Total cost £

Recommended Traditional Inns, Hotels & Restaurants - Great Britain 2001
Publication date: October 2000
I wish to order QUANTITY copy/ies priced at £11.95 each. Total cost £

Historic Houses, Castles & Gardens 2001 (incorporating Museums & Galleries)
Publication date: December 2000
I wish to order QUANTITY copy/ies priced at £7.95 each. Total cost £

Recommended Hotels - Europe & The Mediterranean 2001
Publication date: October 2000
I wish to order QUANTITY copy/ies priced at £16.95 each. Total cost £

Recommended Hotels - North America, Bermuda & The Caribbean 2001
Publication date: October 2000
I wish to order QUANTITY copy/ies priced at £12.95 each. Total cost £

Recommended Hotels, Country Houses & Game Lodges – Southern Africa, Mauritius, The Seychelles 2001 Publ. date: October 2000
I wish to order QUANTITY copy/ies priced at £9.95 each. Total cost £

Recommended Hotels & Lodges Australia, New Zealand, The Pacific 2001
Publication date: October 2000
NEW
I wish to order QUANTITY copy/ies priced at £9.95 each. Total cost £

Recommended Business Meeting Venues 2001
Publication date: February 2001
I wish to order QUANTITY copy/ies priced at £25.00 each. Total cost £

Johansens Pocket Guide 2001
Publication date: January 2001
NEW
I wish to order QUANTITY copy/ies priced at £7.95 each. Total cost £

The Chairman's Collection

order the complete collection of Johansens Recommended Guides for only £99.55 a saving of £35

PLUS FREE P&P worth £4.50

PLUS FREE Luxury Luggage Tag worth £15

PLUS FREE Privilege Card worth £20

The Chairman's Collection contains the following titles:

•Business Meetings Venues •Traditional Inns, Hotels & Restaurants - GB •Hotels - GB & Ireland •Country Houses - GB & Ireland •Historic Houses, Castles & Gardens •Hotels, Country Houses & Game Lodges - Southern Africa •Hotels - North America, Bermuda, The Caribbean •Hotels - Europe & The Mediterranean •Hotels & Lodges - Australia, New Zealand, The Pacific • Johansens Pocket Guide 2001

Now please complete your order and payment details

I have ordered 3 titles - £5 off	–£5.00
I have ordered 4 titles - £10 off	–£10.00
I have ordered 5 titles - £20 off	–£20.00
Total cost of books ordered minus discount (not including the Chairman's Collection)	£
Privilege Card - FREE WITH ANY ORDER Additional cards can be ordered for £20	£
Luxury Luggage Tag - Johansens branded polished steel tag at £15. Quantity and total cost:	£
POSTAGE & PACKING (UK) for a single item add £2.50 / More than one item add £4.50 / (Outside) UK for a single item add £4.00 / More than one item add £6.00	£
I wish to order the Chairman's collection at £99.55 (no P&P required) Enter quantity and total cost:	£
Johansens Gold Blocked SLIP CASE at £5 for the Chairman's Collection. Quantity and total cost:	£
GRAND TOTAL	£

I have chosen my Johansens Guides and (please tick)

I enclose a cheque payable to Johansens ☐

I enclose my order on company letterheading, please invoice (UK only) ☐

Please note that books will be sent upon payment being received

Please debit my credit/charge card account (please tick) ☐

☐ MasterCard ☐ Amex ☐ Visa ☐ Switch (Issue Number)

Card Holders Name (Mr/Mrs/Miss)

Address

Postcode

Telephone

Card No.

Exp Date

Signature

NOW simply detach the order form and send it to Johansens, FREEPOST (CB264), 43 Millharbour, London E14 9BR (no stamp required)

FREE gifts will be dispatched with your order. Fax orders welcome on 0207 537 3594

GUEST SURVEY REPORT

Your own Johansens 'inspection' gives reliability to our guides
and assists in the selection of Award Nominations

Name of Hotel: ______________________________

Location of Hotel: ______________________________

Page No: ______________________________

Date of visit: ______________________________

Name of GUEST: ______________________________

Address of GUEST: ______________________________

______________________________ **Postcode** __________

Please tick one box in each category below:	***Excellent***	***Good***	***Disappointing***	***Poor***
Bedrooms				
Public Rooms				
Restaurant/Cuisine				
Service				
Welcome/Friendliness				
Value For Money				

Occasionally we may allow other reputable organisations to write with offers which may be of interest.
If you prefer not to hear from them, tick this box ☐

To: Johansens, c/o Norwood Mailing CO Ltd, FREEPOST CB264, London SE27 0BR

ORDER FORM

order 3 titles get £5 off • order 4 titles get £10 off • order 5 titles get £20 off

or you can order the Chairman's collection and save £35

Simply indicate the quantity of each title you wish to order, total up the cost and then make your appropriate discount. Complete your order below and choose your preferred method of payment. Then send it to Johansens, FREEPOST (CB 264), 43 Millharbour, London E14 9BR (no stamp required). FREE gifts will automatically be dispatched with your order. Fax orders welcome on 0207 537 3594.

ALTERNATIVELY YOU CAN ORDER IMMEDIATELY ON FREEPHONE 0800 269 397 and quote ref B13

Recommended Hotels - Great Britain & Ireland 2001
Publication date: October 2000
I wish to order QUANTITY copy/ies priced at £19.95 each.
Total cost £

Recommended Country Houses - Great Britain & Ireland 2001
Publication date: October 2000
I wish to order QUANTITY copy/ies priced at £11.95 each.
Total cost £

Recommended Traditional Inns, Hotels & Restaurants - Great Britain 2001
Publication date: October 2000
I wish to order QUANTITY copy/ies priced at £11.95 each.
Total cost £

Historic Houses, Castles & Gardens 2001 (incorporating Museums & Galleries)
Publication date: December 2000
I wish to order QUANTITY copy/ies priced at £7.95 each.
Total cost £

Recommended Hotels - Europe & The Mediterranean 2001
Publication date: October 2000
I wish to order QUANTITY copy/ies priced at £16.95 each.
Total cost £

Recommended Hotels - North America, Bermuda & The Caribbean 2001
Publication date: October 2000
I wish to order QUANTITY copy/ies priced at £12.95 each.
Total cost £

Recommended Hotels, Country Houses & Game Lodges – Southern Africa, Mauritius, The Seychelles 2001 Publ. date: October 2000
I wish to order QUANTITY copy/ies priced at £9.95 each.
Total cost £

Recommended Hotels & Lodges Australia, New Zealand, The Pacific 2001
Publication date: October 2000
NEW
I wish to order QUANTITY copy/ies priced at £9.95 each.
Total cost £

Recommended Business Meeting Venues 2001
Publication date: February 2001
I wish to order QUANTITY copy/ies priced at £25.00 each.
Total cost £

Johansens Pocket Guide 2001
Publication date: January 2001
NEW
I wish to order QUANTITY copy/ies priced at £7.95 each.
Total cost £

The Chairman's Collection

order the complete collection of Johansens Recommended Guides for only £99.55 a saving of £35

PLUS FREE P&P worth £4.50

PLUS FREE Luxury Luggage Tag worth £15

PLUS FREE Privilege Card worth £20

The Chairman's Collection contains the following titles:

•Business Meetings Venues •Traditional Inns, Hotels & Restaurants - GB •Hotels - GB & Ireland •Country Houses - GB & Ireland •Historic Houses, Castles & Gardens •Hotels, Country Houses & Game Lodges - Southern Africa •Hotels - North America, Bermuda, The Caribbean •Hotels - Europe & The Mediterranean •Hotels & Lodges - Australia, New Zealand, The Pacific • Johansens Pocket Guide 2001

Now please complete your order and payment details

I have ordered 3 titles - £5 off −£5.00

I have ordered 4 titles - £10 off −£10.00

I have ordered 5 titles - £20 off −£20.00

Total cost of books ordered minus discount (not including the Chairman's Collection) £

Privilege Card - FREE WITH ANY ORDER Additional cards can be ordered for £20 £

Luxury Luggage Tag - Johansens branded polished steel tag at £15. Quantity and total cost: £

POSTAGE & PACKING
(UK) for a single item add £2.50
More than one item add £4.50
(Outside) UK for a single item add £4.00
More than one item add £6.00
£

I wish to order the Chairman's collection at £99.55 (no P&P required) Enter quantity and total cost: £

Johansens Gold Blocked SLIP CASE at £5 for the Chairman's Collection. Quantity and total cost: £

GRAND TOTAL £

I have chosen my Johansens Guides and (please tick)

I enclose a cheque payable to Johansens ☐

I enclose my order on company letterheading, please invoice (UK only) ☐
Please note that books will be sent upon payment being received

Please debit my credit/charge card account (please tick) ☐

☐ **MasterCard** ☐ **Amex** ☐ **Visa** ☐ **Switch** (Issue Number)

Card Holders Name (Mr/Mrs/Miss)

Address

Postcode

Telephone

Card No.

Exp Date

Signature

NOW simply detach the order form and send it to Johansens, FREEPOST (CB264), 43 Millharbour, London E14 9BR (no stamp required)

FREE gifts will be dispatched with your order. Fax orders welcome on 0207 537 3594

GUEST SURVEY REPORT

Your own Johansens 'inspection' gives reliability to our guides
and assists in the selection of Award Nominations

Name of Hotel: ______________________

Location of Hotel: ______________________

Page No: ______________________

Date of visit: ______________________

Name of GUEST: ______________________

Address of GUEST: ______________________

______________________ **Postcode** __________

Please tick one box in each category below:	*Excellent*	*Good*	*Disappointing*	*Poor*
Bedrooms				
Public Rooms				
Restaurant/Cuisine				
Service				
Welcome/Friendliness				
Value For Money				

Occasionally we may allow other reputable organisations to write with offers which may be of interest.
If you prefer not to hear from them, tick this box ☐

To: Johansens, c/o Norwood Mailing CO Ltd, FREEPOST CB264, London SE27 0BR

ORDER FORM

order 3 titles get £5 off • order 4 titles get £10 off • order 5 titles get £20 off

or you can order the Chairman's collection and save £35

Simply indicate the quantity of each title you wish to order, total up the cost and then make your appropriate discount. Complete your order below and choose your preferred method of payment. Then send it to Johansens, FREEPOST (CB 264), 43 Millharbour, London E14 9BR (no stamp required). FREE gifts will automatically be dispatched with your order. Fax orders welcome on 0207 537 3594.

ALTERNATIVELY YOU CAN ORDER IMMEDIATELY ON FREEPHONE 0800 269 397 and quote ref B13

Title	Publication date	Order
Recommended Hotels - Great Britain & Ireland 2001	Publication date: October 2000	I wish to order [QUANTITY] copy/ies priced at £19.95 each. Total cost £
Recommended Country Houses - Great Britain & Ireland 2001	Publication date: October 2000	I wish to order [QUANTITY] copy/ies priced at £11.95 each. Total cost £
Recommended Traditional Inns, Hotels & Restaurants - Great Britain 2001	Publication date: October 2000	I wish to order [QUANTITY] copy/ies priced at £11.95 each. Total cost £
Historic Houses, Castles & Gardens 2001 (incorporating Museums & Galleries)	Publication date: December 2000	I wish to order [QUANTITY] copy/ies priced at £7.95 each. Total cost £
Recommended Hotels - Europe & The Mediterranean 2001	Publication date: October 2000	I wish to order [QUANTITY] copy/ies priced at £16.95 each. Total cost £
Recommended Hotels - North America, Bermuda & The Caribbean 2001	Publication date: October 2000	I wish to order [QUANTITY] copy/ies priced at £12.95 each. Total cost £
Recommended Hotels, Country Houses & Game Lodges – Southern Africa, Mauritius, The Seychelles 2001	Publ. date: October 2000	I wish to order [QUANTITY] copy/ies priced at £9.95 each. Total cost £
Recommended Hotels & Lodges Australia, New Zealand, The Pacific 2001 (NEW)	Publication date: October 2000	I wish to order [QUANTITY] copy/ies priced at £9.95 each. Total cost £
Recommended Business Meeting Venues 2001	Publication date: February 2001	I wish to order [QUANTITY] copy/ies priced at £25.00 each. Total cost £
Johansens Pocket Guide 2001 (NEW)	Publication date: January 2001	I wish to order [QUANTITY] copy/ies priced at £7.95 each. Total cost £

The Chairman's Collection

order the complete collection of Johansens Recommended Guides for only £99.55 a saving of £35

PLUS FREE P&P worth £4.50

PLUS FREE Luxury Luggage Tag worth £15

PLUS FREE Privilege Card worth £20

The Chairman's Collection contains the following titles:

•Business Meetings Venues •Traditional Inns, Hotels & Restaurants - GB •Hotels - GB & Ireland •Country Houses - GB & Ireland •Historic Houses, Castles & Gardens •Hotels, Country Houses & Game Lodges - Southern Africa •Hotels - North America, Bermuda, The Caribbean •Hotels - Europe & The Mediterranean •Hotels & Lodges - Australia, New Zealand, The Pacific • Johansens Pocket Guide 2001

Now please complete your order and payment details

	Quantity	Amount
I have ordered 3 titles - £5 off		–£5.00
I have ordered 4 titles - £10 off		–£10.00
I have ordered 5 titles - £20 off		–£20.00
Total cost of books ordered minus discount (not including the Chairman's Collection)		£
Privilege Card - FREE WITH ANY ORDER Additional cards can be ordered for £20		£
Luxury Luggage Tag - Johansens branded polished steel tag at £15. Quantity and total cost:		£
POSTAGE & PACKING (UK) for a single item add £2.50 ☐ More than one item add £4.50 ☐ (Outside) UK for a single item add £4.00 ☐ More than one item add £6.00 ☐		£
I wish to order the Chairman's collection at £99.55 (no P&P required) **Enter quantity and total cost:**		£
Johansens Gold Blocked SLIP CASE at £5 for the Chairman's Collection. Quantity and total cost:		£
GRAND TOTAL		£

I have chosen my Johansens Guides and (please tick)

I enclose a cheque payable to Johansens ☐

I enclose my order on company letterheading, please invoice (UK only) ☐

Please note that books will be sent upon payment being received

Please debit my credit/charge card account (please tick) ☐

☐ **MasterCard** ☐ **Amex** ☐ **Visa** ☐ **Switch** (Issue Number) ☐

Card Holders Name (Mr/Mrs/Miss)

Address

Postcode

Telephone

Card No. **Exp Date**

Signature

NOW simply detach the order form and send it to Johansens, FREEPOST (CB264), 43 Millharbour, London E14 9BR (no stamp required)

FREE gifts will be dispatched with your order. Fax orders welcome on 0207 537 3594

GUEST SURVEY REPORT

Your own Johansens 'inspection' gives reliability to our guides and assists in the selection of Award Nominations

Name of Hotel: ______________________

Location of Hotel: ______________________

Page No: ______________________

Date of visit: ______________________

Name of GUEST: ______________________

Address of GUEST: ______________________

______________________ **Postcode** __________

Please tick one box in each category below:	*Excellent*	*Good*	*Disappointing*	*Poor*
Bedrooms				
Public Rooms				
Restaurant/Cuisine				
Service				
Welcome/Friendliness				
Value For Money				

Occasionally we may allow other reputable organisations to write with offers which may be of interest.
If you prefer not to hear from them, tick this box ☐

To: Johansens, c/o Norwood Mailing CO Ltd, FREEPOST CB264, London SE27 0BR

ORDER FORM

order 3 titles get £5 off • order 4 titles get £10 off • order 5 titles get £20 off

or you can order the Chairman's collection and save £35

Simply indicate the quantity of each title you wish to order, total up the cost and then make your appropriate discount. Complete your order below and choose your preferred method of payment. Then send it to Johansens, FREEPOST (CB 264), 43 Millharbour, London E14 9BR (no stamp required). FREE gifts will automatically be dispatched with your order. Fax orders welcome on 0207 537 3594.

ALTERNATIVELY YOU CAN ORDER IMMEDIATELY ON FREEPHONE 0800 269 397 and quote ref B13

Recommended Hotels - Great Britain & Ireland 2001 Publication date: October 2000	I wish to order QUANTITY copy/ies priced at £19.95 each. Total cost £
Recommended Country Houses - Great Britain & Ireland 2001 Publication date: October 2000	I wish to order QUANTITY copy/ies priced at £11.95 each. Total cost £
Recommended Traditional Inns, Hotels & Restaurants - Great Britain 2001 Publication date: October 2000	I wish to order QUANTITY copy/ies priced at £11.95 each. Total cost £
Historic Houses, Castles & Gardens 2001 (incorporating Museums & Galleries) Publication date: December 2000	I wish to order QUANTITY copy/ies priced at £7.95 each. Total cost £
Recommended Hotels - Europe & The Mediterranean 2001 Publication date: October 2000	I wish to order QUANTITY copy/ies priced at £16.95 each. Total cost £
Recommended Hotels - North America, Bermuda & The Caribbean 2001 Publication date: October 2000	I wish to order QUANTITY copy/ies priced at £12.95 each. Total cost £
Recommended Hotels, Country Houses & Game Lodges – Southern Africa, Mauritius, The Seychelles 2001 Publ. date: October 2000	I wish to order QUANTITY copy/ies priced at £9.95 each. Total cost £
NEW **Recommended Hotels & Lodges Australia, New Zealand, The Pacific 2001** Publication date: October 2000	I wish to order QUANTITY copy/ies priced at £9.95 each. Total cost £
Recommended Business Meeting Venues 2001 Publication date: February 2001	I wish to order QUANTITY copy/ies priced at £25.00 each. Total cost £
NEW **Johansens Pocket Guide 2001** Publication date: January 2001	I wish to order QUANTITY copy/ies priced at £7.95 each. Total cost £

The Chairman's Collection

order the complete collection of Johansens Recommended Guides for only £99.55 a saving of £35

PLUS FREE P&P worth £4.50

PLUS FREE Luxury Luggage Tag worth £15

PLUS FREE Privilege Card worth £20

The Chairman's Collection contains the following titles:

•Business Meetings Venues •Traditional Inns, Hotels & Restaurants - GB •Hotels - GB & Ireland •Country Houses - GB & Ireland •Historic Houses, Castles & Gardens •Hotels, Country Houses & Game Lodges - Southern Africa •Hotels - North America, Bermuda, The Caribbean •Hotels - Europe & The Mediterranean •Hotels & Lodges - Australia, New Zealand, The Pacific • Johansens Pocket Guide 2001

Now please complete your order and payment details

I have ordered 3 titles - £5 off		−£5.00
I have ordered 4 titles - £10 off		−£10.00
I have ordered 5 titles - £20 off		−£20.00
Total cost of books ordered minus discount (not including the Chairman's Collection)		£
Privilege Card - FREE WITH ANY ORDER Additional cards can be ordered for £20		£
Luxury Luggage Tag - Johansens branded polished steel tag at £15. Quantity and total cost:		£
POSTAGE & PACKING (UK) for a single item add £2.50; More than one item add £4.50; (Outside) UK for a single item add £4.00; More than one item add £6.00		£
I wish to order the Chairman's collection at £99.55 (no P&P required) Enter quantity and total cost:		£
Johansens Gold Blocked SLIP CASE at £5 for the Chairman's Collection. Quantity and total cost:		£
GRAND TOTAL		£

I have chosen my Johansens Guides and (please tick)

I enclose a cheque payable to Johansens ☐

I enclose my order on company letterheading, please invoice (UK only) ☐

Please note that books will be sent upon payment being received

Please debit my credit/charge card account (please tick) ☐

☐ **MasterCard** ☐ **Amex** ☐ **Visa** ☐ **Switch** (Issue Number)

Card Holders Name (Mr/Mrs/Miss)

Address

Postcode

Telephone

Card No. Exp Date

Signature

NOW simply detach the order form and send it to Johansens, FREEPOST (CB264), 43 Millharbour, London E14 9BR (no stamp required)

FREE gifts will be dispatched with your order. Fax orders welcome on 0207 537 3594

GUEST SURVEY REPORT

Your own Johansens 'inspection' gives reliability to our guides
and assists in the selection of Award Nominations

Name of Hotel: ______________________________

Location of Hotel: ______________________________

Page No: ______________________________

Date of visit: ______________________________

Name of GUEST: ______________________________

Address of GUEST: ______________________________

______________________________ **Postcode** __________

Please tick one box in each category below:	*Excellent*	*Good*	*Disappointing*	*Poor*
Bedrooms				
Public Rooms				
Restaurant/Cuisine				
Service				
Welcome/Friendliness				
Value For Money				

Occasionally we may allow other reputable organisations to write with offers which may be of interest.
If you prefer not to hear from them, tick this box ☐

To: Johansens, c/o Norwood Mailing CO Ltd, FREEPOST CB264, London SE27 0BR

ORDER FORM

order 3 titles get £5 off • order 4 titles get £10 off • order 5 titles get £20 off

or you can order the Chairman's collection and save £35

Simply indicate the quantity of each title you wish to order, total up the cost and then make your appropriate discount. Complete your order below and choose your preferred method of payment. Then send it to Johansens, FREEPOST (CB 264), 43 Millharbour, London E14 9BR (no stamp required). FREE gifts will automatically be dispatched with your order. Fax orders welcome on 0207 537 3594.

ALTERNATIVELY YOU CAN ORDER IMMEDIATELY ON FREEPHONE 0800 269 397 and quote ref B13

Recommended Hotels - Great Britain & Ireland 2001 Publication date: October 2000	I wish to order QUANTITY copy/ies priced at £19.95 each. Total cost £
Recommended Country Houses - Great Britain & Ireland 2001 Publication date: October 2000	I wish to order QUANTITY copy/ies priced at £11.95 each. Total cost £
Recommended Traditional Inns, Hotels & Restaurants - Great Britain 2001 Publication date: October 2000	I wish to order QUANTITY copy/ies priced at £11.95 each. Total cost £
Historic Houses, Castles & Gardens 2001 (incorporating Museums & Galleries) Publication date: December 2000	I wish to order QUANTITY copy/ies priced at £7.95 each. Total cost £
Recommended Hotels - Europe & The Mediterranean 2001 Publication date: October 2000	I wish to order QUANTITY copy/ies priced at £16.95 each. Total cost £
Recommended Hotels - North America, Bermuda & The Caribbean 2001 Publication date: October 2000	I wish to order QUANTITY copy/ies priced at £12.95 each. Total cost £
Recommended Hotels, Country Houses & Game Lodges – Southern Africa, Mauritius, The Seychelles 2001 Publ. date: October 2000	I wish to order QUANTITY copy/ies priced at £9.95 each. Total cost £
Recommended Hotels & Lodges Australia, New Zealand, The Pacific 2001 Publication date: October 2000 (NEW)	I wish to order QUANTITY copy/ies priced at £9.95 each. Total cost £
Recommended Business Meeting Venues 2001 Publication date: February 2001	I wish to order QUANTITY copy/ies priced at £25.00 each. Total cost £
Johansens Pocket Guide 2001 Publication date: January 2001 (NEW)	I wish to order QUANTITY copy/ies priced at £7.95 each. Total cost £

The Chairman's Collection

order the complete collection of Johansens Recommended Guides for only £99.55 a saving of £35

PLUS FREE P&P worth £4.50

PLUS FREE Luxury Luggage Tag worth £15

PLUS FREE Privilege Card worth £20

The Chairman's Collection contains the following titles:

•Business Meetings Venues •Traditional Inns, Hotels & Restaurants - GB •Hotels - GB & Ireland •Country Houses - GB & Ireland •Historic Houses, Castles & Gardens •Hotels, Country Houses & Game Lodges - Southern Africa •Hotels - North America, Bermuda, The Caribbean •Hotels - Europe & The Mediterranean •Hotels & Lodges - Australia, New Zealand, The Pacific • Johansens Pocket Guide 2001

Now please complete your order and payment details

I have ordered 3 titles - £5 off	–£5.00
I have ordered 4 titles - £10 off	–£10.00
I have ordered 5 titles - £20 off	–£20.00
Total cost of books ordered minus discount (not including the Chairman's Collection)	£
Privilege Card - FREE WITH ANY ORDER Additional cards can be ordered for £20	£
Luxury Luggage Tag - Johansens branded polished steel tag at £15. Quantity and total cost:	£
POSTAGE & PACKING (UK) for a single item add £2.50; More than one item add £4.50; (Outside) UK for a single item add £4.00; More than one item add £6.00	£
I wish to order the Chairman's collection at £99.55 (no P&P required) Enter quantity and total cost:	£
Johansens Gold Blocked SLIP CASE at £5 for the Chairman's Collection. Quantity and total cost:	£
GRAND TOTAL	£

I have chosen my Johansens Guides and (please tick)

I enclose a cheque payable to Johansens ☐

I enclose my order on company letterheading, please invoice (UK only) ☐

Please note that books will be sent upon payment being received

Please debit my credit/charge card account (please tick) ☐

☐ **MasterCard** ☐ **Amex** ☐ **Visa** ☐ **Switch** (Issue Number)

Card Holders Name (Mr/Mrs/Miss)

Address

Postcode

Telephone

Card No. **Exp Date**

Signature

NOW simply detach the order form and send it to Johansens, FREEPOST (CB264), 43 Millharbour, London E14 9BR (no stamp required)

FREE gifts will be dispatched with your order. Fax orders welcome on 0207 537 3594

GUEST SURVEY REPORT

Your own Johansens 'inspection' gives reliability to our guides and assists in the selection of Award Nominations

Name of Hotel: ______________________

Location of Hotel: ______________________

Page No: ______________________

Date of visit: ______________________

Name of GUEST: ______________________

Address of GUEST: ______________________

______________________ **Postcode** __________

Please tick one box in each category below:	*Excellent*	*Good*	*Disappointing*	*Poor*
Bedrooms				
Public Rooms				
Restaurant/Cuisine				
Service				
Welcome/Friendliness				
Value For Money				

Occasionally we may allow other reputable organisations to write with offers which may be of interest.
If you prefer not to hear from them, tick this box ☐

To: Johansens, c/o Norwood Mailing CO Ltd, FREEPOST CB264, London SE27 0BR